"There was a time when the w
has now become so vacuous is   ... culture
but represents instead a crisis of vocation. So here we have, none too soon,
a collection of stout essays calling for a new generation of shepherd-
teachers—ecclesial theologians who do their work in the best tradition of
the Church Fathers and the Reformers, in the light of eternity and *pro
Christo et ecclesia.*"

Timothy George, founding dean, Beeson Divinity School, Samford University,
general editor of the Reformation Commentary on Scripture

"A clarion call for pastors to embrace their vocational identity as theologians!
Pastors will surely benefit from the encouragement and challenge these
essays offer, but because the authors celebrate the different callings of other
members of the church, all those who come 'from within the liturgical and
common life of a local congregation'—be they full-time academics or lay-
persons in other fields—will (re)discover ways to think about and support
theology from the church, for the church."

Amy Peeler, associate professor of New Testament, Wheaton College

"This passionate set of essays comes at a crucial time for the church. God's
people are starving for biblical and theological nourishment. Many pastors
long ago abandoned their theological duties, and many theologians work in
a way that is lost on the people of God. Who is left to shape Christians with
the knowledge of God and his Word? Many thanks to Wilson and Hiestand
for this clarion call to pastors to lead their people once again, not so much
as CEOs, therapists or entertainers, but as those who want to help them
know the Lord."

Douglas A. Sweeney, professor of church history and the history of
Christian thought, Trinity Evangelical Divinity School

BECOMING A PASTOR THEOLOGIAN

NEW POSSIBILITIES *for* CHURCH LEADERSHIP

EDITED BY TODD WILSON
& GERALD HIESTAND

An imprint of InterVarsity Press
Downers Grove, Illinois

InterVarsity Press
P.O. Box 1400, Downers Grove, IL 60515-1426
ivpress.com
email@ivpress.com

©2016 by Todd Wilson and Gerald Hiestand

InterVarsity Press® is the book-publishing division of InterVarsity Christian Fellowship/USA®, a movement of students and faculty active on campus at hundreds of universities, colleges and schools of nursing in the United States of America, and a member movement of the International Fellowship of Evangelical Students. For information about local and regional activities, visit intervarsity.org.

Cover design: David Fassett
Interior design: Beth McGill

Image: St. Thomas Aquinas writing before the crucifix by Antonio Rodriguez at Museo Nacional de Arte, Mexico City, Mexico / Bridgeman Images

ISBN 978-0-8308-5171-3 (print)
ISBN 978-0-8308-9336-2 (digital)

Printed in the United States of America ∞

Library of Congress Cataloging-in-Publication Data
A catalog record for this book is available from the Library of Congress.

P	23	22	21	20	19	18	17	16	15	14	13	12	11	10	9	8	7	6	5	4	3	2	1
Y	36	35	34	33	32	31	30	29	28	27	26	25	24	23	22	21	20	19	18	17	16		

To the three Senior Theological Mentors
of the Center for Pastor Theologians:
Scott Hafemann, Doug Sweeney and Paul House

Contents

Acknowledgments

C ICERO ONCE REMARKED THAT EVERY PERSON is best when they stick to their own art. The advantage of a multiauthored volume is that each contributor can do this, and yet the end product is still able to encompass a wide range of expertise and skill. We are deeply grateful to each of the contributors for bringing the best of their art to bear on such an important question. The variegated perspectives, counsel and visions of the pastor theologian detailed by the contributors of this volume provide a composite picture that exceeds any one vision of a single author. To say that we could not have done this book without them is, of course, stating the obvious. But certainly we could not have done it well without the careful thought and talents of our contributors. We are truly grateful to each of them for an excellent volume.

We also owe a debt of gratitude to the Center for Pastor Theologians—the organizer of the conference from which the papers that make up this volume are drawn. The Center has served as a catalyst for our work and a repository of wisdom and counsel on all things pastoral and theological. The leadership of the Center—John Yates, Michael LeFebvre, Jeremy Mann and John Isch— deserve our gratitude and bear a measure of responsibility for any blessing this book brings to the church.

Likewise, we are deeply grateful to Calvary Memorial Church in Oak Park, Illinois, the local congregation where we minister. Calvary has graciously served as ground zero for the CPT and our vision for the pastor theologian. It has happily hosted numerous symposia, as well as the CPT Conference, with grace and hospitality. The good people at Calvary make serving them a joy.

We are thankful to IVP Academic for believing in the usefulness of this project, and especially to our editor, David McNutt, for his enthusiastic participation in the production of this book.

To our families and our wives we remain ever grateful. Their patient endurance in the midst of our already busy schedules is a gift that we do not take lightly. May the Lord pay them back tenfold (yea verily a hundred fold) what they have given to us!

Finally, it is a personal joy to dedicate this volume to the Center for Pastor Theologians's three Senior Theological Mentors: Scott Hafemann, Doug Sweeney and Paul House. We're grateful for their commitment to the CPT's mission, their contribution to its fellowships, and their friendship and encouragement to the two of us.

Introduction

TODD WILSON AND
GERALD HIESTAND

IT WAS AN UNUSUALLY WARM EVENING in early November of 2015. The sanctuary of Calvary Memorial Church in Oak Park, Illinois, where we serve as pastors, began to fill with an admirable and diverse group of pastors, professors, students, non-profit executives, publishers and others—all eagerly gathered for the first-ever conference of the Center for Pastor Theologians. For the next two-and-a-half days, several hundred men and women enjoyed a rewarding feast of fellowship and conversation. While not everyone hailed from the same ecclesial background or theological tradition, they all shared a deep love and concern for the state of theology, the state of the church and the state of the pastorate.

You may know that pastors these days are going through something of an identity crisis. By and large, they don't know who they are or what they're supposed to be doing. Behind the benign pastoral smiles and inspiring sermons and multi-million dollar building campaigns and ever-expanding ministry footprints, there lurks in the hearts and minds of many pastors confusion as to what a pastor is and what a pastor does. In the words of Princeton Seminary president Craig Barnes, the hardest thing about being a pastor today is simply "confusion about what it means to be the pastor."[1]

---

[1]M. Craig Barnes, *The Pastor as Minor Poet: Text and Subtexts in the Ministerial Life* (Grand Rapids: Eerdmans, 2009), 4.

Think about that. There's probably not another profession that suffers from such a lack of clarity as to what the job itself is all about. The net result is that your average pastor has been reduced to little more than what Stanley Hauerwas calls "a quivering mass of availability."[2] This may be why so many pastors resign their posts every year, or leave the ministry and never want to return, or make often-insane attempts to conceal their confusion and burnout with different forms of self-medication, from drinking to pornography to affairs to overeating to obsessing about money or power to complete emotional detachment from the lives of their people—or from God himself.

What makes this crisis of identity among pastors especially tragic is that there used to be such clarity about the pastoral calling. For centuries, the church held out a clear and compelling vision of what a pastor is and what a pastor does. In short, a pastor is a theologian. But this ancient vision has been obscured by the separation of the roles of pastor and theologian—a tragic division of labor that continues to bedevil the Christian ministry and the church.

This is why in 2006 we cofounded an organization devoted to putting the calling of the theologian *back* into the identity of the pastor. We first called it the Society for the Advancement of Ecclesial Theology. But that was way too geeky—even for us—and it was clunky to communicate. So we changed it to the Center for Pastor Theologians. This is not, we admit, a very creative name. But it's clear and its mission is compelling. We exist to resurrect this ancient vision of the pastor *as a theologian*—not as an end in itself, but for the renewal of theology and thus the renewal of the church in its ministry and mission to the world. That's why we decided to host a conference on the theme of "The Pastor Theologian: Identities and Possibilities."

We were so encouraged with the content of the presentations at this conference that we were eager to make them available to the wider public. The five chapters that make up part one were the plenary addresses at the conference, each of which approaches the theme of the pastor theologian from a slightly different yet complementary angle. The four chapters in part two present historical examples from leading pastor theologians like John Calvin

---

[2]Quoted in William Willimon, *Pastor: The Theology and Practice of Ordained Ministry* (Nashville: Abingdon, 2002), 60.

and Thomas Boston. And part three contains six chapters that explore the all-important theme of the pastor theologian and Scripture.

While each of the contributors shares our enthusiasm for the vision of the pastor theologian, there is a wonderful diversity of perspectives and voices represented here. The authors come from a variety of different denominational and theological backgrounds, and we couldn't be more thankful for that. It's part of the very DNA of the Center for Pastor Theologians to carry on this conversation about the pastor theologian within the rich and wide stream of tradition C. S. Lewis (and Richard Baxter before him) called "mere Christianity."

The heartbeat of the Center for Pastor Theologians, as well as the personal pastoral burden behind this book, is the renewal of the church. So we offer you these essays on the important theme of the pastor theologian in the hope and with the prayer that the church's best days are yet to come!

Soli Deo Gloria!

Part One

The IDENTITIES *of the* PASTOR THEOLOGIAN

1

The Pastor Theologian as Biblical Theologian

From the Church for the Church

PETER J. LEITHART

T HE SUBTITLE OF MY CHAPTER, "From the Church for the Church," expresses a vision for an *ecclesial* biblical theology, a biblical theology produced by pastors who serve local congregations for the edification of fellow believers in their own and other churches. In laying out this vision, I expound three points:

1. Over the past few centuries, biblical scholarship has not arisen from the church and is not readily usable by the church.

2. There is a vast, largely unpopulated terrain for the development of a biblical theology from the church for the church.

3. To populate this terrain, pastor theologians have to develop ways of reading and writing that diverge from the methods of academic scholarship.

My treatment of these points is uneven. I will make only brief comments about the first, and the second will be largely implicit. I will spend most of my comments on the third.

THE ENLIGHTENMENT BIBLE

Let me begin with brief, not to say perfunctory, remarks about modern biblical scholarship. This offers occasion for a moment of obligatory Enlightenment-bashing.

In his 2005 book *The Enlightenment Bible*,[1] Jonathan Sheehan describes changes in the Bible's role in Germany and England between the late seventeenth and the middle part of the nineteenth century. Sheehan is not concerned primarily with biblical criticism but with the shifting location of the Bible within European culture. In his account, the Enlightenment is not a philosophy or a secular mood but a "new constellation of practices and institutions"—philology, text criticism, modes of translation, coffee houses, scientific societies, journals—that dislodged the Bible from its central place in the Western imagination. This involved an intellectual revolution. As Europeans became skeptical about divine inspiration, the Bible became post-theological, no longer "Scripture" but an ancient text to be studied alongside *Gilgamesh* and Hesiod's *Theogony*. No longer considered revelation from *outside* this world, the Bible was "reconstituted as a piece of the heritage of the West" and "transformed from a work of theology to a work of culture."[2]

What Sheehan describes is not so much a loss as a reconstruction of biblical authority. This is linked to the Bible's fragmentation, which began long before higher criticism dissolved it among incompatible sources. Scripture was demoted from sacred text to cultural artifact as it was subjected to the probing of new analytical tools. The Enlightenment Bible had authority but its authority "had no essential center," since it was distributed among the disciplines that scrutinized it, each of which "offered its own answer to the question of biblical authority."[3] None of these disciplines, of course, studied the Bible with the tools of precritical exegesis. Prescientific interpretation was precisely what the Enlightenment consigned to the dustbin. Institutionally, the Enlightenment relocated the Bible from the church to the university. Pre-Enlightenment biblical scholarship was largely from the church for the church. The Enlightenment Bible was studied in the academy, its scholarship produced for academics.

---

[1] Jonathan Sheehan, *The Enlightenment Bible: Translation, Scholarship, Culture* (Princeton: Princeton University Press, 2005).
[2] Sheehan, *Enlightenment Bible*, xi, 220. I have been helped by the review of Eric Carlsson in *Fides et historia* 38:2 (2005–2006): 226-28.
[3] Sheehan, *Enlightenment Bible*, 92.

We should not exaggerate the changes, and we should not romanticize premodern biblical study. Neither Europe nor America was ever a continent-wide scriptorium in which each Christian spent his every waking hour poring over, listening to or singing Scripture. And we should not despair about the present either. Though it is no longer the authoritative text for the cultural at large, the Bible remains a basic religious source for many. It is arguably still the most important single book in American public life. For example, in the 2016 campaign for president, John Kasich argued that our nation would be judged by how well it cares for the "least of these." That staunch Presbyterian Donald Trump flashed his personal Bible at rallies, a gift from that other stalwart predestinarian, Norman Vincent Peale.

It is easy to find examples of technical academic work that have little evident value for the church, but even within the academy much biblical scholarship is done by believers who regard Scripture as authoritative and who seek to serve the church in their scholarship. They examine historical, linguistic or grammatical features of the Bible, but are also interested in its spiritual import. A glance at a recent, randomly selected issue of the *Journal of Biblical Literature*—a flagship journal of technical exegesis—includes essays on the following: "Furnace Remelting as the Expression of YHWH's Holiness"; "Circumcision in Israelite and Philistine Societies"; "A Stratified Account of Jephtah's Negotiations and Battle"; "The Politics of Psalmody"; "The Poetry of the Lord's Prayer"; and "Love Conquers All: Song of Songs 8:6b-7 as a Reflex of the Northwest Semitic Combat Myth."[4] No doubt there is much in each of these articles that I would be reluctant to tuck into a sermon,[5] but my main reaction to that table of contents is one of childish glee. I *know* there will be gems here, *preachable* gems.[6]

---

[4] *Journal of Biblical Literature* 234:2 (2015).

[5] Interesting as it may be in its own right, the multi-authored essay on "Computerized Source Criticism of Biblical Texts" does not look pulpit-worthy.

[6] Turns out, I was right about this. Nissim Amzallag's essay on "Furnace Remelting as the Expression of YHWH's Holiness: Evidence of the Meaning of *qanna*' (קנא) in the Divine Context" concludes that "the concepts inspired by the process of furnace remelting seem to be of central importance in biblical theology. They promote the belief that the necessary outcome of a tragic event is the recovery of an improved state, the one closest to the 'revitalized origin.' They also condition the vision of the final issue as an ultimate remelting event bringing back an entirely renewed earth" (252). Anyone who cannot preach that should not be allowed near a pulpit.

Besides, for all the wisdom, charm and interest of precritical exegesis, patristic and medieval biblical commentators suffered from glaring (and entirely *innocent*) limitations. These include ignorance of the historical contexts of both Old and New Testaments and often of the languages of the Bible, as well as—to be blunt—occasional ham-handedness in interpreting literary texts. We would do well to remember that for a millennium most Western theologians were ignorant of Greek, not to mention Hebrew. These limitations sometimes arose from deep sources in premodern theology. In the introduction to his commentary on the Song of Songs, Robert Jenson observes that precritical readers of the poem regularly ascend to a spiritual reading and leave the sensuousness of the poem behind. "The older exegesis indeed did the Song violence," Jenson charges, and he affirms the "vital moment of truth" in what he calls modernity's "rebellion" against precritical interpretation. Whatever else we say, "the poem remains . . . sensual love poetry."[7] It would be a grave mistake for Christians to renounce the disciplines that arose around the Enlightenment Bible so thoroughly that we fail to receive its gifts with gratitude.

Even with these qualifications, I venture a rough caricature of the current state of biblical theology: The library of biblical studies is divided between popular devotional works, on the one hand, and technical, highly specialized studies on the other. There is biblical scholarship from the academy for the academy; there is devotional literature from the church for the church. What is missing—what is currently being filled in by the various branches of the "theological commentary" movement—is serious literary and theological study of the Bible that arises from the church and is written for the church. What is missing is ecclesial biblical theology, with equal emphasis on *ecclesial* and *theology*.

THE NATURE OF ECCLESIAL BIBLICAL THEOLOGY

To fill the empty shelves in our theological libraries, however, pastor theologians cannot mimic the idiom of the university. Academic scholarship is written in technical language, makes heavy use of the biblical languages and other relevant ancient languages and theorizes about history and textual

---

[7]Jenson, *Song of Songs*, Interpretation (Louisville: Westminster John Knox, 2005), 13.

interpretation at a rarefied level. There are good reasons for all this appa-ratus—precision and rigor among them. More questionably, biblical schol-arship, like all scholarship, has its rites of entry and its gestures of mem-bership; every discipline has practitioners who write impenetrable prose to prove they belong in the club. Ecclesial biblical theology must be theology *for* the church. This means that at least it should be written in plain English (or French or Spanish or Swahili or Chinese)—winning, witty, engaging English, but plain for all that. It should be readable by all who want to read it.

Ecclesial biblical theology also comes *from* the church, which is to say it is written by pastor theologians (and others who serve the church) from within the liturgical and common life of a local congregation. The pastor theologian is an endangered species of the genus *pastor*, but we cannot be so worried about reviving the species that we neglect the genus. Whatever we may say about the work of pastor theologians, we must say first and always that pastor theologians are *pastors*, shepherds of the people of God. That is what they are authorized to do by virtue of ordination; that is *all* Jesus authorizes them to do. Pastor theologians may take on specific ministries within the church, may pursue special teaching roles in writing and speaking, but they remain first and foremost ministers of word and sacrament. That is the setting of their theological work. In that sense, all pastors are pastor theologians, all engaged in the work of applying the word of God to the world.[8] Whatever pastor theologians are and do, it is an extension of their fundamental calling.

Ecclesial Biblical Theology: Hermeneutical, Homiletical, Liturgical

In the remainder of this chapter, I offer a set of coordinates that converge toward a biblical theology from the church for the church. First, over against the tools and methods of academic biblical studies, I offer some comments on the old-new hermeneutics required for the cultivation of ecclesial biblical theology. Second, over against certain uses, abuses or *lack* of uses of Scripture in preaching, I offer homiletical encouragement. Finally, over against preaching that is done outside of a Eucharistic setting, I offer sacramental

---

[8]In the background is John Frame's conception of theology as application. See Frame, *Doctrine of the Knowledge of God* (Phillipsburg, NJ: P&R, 1987).

and liturgical observations. The first section imagines the pastor theologian in the study; the second in the pulpit; the third fondly imagines that every pulpit has a table nearby, spread for communion.

Hermeneutical. The hermeneutics of ecclesial biblical theology will draw on precritical sources as well as on the calibrated tools of Enlightenment and post-Enlightenment scholarship. But ecclesial biblical theology will *not* rest on grammatical-historical interpretation.

Limiting analysis of a text to grammatical and historical concerns makes sense in certain settings. Social scientists who want to determine what happened in a particular episode of history will not be interested in the poetic resonances of a text. Anthony Kennedy's majority opinion in *Obergefell v. Hodges* excepted, legal scholars are known more for the logic of their arguments than for the elevated (not to say purple) prose of their opinions. Postmodern theory has taught us to be suspicious of apparently straightforward literalism. Interpretations are already embedded in texts—in the selection and arrangement of the parts, in the minute rhetorical maneuvers that shape a reader's judgment about the substance. All inter-preters are *interested* interpreters. Nowadays, *everyone* is a literary critic. We can set that knot of problems to the side for another day. Whatever we might say about texts in general, we certainly cannot stop with gram-matical and historical analysis of Scripture, and that for two main reasons. The first has to do with the character of Scripture, and the second has to do with the setting in which the results of biblical exegesis are publicized.

The Bible is, so Christians believe, a *unified* book of books with theo-logical and literary coherence. We believe that the Bible is such because the same God who spoke the world into existence spoke again and again through angels and prophets to Israel, spoke again in the last days through his Son who is his eternal Word. This author did not grope from beginning to end, or vice versa, but knew the end at the beginning because he is the Lord who is, who was and who comes.

It is true that Scripture has many authors; it makes use of many sources; it is written—if I may be excused an unhelpful anachronism—in various genres. Academic scholarship has pointed all this out, sometimes with in-sight, often to the point of tedium, often quite erroneously. Academic bib-lical studies has institutionalized this fragmentation with its departments of

Old and New Testament. But the fragmented Enlightenment Bible is not the Bible of the church. Pastors and pastor theologians must learn (again) to read and study the Bible as a single book. No single book or passage can be isolated from the whole. We might wish to draw from the new historicists, but our first aim is to be something closer to the new critics, examining the text in its own terms.

That involves, in the first instance, taking each book as a unity in itself, reading with the grain of the text. In Revelation 17, when the Spirit whisks John into the wilderness, he sees a harlot riding on the back of a scarlet beast. Some biblical scholars will tell us that this chapter is strung together from shiny textual beads. One string consists of 17:1-2, 3b-6a, 7, 18 and a few clauses of verses 8-10. Another includes most of the rest—17:11-13, 17 and 16. In the first, "Semitic" text, the beast symbolizes the Roman Empire; in other fragments the beast is Nero, and in still others he is Nero *redivivus*.[9]

When we break the beast up like this, however, we miss the whole point. Several beasts have appeared in Revelation; it is the Bible's bestiary. But the beasts form a sequence into which the scarlet beast of Revelation 17 fits. In Revelation 13, one beast came from the sea to make war on the saints, another from the land to propagandize for the sea beast. The land beast made an image of the sea beast and forced the people of the land to worship that image. Throughout Scripture, the sea signifies the surging world of the Gentiles, which rages against the land, representing Israel. As they take monstrous form, Gentiles and Jews together strive to overcome the saints.

None of these earlier beasts is described as "scarlet," so we might wonder if the beast of Revelation 17 is yet another beast, dragged from the bullpen in the late innings to finish off the church. But there *is* a red beast earlier in Revelation, the original beast, the dragon who stalks the pregnant woman through the sky, waiting to devour her newborn son (Rev 12:1-3). He fails to eliminate the child—again and again he fails—and he eventually has to delegate, calling up the sea and land beasts to prosecute his war. When the sea beast first emerges, he is a leopard with bear paws and a lion mouth, but he

---

[9]This is not a parody but a faithful summary of R. H. Charles, *Commentary on the Revelation of St. John*, 2 vols. (New York: Scribner's, 1920), 2:55. Source-critical analysis of the chapter is a fossil from the 1920s. See David E. Aune, *Revelation 17–22*, Word Biblical Commentary 52c (Waco: Word, 1998), 917-19.

is not scarlet. In the intervening chapters, he has been scarletized, which means he has become dragonized and satanized. The scarlet beast is the sea beast—Rome—transformed into the image of the serpent of old.

Reading a unified Bible also means reading with the grain of the entire canon. Again, Revelation 17 provides a suitable illustration. Commentators regularly point to the luxuriousness of the harlot's garments, which are scarlet and purple, with gold and precious stones and pearls (Rev 17:4). Many suggest that she wears royal colors and draw the conclusion that the harlot city is Rome riding on the bestial empire. When we read the text within the canon, however, a different conclusion becomes more plausible, almost inescapable. "Purple" (Greek *porphyros*) is one of the dominant colors of the tabernacle curtains and the priestly robes (LXX Ex 25:4; 26:1, 31, 36; 28:5, 8, 15, 33), as is scarlet (Greek *kokkinos*; LXX Ex 26:36; 27:16; 28:5, 8, 15, 33). This pair of color terms occurs together twenty-two times in the Septuagint of the tabernacle texts of Exodus, and otherwise only in the descriptions of the temple in 2 Chronicles (2:6, 13; 3:14). Further, the best-known jeweled robe in Scripture is the breastplate of the high priest, which includes threads of gold as well as inset precious stones.[10] The name plate on the harlot's head seals the case. Beast worshipers in Revelation receive the name of the beast on their forehead and right hand, and the harlot is the queen of beast worshipers. For idolaters and the harlot, the image is drawn from the garb of the Aaronic high priests, who wore a golden plate on the forehead inscribed with "Holy to Yahweh" (Ex 28:36).[11] In an idola-trous twist, harlot Babylon is devoted to no god beyond herself. She is Babylon the great, and her head is consecrated to Babylon the great, mother of harlots and of abominations.

Reading the text with the whole Bible in view, we draw the conclusion that the harlot is *not* an imperial figure but a priestess, and a Jewish one. That she rides on the back of a beast with heads like seven hills indicates she has formed an alliance with the beast of empire.

---

[10] The harlot's pearls make an intriguing divergence. Throughout the Old Testament, land and sea represent Israel and the Gentiles; gems from the earth represent the tribes of Israel, and pearls from the ocean are Gentile stones. The foundation stones of the new Jerusalem are the stones of the breastplate, but the gates are pearl: It is a Jewish-Gentile city that descends from heaven.

[11] Israel is to wear Torah on their foreheads and wrists (Deut 6), precisely where beast worshipers wear their mark.

Reading with the grain of the canon also means becoming attuned to fainter echoes of earlier texts. The second, third and fourth movements of Beethoven's Fifth Symphony do not repeat the same notes as the opening motif, but the theme of each movement is built on the opening motif. The symphony is full of formal, rhythmic echoes of the famous opening phrase.

Scripture is a symphony, replete with repeated themes and variations. So at the end of Revelation 17, the ten horns join with the beast in slaughtering the harlot city Babylon. It is a macabre scene, marked by five relentless verbs—hate, desolate, strip, eat, burn—that describe a bizarre sequence of actions. Many Old Testament texts come into play, including Deuteronomy 13, which requires Israel to carry out the ban against an apostate city, and Leviticus 21, which demands that a priest's daughter who plays the harlot in her father's house be killed and burned. Babylon is an unfaithful city and a harlot. She is, as we have already discovered, a priest's daughter, and so it is fitting that she is not only slaughtered but burned.

But the text comes clear as a whole when we recognize in it the faint outline of a sacrificial ritual. In preparing an ascension offering (Lev 1), the priest would skin the animal, then burn its flesh. Though it is not specified that other offerings were skinned, many would have involved both burning and eating. The treatment of the harlot is a sacrificial sequence, but a twisted one: The horns hate her, desolate her, strip her naked, eat her and, having eaten her, *then* burn her with fire so that the smoke of her sacrifice arises forever and ever (Rev 18:9, 18; 19:3). It is a symmetrical eye-for-eye punishment. For her abominations and desolations, she is desolated. She drank saints' blood, the life of the flesh, and her flesh is given to the beast's horns (as Jezebel was given to dogs). She sacrificed the saints, and in recompense she is sacrificed. It is not an animal offered by a human, but a human offered by a beast and his cohort of kings. As James Jordan has argued, every offering is a gift of "bridal food" (*ishsheh*) to Yahweh the Divine Husband. Every sacrifice is part of an ongoing wedding feast. The slaughter of the harlot is an inverted parody of sacrifice, the slaughter and burning of a harlot rather than a bride.

These examples from Revelation 17 are designed to reinforce this point: Ecclesial biblical theology assumes a unified canon and must develop habits of attentive reading suitable to that assumption. This is the first

reason that ecclesial biblical theology must move beyond strictly gram-
matical and historical and literal analysis.

Homiletical. The second is that the setting for ecclesial biblical theology
is quite different from that of biblical scholarship. Biblical scholars present
their findings in academic seminars, journals, expensive monographs
written for wealthy specialists and research libraries. As I have made clear, I
am far from despising the work of such scholars. It is a great gift. Yet pastor
theologians are not interested in the historical meaning of a text as an end
in itself or for the way it might clarify ancient history or society. They are
interested in the text because they want to deliver the text as gospel to the
people of God. Ecclesial biblical theology must orient its hermeneutics
toward homiletics.

What Scripture *is* determines what Scripture is *for*. It is the Spirit-breathed
gift of God that grants wisdom to salvation and is profitable for teaching,
reproof, correction and training in righteousness, equipping the man of God
for every good work (2 Tim 3:16-17). A pastor theologian teaches these texts
to equip the people of God for the work of ministry and for the mission of
God. A literal, historical reading will not suffice. If the text is to be preachable,
the literal must open into the spiritual senses, into Christological allegory
and tropological exhortation.

I illustrate again with Revelation 17. The harlot Babylon, we are told, is
a mystery (Rev 17:5), one that the angel promises to unravel (17:7). The
term *mystery* is a clue to the sort of evil she represents. In the New Testament, a mystery is something hidden that can be known only by revelation, and for the New Testament writers there is one great mystery, which
Paul describes variously as "Christ in you, the hope of glory" or, more
ecclesially, as the knitting together of Jew and Gentile into one body in
Christ (Col 1:27; Eph 3:6). In the categories of the Apocalypse, the evangelical mystery is the gathering of the inhabitants of the land with those
from every tribe, tongue, nation and people. That mystery is finished
during the time of the seventh trumpet (Rev 10:7), when the 144,000
martyrs are hounded and harvested, when those who shed their blood are
raised above the firmament to join Jesus on heavenly thrones. The gospel
mystery comes to its climax in a marriage supper, the feast of the Bride
and the heavenly Lamb, after a new Eve has been formed for the last Adam.

Of all this the harlot is a parody. She is the final expression of the Babel project, the gathering of the human race to build a city and a tower. As prostitute-priestess, she is a counterfeit church. The Reformers who interpreted the harlot as the church of Rome were right to this extent: She is not a political figure but an ecclesial one. In the first-century context, her alliance with the beast represents a counterfeit of the union of Jews and Gentiles in the church. And throughout the ages, the harlot represents the continuing threat of an unfaithful bride who climbs into bed with bestial powers.

The text preaches itself. We are not living under a Soviet regime, when many in the Orthodox Church cozied up to the brutes who ran the Gulag, when the Orthodox hierarchy was salted with KGB operatives. We do not live in Nazi Germany, when the Protestant church prostituted herself to Hitler. But we are living in an age when many churches, liberal ones, are intent on making their peace with the sexual libertinism of our age, and when others, conservative ones, ride cheerily on the back of an American tank.

And when we recognize that the harlot is a false bride, we also take note of the cup in her hand. She is a *pornē* who drinks a cup full of abominations and the unclean things of her *porneia*. In Torah, abomination has a specific connotation: *Unclean* things defile the sanctuary so that it needs to be purged, but *abominations* pollute the land until the land can be purged only by the expulsion of its inhabitants. First Canaanites, then Canaanito-Israelites, were vomited from the land because of their abominations. Three sins pollute the land: idolatry, sexual immortality and the shedding of innocent blood. The harlot is guilty of all three. She is a purveyor of sexual sin, here an image of spiritual and liturgical infidelity, and she drinks the blood of witnesses to Jesus (Rev 17:6). For John's original readers, the setting would be clear: Jerusalem was the source of murderous opposition to the early church; eventually the dragon turned Rome scarlet and it became an enemy of Christ. Both attack the saints, but the harlot drinks holy blood. The one who most relishes the blood of martyrs is not the oppressive empire but the prostituted church. Even to the present, our enemies will be members of our own household.

There is encouragement for martyrs as well, because the harlot's gold cup is not the only cup in the book of Revelation. She drinks from a gold *potērion*, full of the blood of the saints, but only a few verses earlier we are told that

God gives her the "*potērion* of the wine of His fierce wrath" (Rev 16:19). Two cups, but they are ultimately one. The harlot drinks down the blood of the saints with gusto, but the cup of holy blood that is part of her victory feast is the cup of the fierce wrath of God. In an application of the *lex talionis*, God gives blood to the bloodthirsty: "Righteous are you, who are and who were, O Holy One, because You judged these things; for they poured out the blood of saints and prophets, and You have given them blood to drink" (Rev 16:5-6 NASB). Drinking holy blood, she becomes drunk, and drunk cities are, like real drunks, unsteady on their feet. Drunks eventually stumble and fall (compare Jer 25).[12] The whore and the beast join in a common purpose, but as they execute their common purpose they execute God's purpose. Thus they fall into the very trap that they set for the saints.

Ecclesial biblical theologians are thus inevitably, naturally, public and political theologians. Public theology is embedded within their task as ministers of word and sacrament. If they are going to preach the text of Scripture, they cannot avoid talking about beasts and whores and their alliances and their triumphs and defeats. And the text alerts us to a dimension of political theology that we may otherwise miss. Our interest in the political and cultural ramifications of the faith may distract us from the enmity that counterfeit, prostituted churches bear toward the faithful.

I am trying to demonstrate how Revelation 17, read within the sweep of Revelation and the whole Bible, becomes preachable. I am illustrating how a whole-Bible hermeneutics leads into a public homiletics. To do that well, the pastor theologian must trace the edges and contours of the text, not only in the study but in the pulpit. We will miss much of the import of the passage if we do not recognize that the harlot is dressed like a priest. We will skim over the theological profundity if we do not take seriously how the common purpose of the horns is enclosed within and overridden by God's word and purpose. We cannot preach this passage responsibly without attending to its details.

---

[12] The end of the chapter highlights the same point. The horns of the beast turn against the harlot. They form a common purpose against the harlot to strip, kill, eat and burn her. But that common purpose is enclosed in God's purpose for the beast and the harlot. He puts a purpose in their hearts to execute his purpose in their common purpose. When they give their kingdom to the beast, when the horns offer their power to the beast for his use, they are fulfilling the words of God and executing God's own purpose (Rev 17:17).

And that means that the sermon has to be a Bible study. It does not need to be a study of the Greek grammar, but it does need to engage the text of Scripture. Ecclesial biblical theology, in short, does not tolerate jaunty sermons that collapse into a pious version of self-help. Let me say it bluntly: Preachers who spend their sermon time telling cute anecdotes or reviewing the news or commenting on the World Series are guilty of pastoral malpractice. You are commissioned by the Lord Jesus to be a minister of the Word. So *minister* it.

Liturgical. I have established two of my coordinates: Ecclesial biblical theology demands the development of new-old ways of reading Scripture, and the pastor theologian's most important theological publication is the sermon delivered to the local congregation. To those I want to add a third coordinate: The sermon itself takes place in a liturgical setting. The pastor does not prepare or deliver a sermon for an academic conference, gathering information to relay to the people. The Lord's service is a different sort of event. Pastors speak from the table of the Lord, and the words they speak, as much as the bread and wine, are food and drink. Ecclesial biblical theology is necessarily also liturgical and sacramental theology.[13]

Revelation 17 again illustrates. I have indicated that the harlot is a priestly figure, robed in priestly garments and adorned with priestly jewelry. She is clearly a counterfeit priestess; she is, after all, a whore. Several details reinforce her anti-priestly status. For starters, she is seated, and she claims her seat is permanent: "I sit as a queen and I am not a widow, and will never see mourning" (Rev 18:7 NASB).[14] Aaron and his sons were ordained to *stand* and serve; as Hebrews points out, the Aaronic priests never sat down because their work was never done. They never entered Sabbath rest, because the blood of bulls and goats that they slung and sprinkled around the sanctuary

---

[13]Premodern interpreters recognized this, moving easily from Christological allegory to sacramental tropology. It is a biblical move. According to Jesus, the entire Bible is about the suffering and glory of the Christ. But the Christ about whom the Scripture speaks is not simply the dead and risen Jesus but the whole Christ. This is clear in the various places where Paul deals directly with sacramental typologies. The exodus is not merely a type of Jesus' passage from death to life, but a type of the passage of the church through the waters of baptism into the pilgrimage through the wilderness. The whole Christ is the assembly of people who are marked by the seals of baptism and the Supper. The whole Scripture that speaks about the whole Christ therefore also speaks about the Eucharistic feast where Christ offers himself to us by His Spirit.

[14]It is an ironic declaration. The harlot quotes from Is 47:7, a passage about the *fall* of Babylon.

could never take away sin. Until the heavenly sanctuary was cleansed by the blood of God, there was no rest for the weary priest. *This* priestess has settled in, as if she has entered the eschaton, as if she has reached sabbath.

The angel promises to show a harlot who "sits on many waters," and later explains that the waters represent the "peoples and multitudes and nations and tongues" (Rev 17:1, 15 NASB). Her temple is a house of prayer for all nations, but only because it has become a house of prayer to all the gods of the nations. When John actually sees her in the wilderness, though, she is not on the waters but seated on some rough, slouching beast. She is in bed with a beast, and her *porneia* includes spiritual bestiality. The more damning point is more subtle. In Scripture, there is another royal figure who rides enthroned on the back of composite beasts: Yahweh himself, enthroned above the four-faced cherubim, who rides on the cherub-chariot that is his storm cloud. This priestess/goddess has not only taken rest, but she has taken rest on a counterfeit cherub throne. It is as if this priestess has marched into the most holy place and plopped herself on Yahweh's own seat above the cherubim.[15] It is appropriate that she wears the name of her patron goddess—that is, herself—on her forehead, for on her beast she is more the enthroned goddess than the servant who stands in attendance.

A final detail also highlights her effort to immanentize the eschaton: She violates the rules of priestly service not only by sitting but by *drinking*. Wine was strictly forbidden in the sanctuary for the same reason as sitting was prohibited. As James Jordan has put it, wine is omega drink, the drink of sabbath rest, the drink of completed work. Since the priests' work was never completed, they were never to drink wine in the presence of Yahweh. The harlot priestess, though, drinks from a wine goblet as she sits complacently on her cherub throne. Worse still, she drinks blood. She commits continuous sacrilege by drinking holy blood (compare Lev 17).

If the whore sits enthroned, drinks, and drinks blood, then we might imagine the bride must do the opposite—she must stand, refuse wine and renounce the consumption of blood. But the harlot priestess in her false sabbath is a parody of the genuine sabbath of the bride. When Jesus feeds

---

[15]Like the man of sin, exalting himself to be God and taking his position in the temple.

multitudes, he invites them to sit. He gives sabbath wine at the Last Supper and Paul tells us to continue drinking the wine of gladness until Jesus comes again. Just as much as the harlot, we drink blood, *martyr* blood, the blood of the first and truest witness, Jesus. Drinking this blood, we commit ourselves to shed our own, following Jesus to the cross.[16] A pastor theologian preaching this text will have a ready application. Do not feast at the table of demons or whores; come, enjoy the sabbath wine of Jesus, the witness and firstborn of the dead.

Detached from the Eucharistic liturgy, preaching is at sea. We announce the gospel and call our people to faith. We also want to give them something to do. There are dangers on both sides. We may so much emphasize the grace of God that we provide sophisticated excuses for passivity and inaction, if not sin; or we may so emphasize the duties of the Christian life that our preaching becomes little more than moralizing. We want to tell our people to *do* something; we want an altar call. But we do not want them to think that they are somehow achieving status with God by doing what we call them to.

The best altar call is . . . well, an altar call—a call to the altar-table of Jesus, where he offers himself to us by his Spirit through bread and wine. Liturgical biblical theology has a ready-made application: "Do *this*!" This is clearly not a meritorious doing, because the command is an order to receive a gift. If we think that is too little to call people to do, we do not grasp what it is we are doing. For in calling the congregation to do this, we are calling them to abide in Jesus, to eat and drink and breathe him, to share in his death as faithful witnesses, to renounce the table of demons, to share bread with the hungry and all their goods and gifts for the common good, to rejoice with thanksgiving in all things, to live together as Christ's Spirit-filled body, to mount resistance to the violent, to be the political body of the age to come in the present age. All that, and far more, is entailed every time we call on the congregation to the broken bread and the cup of the Lord.

If you are preaching without bread and wine, then your first task is to put an end to that anomaly as quickly as possible.

---

[16]We might even notice a macabre echo of our Eucharistic feast in the feast of the horns at the end of the chapter, the horns who turn against the harlot to desolate, strip, burn and eat her (Rev 17:17; *not* in that exact order!).

Conclusion

Pastoral ministry is the most wide-ranging, challenging vocation known to mortals. The ideal pastor would have the rhetorical panache of a Churchill, the compassion of Mother Teresa, the tenacity and courage of a Navy Seal, the intellect of a lawyer, the patience of Job and the vision of Ezekiel, the creativity of an entrepreneur and the management skill of a CEO and the magnetic energy of a rock star. They must be exemplary in their devotion to Jesus and the uprightness of their character. And they must be everywhere for everything. A doctor comes when you are ill or injured; you ask for a lawyer when you face legal challenges; you hire a consultant to revive or expand your business; you call in the nurse or the hospice worker to care for an aging parent. We have specialists for every moment and stage of life, but pastors are generalists. They are there at birth, at the bedside, through the trial and the lawsuit, when a child is fighting for life and when a parent is slipping into the grave. Pastors are generalists in all the forms and varieties of human misery. If pastors are specialists, they are specialists in death, in actual physical death and in all the lesser shocks of death that flesh is heir to. They are present at all of these gravesides as a representative of the Good Shepherd. They are the visible, tangible presence of Christ and the church at every moment of crisis. Pastors have one word to speak—the word of the gospel, the word of life in the midst of death, the promise of a life that *begins* rather than *ends* with death. They have one thing to do—to offer the challenge and consolation of the word, sensibly conferred in water, bread and wine.

I might have written a chapter on ecclesial biblical theology that made the hospital room or the counseling session the primary context for reflection. I kept it simple by imagining ecclesial biblical theology in the context of sermon preparation and delivery. This is the primary context for biblical theology, not mainly because the work must be delivered as a sermon before it reaches a wider public. Ecclesial biblical theology is not done only in sermon preparation or in the book or article that emerges from the sermon. It is also done when the Lord's servant speaks the word of the Lord to the Lord's people who are gathered by the Lord's Spirit at the Lord's table on the Lord's day in the presence of the Lord. That, *above all*, is where and when ecclesial biblical theology is *done*.

2

The Pastor Theologian
as Political Theologian

Ministry Amidst the Earthly City

JAMES K. A. SMITH

W HILE WE OFTEN SPEAK OF THE "PUBLIC SQUARE," the metaphor is antiquated and unhelpful. Our political lives are not sequestered to a particular sphere; there is no square with discernible gates. The political is less a space and more a way of life. The political is not restricted to our capitols; there's no square there.[1]

The political is less a realm and more a *project*. When we reduce the political through a twofold spatialization and rationalization, what is lost and forgotten is an appreciation of the way the polis is a *formative* community. We do well to remember that, according to the very first line of Aristotle's *Politics*, "every *polis* is a *koinonia*, and every *koinonia* is established with a view to some good."[2] Political participation requires and assumes just such

---

[1] Nor is it a stage that we can either be "on" or "off," like a stage where the microphone becomes hot as soon as you step on stage and is muted as soon as you step off.

[2] Aristotle, *Politics* 1252a, in *The Basic Works of Aristotle*, ed. Richard McKeon, trans. Benjamin Jowett (New York: Random House, 1941), 1127. What Aristotle couldn't quite imagine is a territory that was effectively a terrain of competing *poleis*. He could only imagine one where an overarching "state" (*polis*) articulated a substantive vision of the good that was taken to be *the* Good for those in that territory—that is, the state/*polis* was the "highest *koinonia* of all" in the territory. In short, Aristotle could imagine international pluralism, but not the intranational pluralism in which we find ourselves. Augustine, on the other hand, was intimately aware of the fracture and competition that characterized our public life.

formation—a citizenry with habits and practices to live in common and toward a certain end, oriented toward a telos. Even if this Aristotelian (and Augustinian) intuition has been buried by the rationalistic proceduralism of modern liberalism, that doesn't mean it isn't true. Political animals are *made*, not born.[3]

This is why our political theologies need to worry less about policing boundaries and securing a platform for expressing our beliefs. Instead, they should carefully consider the ways political life is bound up with the formation of habits and desires that make us who we are. What if we aren't fundamentally thinking things who enter the "space" of politics with ideas to get off our chests? What if we are creatures of craving, defined by our desires, who make our way in the world governed by what we long for? And what if the political is not just some procedural gambit to manage our mundane affairs but an expression of a creational desire and need, a structural feature of creaturely life that signals something about the sociality of human nature? What if politics, as John von Heyking puts it, is really about "longing in the world?"[4]

Politics, then, both forms us and requires formation. The political is more like a repertoire of rites than a space for expressing ideas. Laws, then, are not just boundary markers; they are social nudges that makes us a certain kind of people. Institutions are not just abstract placeholders for various functions; they are incubators of habituation that shape character and identity.

When we recover an appreciation of politics as a repertoire of formative rites—as a nexus of habit-forming practices that not only govern us but also form us—then we will remember that politics is bound up with matters of virtue.[5] And truly appreciating the dynamics of virtue requires recovering a sense of teleology, a purview on the political that takes into account the *ends* we are pursuing, the vision of the Good that animates our collaboration and common life.

---

[3]And even if we (rightly) want to argue that human beings are "by nature" political animals, that is still a claim about a capacity that requires cultivation and training—and that can be malformed.
[4]John von Heyking, *Augustine and Politics as Longing in the World* (Columbia: University of Missouri Press, 2001).
[5]Though not *only* politics, contra the political-centrism of James Davison Hunter, *To Change the World* (Oxford: Oxford University Press, 2010).

For Christian thought, zooming out to take account of teleology is intimately bound up with eschatology. Our teleology *is* an eschatology: a hope for kingdom come that arrives by the grace of Providence and doesn't arrive without the return of the risen King. This changes everything. A teleology that is at once an eschatology will be countercultural to every political pretension that assumes a Whiggish confidence in human ingenuity and progress. And precisely because Christian eschatology is a teleology of *hope*, it will also run counter to cynical political ideologies of despair that reduce our common life to machinations of power and domination. Furthermore, a Christian political theology attuned to eschatology will run counter to a kind of postmillennial progressivism to which the so-called justice generation seems prone.

But if Christian hope reframes the political in light of eternity, we might say that Christian faith resituates the political in light of creation. If eschatology relativizes the political from above and beyond, a biblical theology of creation and culture also relativizes the political from below. This is why my quarry is not just a *political* theology but more broadly a *public* theology. I want to encourage us to overcome a narrow fixation on certain modes of electoral politics and realize that much of what constitutes the life of the *polis* are modes of life in common that fall outside the narrow interests of state and government.[6] So a Christian account of our shared socioeconomic-political life might be described more properly as a public theology—an account of how to live in common with neighbors who don't believe what we believe, don't love what we love, don't hope for what we await. The institutions of government are a part of that life in common, but only a slice of a much wider web of institutions and practices that govern our common life. We might say that it is not only government that governs; the state is not the only—or even the most primordial—mode of solidarity.

A LITURGICAL LENS ON THE POLITICAL

My task, then, is to look at the political through the lens of liturgy. What difference will it make for our theological reflection on politics if we begin from the assumption that the same human beings who are, by nature, *zoon politikon* (political animals) are also *homo adorans* (liturgical animals)?

---

[6]Compare Hunter's point in *To Change the World*.

What if citizens are not just thinkers or believers but *lovers*? How will our analysis of political institutions look different if we attend to them as incubators of love-shaping practices, not merely governing us but forming what we love? How will our political engagement change if we are not only looking for permission to express our views in the political sphere but actually hope to shape the ethos of a nation, a state, a municipality to foster a way of life that bends toward shalom?

But my concern in this essay is more specifically with the role of the *pastor* in such an ecclesial understanding of the political. Even more specifically, I want to ask what the role of the ecclesial pastor theologian is in the church as polis. Does this turn into some vision of the pastor as "mayor," a reversion to the prince-bishop?

The pastor is always already a political theologian. What's needed is not the adoption of a role but intentionality and sophistication about that role. In suggesting the role of the pastor as political theologian, I'm *not* advocating the pastor as partisan endorser or electoral meddler. To the contrary, I am suggesting that a robustly orthodox political theology will relativize the cult of electoral politics, retooling our very conception of the political while making us attentive to the formative rites of the regnant polis that have nothing to do with the state. At the same time, I will argue that citizens of the city of God are nonetheless *sent* as ambassadors and emissaries to the earthly city, taking up their human vocation to cultivate creation and love their neighbors. So the pastor theologian is not the mayor of some pure alternative polis that prides itself on escaping the *permixtum*; to the contrary, the pastor as political theologian is a shepherd of the *sent* church, equipping the saints for the messy work of living in the *saeculum*.

I will suggest that the work of the pastor as political theologian can be summarized in two key roles: first, the pastor as ethnographer, exegeting the cultural rites of the empire; and second, the pastor as liturgical catechist, explicating the vision of the Good that is carried in the practices of Christian worship. In the spirit of Gerald Hiestand and Todd Wilson's desire to "resurrect an ancient vision," I will close by considering St. Augustine as a case study.[7]

---

[7]Gerald Hiestand and Todd Wilson, *The Pastor Theologian: Resurrecting an Ancient Vision* (Grand Rapids: Zondervan, 2015).

In suggesting a role for the pastor as political theologian, I will also be focusing on a role the pastor plays as *local* theologian, to use Hiestand and Wilson's term.[8] However, I'm not sure I share their implicit ranking of the pastor theologian's role—from local, to popular, to ecclesial. In particular, I'm not sure I buy their claim that "evangelicalism will never reclaim the emerging generation of theologians for the pastorate if our only conception of the pastor theologian is that of a local or popular theologian."[9] I think there are pastors who find the unique challenges of local theology to be exactly the intellectual challenge they've been looking for; I don't see the priority of local theology as diminishing. And I think the particularly local, contextualized challenges of political theology pose a challenge worth tackling.

Cultural Exegesis of the Rites of Empire

The first task of the pastor as political theologian is to serve congregations by being ethnographers of the rites of the empire that surround them, teaching them to read the rituals of late modern democracy through a biblical, theological lens.

As I mentioned above, the political is not just the administration of law— as if political life boiled down to trash removal service and keeping the traffic lights operational. The political is not merely procedural; it is formative. The polis is a koinonia that is animated by a vision of the Good. And while Aristotle couldn't imagine competing visions of the Good within the territory of the walled city, this reality of competing poleis and rival goods was something Christians appreciated from the beginning. There are rival poleis within the confines of the nation-state. The formative power of the polis is not embodied in its sword but in its rituals. In this respect, the reach of the polis's vision of the good life is carried in all kinds of non-state rhythms and routines that reinforce, say, the *libido dominandi* of the earthly city, or the ultimate mythology of independence and autonomy that is not only articulated in a constitution but enshrined in a million micro-liturgies that reinforce our egoism.

So part of the pastor-as-political-theologian's role is apocalyptic: to unveil and unmask the idolatrous pretensions of the polis that can be all too easily

---

[8]Ibid., 81-83.
[9]Ibid., 85.

missed since they constitute the status quo wallpaper of our everyday environment.[10] It requires thoughtful, rigorous, theological work to pierce through the everyday rituals we go through on autopilot and see them for what they are: ways we are lulled into paying homage to rival kings. This requires what Richard Bauckham calls a "purging of the Christian imagination."[11] At stake here is nothing less than true versus false *worship*.[12]

So part of the pastor theologian's *political* work is to enable the people of God to "read" the practices of the regnant polis, to exegete the liturgies of the earthly city in which we are immersed. This is an essentially local, contextualized task, both in time and space: the political idolatries that tempt us and threaten to deform us are localized. The political hubris of today is not the same as the political hubris of even eighty years ago, let alone of fifth-century Africa or sixteenth-century New England. Such cultural exegesis has to be local and contextual, but it also has to be theological—and, I might suggest, theologically *sociological*.[13] If you want to deepen the theological capacity of the church, try offering a theological ethnography of Independence Day.[14]

Again, we can find ancient exemplars of this. One standout is a sermon Augustine preached on New Year's Day in 404, likely in Carthage, in which he offers a theological and cultural exegesis of the pagan festivals that would dominate the city that day.[15] He takes as his text a line of Psalm 106 they've just sung: "Save us, Lord our God, and gather us from among the nations, that we may confess your holy name" (Ps 106:47). How do you know if you're "gathered from among the nations," Augustine asks? "If the festival of the nations which is taking place today in the joys of the world and the flesh, with the din of silly and disgraceful songs, with the celebration of this false

---

[10]For work by a pastor theologian that does this, see T. Scott Daniels, *Seven Deadly Spirits: The Message of Revelation's Letters for Today's Church* (Grand Rapids: Baker Academic, 2009).

[11]Richard Bauckham, *The Theology of the Book of Revelation* (Cambridge: Cambridge University Press, 1993), 17.

[12]Ibid., 35.

[13]See the Eerdmans series Studies in Ecclesiology and Ethnography. I might note that the church doesn't just need ecclesial *theologians*. We need ecclesial *scholars*.

[14]Admittedly, it might also be a good way to *shrink* a church.

[15]Augustine, Sermon 198; in *Sermons*, vol. III/6, The Works of Saint Augustine, ed. Edmund Hill (New York: New City Press, 1993). This might also explain why his sermon was three hours long—a kind of filibuster to keep his parishioners away from the temptations as long as he could. Suffice it to say, Augustine wouldn't be hosting Super Bowl parties in the cathedral.

feast day—if the things the Gentiles are doing today do not meet with your approval"—well, *then* you're gathered from the nations.

But this isn't just pietistic moralizing. Augustine launches into a theological and philosophical analysis of the rites of pagan feasts. At stake, he argues, is faith, hope and love:

> If you believe, hope, and love, it doesn't mean that you are immediately declared safe and sound and saved. It makes a difference, you see, what you believe, what you hope for, what you love. Nobody in fact can live any style of life without those three sentiments of the soul, of believing, hoping, loving. If you don't believe what the nations believe, and don't hope for what the nations hope for, and don't love what the nations love, then you are gathered from among the nations. And don't let your being physically mixed up with them alarm you, when there is such a wide separation of minds. What after all could be so widely separated as that they believe demons are gods, you on the other hand believe in the God who is the true God? . . . So if you believe something different from them, hope for something different, love something different, you should prove it by your life, demonstrate it by your actions. (Sermon 198.2)

The remainder of Augustine's sermon is a sustained cultural exegesis that aims to make implicit the (pagan) faith, hope and love that is carried in the city's feasts and rituals, which too many of his parishioners merely considered things to do rather than rites that do something *to* them. The burden of Augustine's theological analysis is to highlight the incoherence of singing the psalm and participating in the festivals.

This is an ongoing task. One of the responsibilities of the pastor as political theologian, then, is to help the people of God read the festivals of their own polis—whether it be the annual militarized Thanksgiving festivals that feature gladiators from Dallas and Detroit or the rituals of mutual display and haughty purity that suffuse online regions of "social justice." Our politics is never merely electoral. The polis doesn't just rear to life on the first Tuesday of November. Elections are not liturgies; they are events. The politics of the earthly city is carried in a web of rituals strung between the occasional ballot box. Good political theology pierces through this, unveils it—not to help the people of God withdraw but in order to equip them to be sent into the thick of it. When we are centered in the formative rites of the city of God, Augustine reminds his hearers, "even if you go out and mix with them in general social intercourse . . . you will remain gathered from among the Gentiles, wherever you may actually be" (Sermon 198.7).

LITURGICAL CATECHESIS AS POLITICAL THEOLOGY

This points to the second, constructive function of the pastor-as-political-theologian. It is not sufficient to unmask the rites of earthly city politics. We also need to help the people of God *cultivate* their heavenly citizenship. Citizenship is not just a status or a property that one holds; it is a calling and a vocation.[16] I can hold a Canadian passport and a Canadian birth certificate and yet fail to be a *good* Canadian citizen. Citizenship is not only a right; it is a virtue to be cultivated. The pastor as political theologian plays a role in shepherding civic virtue in citizens of the city of God (compare Phil 3:20).[17]

If Christian worship constitutes the civics of the city of God, then liturgical catechesis is the theological exercise by which we come to understand our heavenly citizenship. In other words, a key theological work that is charged with political significance is to help the people of God understand why we do what we do when we worship. Liturgical theology *is* political theology. Cultural exegesis of Christian worship makes explicit the political vision that is carried in our liturgy. The pastor theologian has responsibility to unpack the telos—the substantive, biblical vision of the Good—that is implicit in Christian worship.

Baptism, for example, signals our initiation into a people. Through baptism God constitutes a peculiar people that makes up a new polis, a new religio-political reality—what Peter Leithart calls a "baptismal city."[18] This new polis is marked by the obliteration of social class and aristocracies of blood. It is a motley crew: "Not many of you are wise by human standards, not many were powerful, not many were of noble birth," as Paul points out to the Christians in Corinth (1 Cor. 1:26 NRSV). But that is the mark of the city of God, God's upside-down kingdom: "God chose what is foolish in the

---

[16]See Ronald Beiner, *Theorizing Citizenship* (Albany: SUNY Press, 1994). Compare Aristotle, *Politics*, book 3.

[17]I should note that since I endorse Presbyterian forms of church government, I would not want to limit this role to the *teaching* pastor. Indeed, I do worry that the picture of the pastor theologian in Hiestand and Wilson, *Pastor Theologian*, seems to assume either a Baptistic or Episcopal model.

[18]Peter Leithart, *The Priesthood of the Plebs: A Theology of Baptism* (Eugene, OR: Wipf and Stock, 2003), 210.   •

world to shame the wise; God chose what is weak in the world to shame the strong; God chose what is low and despised in the world, things that are not, to reduce to nothing things that are" (1 Cor 1:27-28 NRSV). The citizens of the baptismal city are not just "have-nots"; they're "are-nots"! And yet they are chosen and commissioned as God's image bearers, God's princesses and priests who are empowered to be witnesses of a coming kingdom and charged with the renewal of the world.[19]

So baptism both makes and signifies a social reality, which is why it is situated in the context of gathered worship. While perhaps only one person is being baptized, all of us participate in this sacrament. We, the congregation, are not there merely as spectators. On a minimal level, the ritual should call to mind our own baptism, reminding us that we are citizens of another city. This is also why some churches have water at their entry, providing a tangible occasion for recalling *whose* we are. As we enter for prayer or worship, the stirring, touching and perhaps self-anointing with water is a visceral reminder that we are a marked people. Baptism is a practice that reconstitutes our relation to other social bodies such as the family and the state.

Similarly, in the culmination of worship in the Eucharist, we are invited to sit down for supper with the Creator of the universe, to dine with the King. But we are *all* invited to do so, which means we need to be reconciled to one another as well. Our communion with Christ spills over into communion as his body. There is a *social*, even *political*, reality enacted here: there are no box seats at this table, no reservations for VIPs, no filet mignon for those who can afford it while the rest eat crumbs from their table. The Lord's Table is a leveling reality in a world of increasing inequalities, an enacted vision of "a feast of rich food for all peoples, a banquet of aged wine" (Is 25:6 NIV). This strange feast is the civic rite of another city—the heavenly city—which is why it includes our pledge of allegiance, the Creed. In this communion our hearts are drawn into the very heart of God's triune life. Thus, in some ways the fulcrum of the liturgy is the *sursum corda*: "Lift up your hearts." In worship, "we lift them up to the Lord." The Lord's Supper isn't just a way to remember something that was accomplished in the past; it is a feast that nourishes our hearts. Here is an existential meal that retrains our deepest, most human hungers.

---

[19]See James K. A. Smith, *Desiring the Kingdom: Worship, Worldview, and Cultural Formation* (Grand Rapids: Baker Academic, 2009), 184-85.

Having been invited into the very life of the triune God—having been recreated in Christ, counseled by his word, and nourished by the bread of life—we are then sent into the world to tend and till God's good creation and to make disciples of every nation. The sending at the end of the worship service is a replay of the original commissioning of humanity as God's image bearers because in Christ—and in the practices of Christian worship—we can finally be the humans we were made to be. So we are sent out to inhabit the sanctuary of his creation as living, breathing images of God. We bear his image by carrying out our mission to cultivate creation and invite others to find their humanity in this Story. Thus worship concludes with a benediction that is both a blessing and a charge to go, but to go *in* and *with* the presence of the Son who will never leave us nor forsake us—to "go in peace to love and serve the Lord."

A CASE STUDY: AUGUSTINE AND BONIFACE

The pastor as political theologian—actually, every pastor—is a pastor not only of the *gathered* church but of the *sent* church. In Abraham Kuyper's terms, the pastor is called to shepherd not only the church as institute but the church as organism. The pastor theologian shepherds the work of citizens of the city of God who answer the call to enter the messy *permixtum* of the *saeculum*.

We can see a case study of this role in Augustine's ongoing relationship with Boniface. Boniface was a Roman general and African governor. In their ongoing correspondence we see a spiritual friendship in which Augustine the pastor theologian is not afraid to challenge and exhort the imperial soldier. But we also see a political practitioner who is hungry for theological wisdom, and not merely blessing or permission. In fact Boniface was the recipient of a long, intricate theological letter (Letter 185) about the Donatists that Augustine later, in his *retractationes*, described as a book (*The Correction of the Donatists*). After this long letter Augustine sent Boniface a short, simple note: "It is highly pleasing to me that amid your civic duties you do not neglect also to show concern for religion and desire that people found in separation and division be called back to the path of salvation and peace."[20]

---

[20]Augustine, *Letters 156–210*, ed. Boniface Ramsey, trans. Roland Teske, SJ, The Works of Saint Augustine, vol. II/3 (Hyde Park, NY: New City Press, 2004), 207 (*epist.* 185a). The quotations from Augustine's letters in the following paragraphs are from this edition.

In Letter 189, Augustine dashes off an eloquent articulation of the faith fused with theological counsel in response to a pressing request from Boniface for help (189.1). Augustine begins where he always does: with love. "This, then, I can say briefly: *Love the Lord your God with your whole heart and with your whole soul and with your whole strength*, and *Love your neighbor as yourself*. For this is the word that the Lord has shortened upon the earth [alluding to Rom 9:28]." He exhorts Boniface to "make progress" in this love by prayer and good works, bringing to fullness the love that has been shed abroad in our hearts (189.2). For it is "by this love," Augustine reminds him, that "all our holy forefathers, the patriarchs, prophets, and apostles pleased God. By this love all true martyrs fought against the devil to the point of shedding their blood, and because this love neither grew cold nor gave out in them, they conquered" (189.3). And it is the same love that is at work in Boniface, Augustine points out: "By this love all good believers daily make progress, desiring not to come to a kingdom of mortal beings but to the kingdom of heaven."

Augustine then speaks directly to some of Boniface's doubts and questions: "Do not suppose that no one can please God who as a soldier carries the weapons of war" (189.4). Augustine offers exemplars for Boniface to emulate: "Holy David"; the centurion who displayed great faith; the prayerful Cornelius who welcomed Peter; and others. But Augustine also offers vocational wisdom that is rooted in some fine points of eschatology. While some are called to lives of chastity and perfect continence and cloistered devotion, "*each person*, as the apostle says, *has his own gift from God, one this gift, another that* (1 Cor 7:7). Hence others fight invisible enemies by praying for you; you struggle against visible barbarians by fighting for them" (189.5). While we might long for the day when neither sort of battle is necessary— neither prayer warriors nor weaponized soldiers—we need a more nuanced eschatology, Augustine counsels. "Because in this world it is necessary that the citizens of the kingdom of heaven suffer temptation among those who are in error and are wicked so that they may be exercised and put to the test like gold in a furnace," Augustine says, "we ought not to want to live ahead of time with only the saints and the righteous." This is Augustine's way of saying, "Don't fall for the temptation of a realized eschatology."

So answer your call, Boniface, but take up your vocation in ways that are faithful, in a way that longs for kingdom come without thinking *you* can make it arrive. "Be, therefore, a peacemaker even in war in order that by conquering you might bring to the benefit of peace those whom you fight" (189.6). As he begins to draw the letter to a close, Augustine seems attentive to the unique temptations the soldier faces, attuned to the cultural liturgies of military life: "Let marital chastity adorn your conduct; let sobriety and frugality adorn it as well. For it is very shameful that lust conquer a man who is not conquered by another man and that he who is not conquered by the sword is overcome by wine" (189.7). He closes with an exercise in liturgical catechesis. Appealing to the Preface of the Mass ("Lift up your hearts." | "We lift them up to the Lord."), Augustine encourages Boniface to find in that a posture for life, for his work and vocation: "And, of course, when we hear that we should lift up our heart, we ought to respond truthfully what you know that we respond" (189.7). In other words: don't just *say* "we lift up our hearts"; *lift up your heart* in your work.

Augustine's affection for Boniface did not preclude admonishment. Letter 220 is an intriguing case. After the death of his wife, Boniface seems to be lost. He seems to be wavering in his sense of calling as a soldier and imperial servant, but he also seems wayward in his grief, making bad decisions. When they had last seen each other in Hippo, Augustine was so depleted by exhaustion he could barely speak. And so he follows up with a letter "to do with you what I ought to do with a man I love greatly in Christ" (220.2).[21]

After the death of his wife, Boniface wanted to abandon his public life and retreat to a monastery to devote himself to "holy leisure." But when he expressed this to Augustine and Alypius in private, they counseled otherwise. "What held you back from doing this," Augustine reminds him, "except that you considered, when we pointed it out, how much what you were doing was benefitting the churches of Christ? You were acting with this intention alone, namely, that they might lead *a quiet and tranquil life*, as the apostle says, *in all piety and chastity* (1 Tim. 2:2),[22] defended from the attacks of the

---

[21] Augustine, *Letters*, vol. II/4 (Hyde Park, NY: New City Press, 2005).
[22] Augustine often appeals to 1 Tim 2:2 as the goal of Christian involvement in public life, as he does in *City of God* 19.26: "It is important for us also that this people should possess this peace in this life, since so long as the two cities are intermingled, we also make us of the peace of Babylon—although the People of God is by faith set free from Babylon, so that in the meantime they are only pilgrims in the midst of her. That is why the Apostle instructs the Church to pray for kings of that city and those in high positions, adding these words: 'that we may lead a quiet and peaceful life with all devotion and love.'" Augustine, *City of God*, trans. Henry Bettenson, ed. G. R. Evans (New York: Penguin, 2003).

barbarians" (220.3). These pastor theologians exhorted him to remain steadfast in his public life; indeed, in some ways *their* pastoral/theological work depended on his public work as governor and defender.

Though Boniface continued to answer the call to public office, the weakness of grief seemed to compromise his moral judgment. Thus Augustine confronts him for abandoning continence, for being "conquered by concupiscence" (220.4), and for becoming embroiled in webs of intrigue. Augustine forthrightly reminds him of the need for repentance and penance. And then Augustine the pastor theologian presses Boniface theologically to be more resolute in the execution of his public duties: "What am I to say about the plundering of Africa that the African barbarians carry out with no opposition, while you are tied up in your difficulties and make no arrangement by which this disaster might be averted?" (220.7). While Boniface is trying to secure his status in a contested imperial court, he is in fact shirking his duties to the common good (see: election season). "Who would have believed," Augustine asks,

> who would have feared, that with Boniface as head of the imperial body-guards and stationed in Africa as count of Africa with so great an army and such great power, who as a tribune pacified all those peoples by battling them and terrifying them with a few allies, the barbarians would now have become so venturesome, would have made such advances, would have ravaged, robbed, and devastated such large areas full of people? Who did not say, when you assumed power as count, that the barbarians of Africa would not only be subdued but would even be tributaries of the Roman state? (220.7)

Augustine the pastor theologian is mounting a theological case for the Roman general to man his station, do his job, be faithfully present as count and governor. Behind his counsel is a crucial theological distinction between the earthly city and the city of God. There is not a hint of the "Holy Roman Empire"-ism for which Augustine is often mistakenly blamed. To the contrary, Augustine relativizes Rome without demonizing it. So whatever disputes or frustrations Boniface might have with Rome, he still owes a debt: "If the Roman empire has given you good things," Augustine says, "albeit earthly and transitory ones, because it is earthly, not heavenly, and cannot give save what it has in its control—if, then it has conferred good things upon you, do not repay evil with evil" (220.8).

In these letters we hear something of Augustine's hopes for Boniface and those like him: the hope for faithful agents of the coming kingdom who answer the call to public life, who administer the common good, in this *saeculum* of our waiting. Such public servants bear heavy burdens on our behalf and find themselves pressed on every side. Many, like Boniface, are honestly hungry for theological counsel and scriptural wisdom for a messy world. The pastor theologian needs not only the theological chops to answer their questions with a robust theology of public life; above all, the pastor theologian needs to love. Thus Augustine closes his letter to Boniface: "Love commanded me to write these things to you, my most beloved son; by that love I love you by God's standards, not by those of the world" (220.12). If Augustine enjoins Boniface to love not the world, it's because he loves him, and loves him enough to equip him with a rich political theology.

3

The Pastor Theologian as Public Theologian

KEVIN J. VANHOOZER

"FEED MY SHEEP" (JN 21:17).[1] *Feed* my sheep. You've heard of the sous-chef, the second-in-command in a kitchen under the head chef. Well, pastors are *sous-shepherds*, seconds to the Lord Jesus. Jesus is "the good shepherd [who] lays down his life for the sheep" (Jn 10:11; compare 10:14). According to Hebrews 13:20, he is "the great shepherd of the sheep" and, as the great shepherd, Jesus self-identifies with God in his relation to Israel: "He will tend his flock like a shepherd" (Is 40:11). With David we therefore confess, "The LORD is my shepherd" (Ps 23:1). His sheep hear his voice (Jn 10:27), which is why pastors must minister his word rather than somebody else's. Pastors participate in the all-important task of good shepherding by watching over places where *people*, the sheep in question, fellowship in God's presence, enjoy his mercies and glorify his name.[2] To feed Jesus' sheep is to guard, nurture and lead *people*—all those who gather together as followers of the Way.

"The pastor-theologian should be evangelicalism's default public intellectual, with preaching the preferred public mode of theological interpretation of

---

[1]Unless otherwise indicated, Scripture quotations in this chapter are from the English Standard Version.

[2]Ryan Lister associates place with *dominion*, people with *dynasty* and God's presence with *dwelling* (Lister, *The Presence of God: Its Place in the Storyline of Scripture and the Story of Our Lives* [Wheaton, IL: Crossway, 2015], 65). Lister borrows the notions of *dominion* and *dynasty* from Stephen G. Dempster's *Dominion and Dynasty: A Theology of the Hebrew Bible* (Downers Grove, IL: InterVarsity Press, 2003) but notes that Dempster does not appreciate the centrality of *dwelling/presence*.

Scripture."[3] The well-being of the church, and its mission, depends on pastors recovering their vocation and identity as local public theologians. This involves thinking hard not only about pastors but also about churches. We must ask what pastors are for, but also, "Why is there church rather than nothing?"

"LOCATION, LOCATION, LOCATION" AS ECCLESIOLOGICAL AXIOM

The church is a gathering of people, an assembly brought near to God by the blood of Jesus Christ (Eph 2:13), raised up with Christ "and seated . . . with him in the heavenly places" (Eph 2:6). To be part of Christ's church is to belong to a fellowship gathered around God's heavenly throne.[4] This same fellowship also exists on earth in any number of particular places.

In selling property, and in doing church, the basic principle is "location, location, location." Three "locations" in one "property" (*ousia*): this is not simply proverbial but Trinitarian wisdom! The church is one but exists in three locations: in heaven, triumphant; on earth, militant; in particular earthly places, *habitant*.

In recent topology, place is less a physical location than a structure of lived human experience, a way of being in the world. Why is there church rather than nothing? Because the risen Lord, the Prince of Peace, wants local embassies, people in particular places, to bear witness to and extend on earth the kingdom that is now in heaven.[5] "For where two or three are gathered in my name, there am I among them" (Mt 18:20). The local church is "wholly the church, but not the whole church."[6] The people—especially the space *between* people—are the place where Christ reigns, his domain or sphere of influence, for it is in and among and through the people that Christ's exercises his lordly influence and manifests the power of resurrection life.

Place enables bodies to dwell in and engage the world.[7] Unlike empty space (if such a thing exists), place is location overwritten by human action

[3]Kevin J. Vanhoozer, "Interpreting Scripture between the Rock of Biblical Studies and the Hard Place of Systematic Theology: The State of the Evangelical (dis)Union," in Richard Lints, ed., *Renewing the Evangelical Mission* (Grand Rapids: Eerdmans, 2013), 224.

[4]See D. Broughton Knox, "The Church," in *Selected Works, Volume II: Church and Ministry* (Kingsford, Australia: Matthias Media, 2003), 19-22.

[5]See further Jonathan Leeman, *Political Church: The Local Assembly as Embassy of Christ's Rule* (Downers Grove, IL: InterVarsity Press, 2016).

[6]Jean Jacques von Allmen, "L'église locale parmi les autres églises locales," *Irénikon* 43 (1970): 512.

[7]See the essays in Wilfred M. McClay and Ted V. McAllister, eds., *Why Place Matters: Geography, Identity, and Civic Life in Modern America* (New York: Encounter Books, 2014).

and experience. The pastor is a social geographer, one who wants to "write" the gospel onto the minds and hearts of a people gathered in a particular place. The pastor of a local church is a place-maker whose mission is to make a congregation into a fit dwelling place for the Spirit of Christ, a place in which certain activities will enact corporate heavenly citizenship under historical earthly conditions. The pastor wants to help each member of the flock to find his or her place in the world, to know how to follow Christ here and now as his disciple.

"And in the same region there were shepherds out in the field, keeping watch over their flock by night" (Lk 2:8). This familiar verse from the Christmas story is also a beautiful picture of the pastor theologian at work. "In the same region," in a certain place; "there were shepherds," pastors; "keeping watch over," pastoring; "their flock," a local congregations of believers.

Pastors are shepherds who lead local flocks, sometimes "beside still waters" (Ps 23:2), but more often through rough waters. In particular, pastors ought to lead their flocks deeper into the waters of baptism, deeper into what the triune God is doing in and through Jesus' death and resurrection. This is the way they fulfill the Great Commission to "make disciples of all nations, baptizing them in the name of the Father and of the Son and of the Holy Spirit, teaching them to observe all that I have commanded you" (Mt 28:19-20). Pastors make disciples by leading people into what the triune God is doing in Christ. To put it in more contemporary terms, *pastors teach people to lean into Christ and to live out Christ's life*. To lean into Christ is to "grow up in every way into him who is the head" (Eph 4:15). To lean into Christ is to learn to lean *on* the everlasting arms, as the old hymn puts it (compare Deut 33:27)— to "trust in the LORD with all your heart and lean *not* on your own understanding" (Prov 3:5 NIV, emphasis added). Pastors lead their flocks into maturity in Christ. It's a matter of learning to live *into* Christ in order to live Christ *out*.

WHY CALL PASTORS PUBLIC THEOLOGIANS?

Given the fact that all pastoral ministry is local church ministry, why should we describe pastors using the additional words *theologian* and *public*?

Theologian. We have for too long been operating with a dichotomy between the academy and the church. We have boxed theology into a theoretical science, a specialization, and the pastorate into a practical sphere, a professionalization. The result is that we no longer encourage the smartest students in seminary to get their PhDs so that they might serve the church, and at the same time getting a PhD to serve in the academy is viewed as not all that useful. I like the story of the mother who introduces her little girl to a newly minted PhD in theology. "Can you operate on people now?" asks the little girl. To which the mother (too) quickly replies: "Oh no, he's the kind of doctor that can't help anyone." So much for theologians as doctors of the church!

Jerusalem, we have a problem. On the one hand, we have impractical theologians. On the other hand, we have pastors who are part of what Gerald Hiestand and Todd Wilson describe as "intellectual middle management": they can translate scholarship but can't do it themselves.[8] Healthy bodies of Christ need both the red blood cells of pastoral vitality and the little gray cells of theological intelligence.

At this point rich rulers—or rather poor pastors—may become exceeding sorrowful, for they are very busy (compare Lk 18:23). Being a pastor is hard enough as it is: the *New York Times* reported in 2010 that 50 percent of pastors feel unable to meet the needs of the job, with 90 percent saying they feel unqualified or poorly prepared for ministry. How dare I suggest one more thing pastors need to do! It would take several weeks to work through Herman Bavinck's *Reformed Dogmatics* and at least several months to read Karl Barth's *Church Dogmatics*, even if there were nothing else to do.

Andrew Wilson published an article on the *Christianity Today* website in September 2015 called "Why Being a Pastor-Scholar Is Nearly Impossible."[9] In it, he pointed out that time is only one issue. He goes on to identify three tensions that have contributed to pastor-scholars becoming an endangered species: (1) the university-church tension, (2) the specialist-generalist tension and (3) the theoretical-practical tension (what motivates scholars is usually not the question, "What shall we do?").

These are fair points, but Wilson is speaking of pastor-scholars, not pastor theologians. In suggesting that pastors are theologians, I am not

---

[8]See Gerald Hiestand and Todd Wilson, *The Pastor Theologian: Resurrecting an Ancient Vision* (Grand Rapids: Zondervan, 2015), 11.
[9]Andrew Wilson, "Why Being a Pastor-Scholar Is Nearly Impossible," www.christianitytoday.com /ct/2015/september-web-only/why-being-pastor-scholar-is-nearly-impossible.html.

saying they should be scholars. Theology is the project of seeking, speaking and showing understanding of what the triune God is doing in and through Jesus Christ for the sake of the whole world, and this is far too important to be left to academics.

Public. Why qualify pastor theologians with a further adjective: *public?* "Public" means having to do with people in general or in community. Pastors are public theologians because they work in and for local assemblies of the people of God for the sake of people everywhere. People are the medium with which the pastor works to form God-glorifying lives, both in individuals (saints) and communities (the communion of saints). Theology is a local public work; it's first and foremost *God's* work "to bring into being a people under his rule in his place."[10] The church is a living temple; what the church enacts in its life together is a theological building project—the formation of a people set apart to love God and their neighbors as themselves. Pastors are public theologians because they work with people to do lived theology. This is hard work; it's harder to work with people than ideas. If you want a real challenge, don't go into academic theology; go into the pastorate. But God's people—local churches—are the public places where the life of Christ is remembered, celebrated, explored and exhibited. Stated simply, the pastor's task is to help congregations become what they are in Christ.

Pastors should be evangelicalism's default *public intellectuals*, as distinguished from academic scholars.[11] The mandate of the public intellectual is to speak meaningfully about broad topics of ultimate social concern and to address central issues about what it means to flourish as human individuals and communities. Alexander Solzhenitsyn was speaking as a public intellectual in his 1978 commencement address at Harvard University. It was a prophetic talk, a searching critique of the spirituality of modern Western culture. He spoke of Evil (with a capital *E*!) and criticized the West's tendency to posit the autonomy of human beings over against human responsibility to God.

There are intellectuals in both the academy and society, but they are few and far between. Most scholars are specialists who know a lot about a little,

---

[10]J. G. Millar, "People of God," in *New Dictionary of Biblical Theology*, ed. T. D. Alexander and Brian S. Rosner (Downers Grove, IL: InterVarsity Press, 2000), 684.

[11]For a helpful typology of the various ways one can combine the roles of pastor and scholar, see Michael Kruger's "Should You be a Pastor or a Professor?," http://michaeljkruger.com/should-you-be-a-pastor-or-a-professor-thinking-through-the-options.

but are tongue tied when it comes to the big questions. Pastors address the big questions—of life and death, meaning and meaninglessness, the physical and the spiritual—on a regular basis, and have to do so in a way that communicates to non-academics.

What does this have to do with shepherding? One distinguishing mark of the shepherd also characterizes intellectuals: "The shepherd characteristically is 'out ahead' of [the sheep], not only guiding them, but looking out, by way of anticipation, for their welfare."[12] What threatens the flock of Jesus Christ is not lions, bears or wolves (1 Sam 17:34-35) but false religion, incorrect doctrine and ungodly practices. Those who lead need in some ways to be out ahead of their congregations. Pastors don't have to be academic scholars, but they do have to be grounded in biblical theology, the big redemptive-historical picture that ties Old and New Testament together and focuses on Christ. It also helps to be culturally competent. Paul knew the cultural situation at Corinth, to be sure, but he was grounded in the gospel: "For I decided to know nothing among you except Jesus Christ and him crucified" (1 Cor 2:2).

Think of pastor theologians also as *organic intellectuals*.[13] An organic intellectual is neither a scholar nor a genius but someone who is able to articulate the needs, convictions and aspirations of the community to which he or she belongs, the evangelical mind of the body of Christ. Pope Francis describes the theologian as "primarily a son of his people. He cannot and does not wish to ignore them. He knows his people, their language, their roots, their histories, their tradition."[14] The organic intellectual knows that ideas matter—they have the power to give shape to certain forms of life. But the organic intellectual is less an abstract theorist and more a social activist, one who organizes and preserves the integrity of the church as the city of God by helping congregations to read cultures and adopt practices befitting citizens of the gospel.

---

[12]Thomas Oden, *Pastoral Theology: Essentials of Ministry* (New York: HarperOne, 1983), 51.

[13]I am borrowing the term *organic intellectual* from Antonio Gramsci, a twentieth century Italian literary and social critic. See especially his *Selections from the Prison Notebooks*, ed. Quentin Hoare and Geoffrey Newell Smith (New York: International Publishers, 1971).

[14]"Video Message of His Holiness Pope Francis to Participants in an International Theological Congress Held at the Pontifical Catholic University of Argentina," http://w2.vatican.va /content/francesco/en/messages/pont-messages/2015/documents/papa-francesco_20150903 _videomessaggio-teologia-buenos-aires.html.

Pastor theologians don't have to be the smartest people in the room—but then again, neither did the apostles. When Peter and John were arrested for preaching the gospel and dragged before the Sanhedrin, they had to do some impromptu—and inspired—public speaking: "This Jesus is the stone that was rejected by you, the builders, which has become the cornerstone. And there is salvation in no one else" (Acts 4:11-12). When the high priests, elders and scribes—all highly trained in rabbinic schools—saw the boldness of Peter and John, they were astonished, for they "perceived that they were uneducated, common men" (Acts 4:13). Peter and John were not geniuses but apostles: they knew something that the Sanhedrin did not know ("He is risen!"), and they knew it not because they were clever but because they had been told.

Pastor theologians also know something others don't, and they know it because the Bible tells them so. What they know is something quite particular, but it has enormous, even universal, implications. The organic intellectual pastor theologian knows one big thing: what the triune God is doing in Christ through the Spirit to create a people for his treasured possession (Ex 19:5; Deut 7:6; 14:2; 26:8; Mal 3:17; Tit 2:14; 1 Pet 2:9). Like Solzhenitsyn, pastor theologians are generalists who give voice to faith's understanding of the meaning of life—the life hidden in Christ (Col 3:3). Yes, pastor theologians know something particular and definite, but strictly speaking it is not "specialized" knowledge. The pastor theologian is rather *a generalist who specializes in relating all things to the gospel of Jesus Christ*. Pastors are local public theologians—organic intellectuals who represent the mind of Christ in order to animate, and watch over, local assemblies of Christ's body.

What Public Theologians (Pastors) Are For

According to C. S. Lewis, the church exists for no other reason "but to draw men and women into Christ, to make them little Christs. If they are not doing that, all the cathedrals, clergy, mission, sermons, even the Bible itself, are simply a waste of time."[15] Call it the Great Pastoral Commission: to make disciples who come to share the heart, mind and hands of Jesus Christ.

In general: making disciples. Let me begin by making a few general observations about how pastors go about fulfilling this commission.

---

[15]C. S. Lewis, *Mere Christianity* (New York: Touchstone, 1996), 171.

Pastor theologians minister reality. In philosophy, metaphysics is the study of reality: what is. Pastor theologians minister reality insofar as they communicate *what is* in Christ. What pastor theologians have to say that no one else has to say concerns what the triune God is doing in Jesus Christ through the Spirit to renew creation.

To minister the gospel is to minister reality: new life in Christ. Whereas philosophy for Martin Heidegger was all about being-towards-death—learning to cope authentically with mortality—it is the great privilege of pastor theologians to represent in word and deed the joy that accompanies the proclamation of the gospel: call it being-towards-resurrection. Pastor theologians are representatives of the strange new reality of the gospel, emissaries of the kingdom of God that has already broken in to the old order of things. Pastors minister reality because they bear witness to *what is in Christ*, and there is no more enduring reality than that.

Pastor theologians minister understanding. "Feed my sheep." Sheep shall not live by grass alone, but by every word that comes from the mouth of God (compare Mt 4:4). The pastor theologian's first and foremost task is the ministry of the word (*diakonia tou logou;* Acts 6:4). Theologians minister understanding by helping followers of Jesus to be better followers of Scripture, and that means grasping its overarching story. Pastors help people to become biblically literate, to understand the big redemptive-historical picture and their own place in the story, especially their identity in Christ.

It is not enough to know facts about the Bible. Disciples need *canon sense*: the ability to interpret particular passages of Scripture in light of the whole. Canon sense means knowing where we are in the flow of redemptive history. To summarize the plot as simply as possible: God "meets" (creates) world; God loses world; God gets world back; God and world live happily ever after. Biblical literacy also means helping people to read their own world—their own particular cultural context—in light of the overarching drama of redemption.

To minister understanding is to help people make connections: between the parts of the Bible and the overarching story; between the Bible and the world in which they live; between who they are and who God calls them to be. Pastors are called not to practice academic theology but to minister theological understanding, helping people to interpret the Scriptures, their cultures and their own lives in relation to God's great work of redemption summed up *in Christ*. Again, the theologian is a generalist who speaks about things in general (the renewed created order) in relation to one thing in particular: the gospel of Jesus Christ.

Too often we associate theology with past doctrinal formulations and the pastoral ministry with exciting new ways of doing things. Pastor theologians must guard against two temptations: on the one hand, a pride in the past (our way of doing things) that condemns everything new; on the other, an indifference to or embarrassment about the past that condones everything new. The faithful way forward is to take our bearings from Scripture as we navigate our way through the present. Biblical literacy should lead to cultural literacy.

Culture is the world of meaning in which people dwell, a world that consists in various works of meaning that communicate a society's beliefs and values (for example, books, films, paintings, ads, songs, fashion, cars, sports, buildings, meals, games and so on). The institutions of society are its hardware, but culture is society's software, its "program" for cultivating humanity and shaping its freedom. Pastor theologians must educate their people about culture, for culture is in the full-time business of educating people, cultivating their humanity. In other words, culture is in the business of spiritual formation; what culture ultimately educates and forms is not only the mind, but the heart.[16]

Cultural literacy is the ability to make sense of what is happening in contemporary society, the ability to read cultural texts and make sense of cultural trends. The purpose of cultural literacy is to achieve understanding of the present moment. We need rightly to understand what is happening, here and now, in our locale, in order to know how those whose citizenship is in heaven ought rightly to respond. Cultural literacy refers to what Christians need to know about their everyday culture in order to be effective cultural agents for Christ's kingdom. Cultural literacy is part and parcel of a Christian's dual citizenship, being in the world (being-towards-death) but not of it (being-towards-resurrection).

I've said that it's important for pastors to understand God's word and God's world, but it's also important to understand people and the challenges they face in their particular places. That's why the *local* church is so important.

---

[16]See further James K. A. Smith, *Desiring the Kingdom: Worship, Worldview, and Cultural Formation* (Grand Rapids: Baker, 2009).

People are the medium with which pastors do theology, and people are finite; they occupy only one place and time at a time. One valuable way to understand culture and people is by reading fiction; I wish more pastors did so. Neil Plantinga encourages us to start small: one novel a year.[17] Newcomers can start with Marilynne Robinson's *Gilead*.

Pastor theologians minister wisdom. One of the main tasks of the pastor theologian is to deliberate, discern and then demonstrate what it means to be a disciple in today's world, in the time and place where people live. Pastor theologians make disciples by helping people who appreciate every spiritual blessing they have in Christ (Eph 1:3), people who learn how to participate in the reality of the risen Christ, to live into—and then through his Spirit live *out*—the life of Christ in their particular places.

This is the goal of understanding: to embody the heart and mind of Christ by living out the life of Christ in us. The gospel indicative—"you *are* in Christ"—contains a tacit imperative: conform to Christ. Joyfully participate in what the triune God is doing in Christ. Living to God, living into Christ, living out the life of Christ through the Spirit: this is the essence of Trinitarian (and pastoral) theology.

In particular: ministering Christ in three thoroughly theological acts. I turn now to consider some particular ways in which pastors do public theology, focusing on the sermon, liturgy and the local church.

The sermon proclaims what the triune God is doing in Christ. Theology's special vocation is to proclaim and explain what the triune God is doing in Christ to make all things new: "In Christ God was reconciling the world to himself" (2 Cor 5:19). Most fundamentally, what is in Christ is the fullness of the deity (Col 2:9), God going out of himself in order to draw what is not God (human beings) into God's own life. In Christ there is true deity, true humanity, the reconciliation of God and humanity, the light, life and love of God, the church and much more.

Pastors are evangelists—proclaimers of the gospel—and there is nothing more theological than the gospel of Jesus Christ. Proclamation is more than verbal; pastors must embody the compassion of God and the truth of the gospel, especially the love of other people and the joy of being-towards-

---

[17]Cornelius Plantinga, *Reading for Preaching: The Preacher in Conversation with Storytellers, Biographers, Poets, and Journalists* (Grand Rapids: Eerdmans, 2014), 42.

resurrection. In the book I coauthored with Owen Strachan, *The Pastor as Public Theologian*, I wrote about how pastors minister the gospel word of reconciliation through personal counseling and pastoral visitation; here I want to say something about proclamation as preaching (and teaching).

Preaching is a microcosm of pastoral ministry, "the most public of pastoral acts."[18] As the sermon goes, so goes the (holy) nation. Shallow sermons foster shallow congregations. Words are our most sophisticated medium of communication; through words we can share both simple experiences and complex ideas. Pastor theologians minister the word because that is precisely what Jesus did: "Jesus came . . . preaching the gospel of God" (Mk 1:14 RSV). I have time here only to highlight three functions that explain why the sermon is the cutting edge of public theology, three reasons why the pulpit "leads the world" and may be the best means of staying out ahead of the flock.

First, preaching fosters biblical literacy, biblical-theological competency and canon sense. There is nothing like the disciplined exposition of Scripture to help congregations learn to understand how the various parts of Scripture relate to the whole and to the person who stands at the center of it all: Jesus Christ.

Second, preaching fosters theological literacy, the ability to read (and, if necessary, critique) our world—our history, our culture—in the light of God's presence and activity. While the primary task of preaching is to unfold God's Word, throwing light on the church's contemporary situation is often an important byproduct. In expositing God's Word, pastor theologians give their congregations a powerful means to discern, and then cast down, the idols of our time. Those who are unaware of culture are doomed to repeat it.

Third, preaching draws the local church, here and now, into relationship with the bracing reality of Jesus Christ, directing disciples to adopt beliefs, values and practices that correspond to what is in Christ in order to get real. The sermon is not a secondhand description of what is happening in a historical galaxy far, far away. No, gospel preaching proclaims the true story of the world, acknowledging that all things are "from him and through him and to him" (Rom 11:36). The sermon is the heavy artillery in the pastor

---

[18]Oden, *Pastoral Theology*, 127.

theologian's arsenal; it is the best frontal assault on imaginations held captive by other stories promising other ways to the good life.

A sermon must not only say *what is in Christ* but also communicate its *excellence*. Preaching must not simply inform but transport us. To say *what is in Christ* is to enumerate and explore every spiritual blessing with which we have been blessed (Eph 1:3; compare Rom 15:27). A sermon that describes our life "hidden with Christ in God" (Col 3:3) appeals to our imagination so that we can see, and practically *taste*, reality as it truly is: not a mechanical universe in perpetual motion but a divine creation in the midst of labor pains, where the new in Christ is coming forth from the old in Adam. Preaching *inscribes* the gospel on listening hearts and *inserts* listeners into the story. Preaching is a practice "by which the church is taken into the very life of God."[19]

Liturgy celebrates what the triune God is doing in Christ. Pastor theologians are ministers of understanding, first, of the Word, but secondly, of sacrament. Alongside the sermon, the liturgy too is a quintessentially theological act. Pastor theologians are responsible for leading congregations in celebrating what is in Christ. Many pastors may not think of themselves as liturgists, but technically this is what rightly ordered corporate worship is. Liturgy literally means "the work of the people," from the Greek *leitourgia* (= *leitos*, "public" + *ergos*, "work"). Liturgy is public theology, ordering corporate expressions of Christian praise and worship.

The people of God gather together in particular places to celebrate what the triune God is doing in Christ and to be built up in Christ so that they can become the kind of people who can worship God in spirit and truth in all places. To celebrate what is in Christ is to reorder our ideas about and realign our hearts toward what is ultimately real.

I would be remiss not to mention the Lord's Supper, which is both proclamation and celebration of the gospel (1 Cor 11:26). When we remember Jesus' atoning death on the cross by sharing the bread and wine, thereby recalling Israel's Passover meal as well, we act out a verbal, visual and altogether visceral summary of the whole drama of redemption. Moreover, to celebrate the Lord's Supper is literally to get a precious taste of ultimate

---

[19]L. Roger Owens, *The Shape of Participation: A Theology of Church Practices* (Eugene, OR: Cascade, 2010), 67.

reality. For what is in Christ, what is ultimately real, is *communion,* with God and with one another. The Lord's Supper is a dramatic exhibit of the unity that exists in Christ. It is a powerful act of public theology that gets at the heart of what the gospel is all about. As such, it too is a quintessentially theological act.

The local church demonstrates what the triune God is doing in Christ. I hope you now see why I think theology is less an intellectual achievement to admire from afar than an embodied interpretation of our faith, staged by local churches and overseen by pastors—theologians who work on, with and among people. We are, as Paul says, to "put on" Christ (Rom 13:14; Gal 3:27). This putting on refers to a *costume*: we are to be clothed in righteousness (Eph 6:14) and humility (1 Pet 5:5). It also refers to a *production*: "Be imitators of me, as I am of Christ" (1 Cor 11:1). This is perhaps the ultimate vocation of the pastor theologian: to help dress and direct the church, assisting believers to get into their God-given roles and equipping them actively to play their parts. Theology ultimately exists to serve and preserve the integrity of the church's "exhibit" to the world (1 Cor 4:9).

Pastors, as *sous-shepherds*, lead God's people into becoming local congregations whose community life and practices bodily display the realities of the gospel, especially reconciliation in Christ. This is why the church exists: to make disciples who, by their life together, witness to redemption in Christ, the forgiveness of sins and multiethnic reconciliation. We do this by mounting local productions of peace and reconciliation, justice and truth. The pastor is an assistant director of what is ultimately a local theater of the gospel, helping individual disciples and believing communities to learn and then perform their parts: to act out the heart and mind of Christ as the body of Christ. The pastor theologian forms the local congregation to be a Christ to its community. The church public exists for the world public.

The local church is a practical demonstration of what is in Christ, an embodied apology for the wisdom of the cross. When the church becomes what it is—a fellowship of the Holy Spirit—it becomes a lived plausibility structure. Christian faith proves true when the people of God willingly submit to every kind of critical testing, intellectual and existential, and endure to the end, rejoicing in the assurance that suffering produces endurance, character and a hope that does not disappoint (Rom 5:3-5).

The Lord's Supper is both summation and demonstration, *summa* and *apologia,* of the gospel, for in celebrating the Supper the church not only proclaims but enacts in embodied fashion both union and communion, the ultimate reality of *what is in Christ.* Jesus himself taught about the importance of this aspect of public theology: "By this all people will know that you are my disciples, if you have love for one another" (Jn 13:35). In the final analysis, the best apologetic is the whole people of God doing communion as church and performing works of love to the world, demonstrating the truth of what is, and what will be, in Christ.

CONCLUSION: THE PASTOR THEOLOGIAN IN THE ECONOMY OF PUBLIC WORKS

Pastors are local theologians in the triune economy of public works. The challenge is to understand what it is that pastors have to say and do that is distinct from all other types of public service. Arguably there is no more urgent need than for pastors who know how to keep watch over and stay ahead of their flock, by day and by night. There is no greater challenge than to build people up into Christ. The smartest people in any room would therefore do well to consider becoming pastors rather than professors—if, that is, they want to do something really challenging and truly important.

The ultimate end of theology, as with all things human, is the glory of God. However, theology's proximate end is to build up the people of God precisely to equip them to realize their ultimate end: glorifying God in everything that they do, say and suffer. Pastor theologians are artisans in the house of God, overseeing a work not merely of urban but cosmic renewal as they anticipate, through diverse practices of reconciliation, the time when Christ will be all in all.

The pastor is the resident theologian of a local church whose great privilege and responsibility is working with people, ministering the reality of Jesus Christ in order to build people up into the house of God. To minister the reality of Christ is to do more (but not less) than inform others about him. The apostle Paul speaks of the "surpassing worth" of knowing Christ (Phil 3:8). Paul wants to know the Christ, the whole Christ, and nothing but the Christ. The pastor theologian communicates this knowledge not to swell people's heads but to transform their hearts. Ultimately what pastor theologians want people to know is "the love of Christ that surpasses knowledge" (Eph 3:19).

The pastor theologian is the organic intellectual of the body of Christ. We might be tempted to say the pastor theologian is the "brains" of the operation—the body of Christ—but this is only partially correct. Better to see the pastor as embodying the mind, heart and hands of Jesus in order to communicate the fullness of Christ. Alistair Roberts, a British blogger, goes further and suggests that the pastor theologian is the backbone and immune system of the church too. As the backbone, the pastor ensures that the body is communicating with its Head. The backbone is also "responsible for maintaining the form of the body," its good posture, so to speak. Theology strengthens the backbone of the church by encouraging pastors to stand tall, resisting the winds of prevailing cultural doctrines and the waves of social pressure that challenge the church today. And as the immune system, the pastor theologian is responsible for ensuring the body's healthy operation, especially by identifying and attacking bacteria and viruses that threaten to invade and weaken it.

Sous-shepherds, organic intellectuals, ministers of reality, ecclesial backbones. These are some of the images I've used to describe pastors as public theologians who lead local congregations. I don't know which, if any, of these comparisons is the most memorable or striking. But, whichever image you prefer, do remember and rejoice in the ascended Christ's gift of pastor teachers to the church (Eph 4:11)—disciple-making and body-building theologians who proclaim what is in Christ and help people grow up into the fullness of Christ (Eph 4:15). "Feed my sheep."

4

The Pastor Theologian as Ecclesial Theologian

GERALD HIESTAND

WITH A BIT OF OPTIMISM, FUTURE GENERATIONS might generously term 2015 the "Year of the Pastor Theologian." The conference at which these papers were presented, the publication of two monographs,[1] and a flurry of online essays all indicated a renewed interest in the idea of the pastor theologian.

However, not all of this attention was uncritically positive. Two essays in particular called into question the viability of the pastor scholar. Andrew Wilson wrote an essay for *Christianity Today* entitled "Why Being a Pastor Scholar is Nearly Impossible," and Mark Jones wrote a similarly themed piece for *Reformation 21* and called it "Pastor Scholar? Not Likely."[2] A primary point of both essays was that the work of an academic scholar is of such a demanding nature that it cannot easily (Wilson) or realistically (Jones) be combined with the work of a pastor—also a demanding vocation. Something has to give; either one will be an effective scholar and a poor pastor or a poor scholar and an effective pastor.

---

[1]Gerald Hiestand and Todd Wilson, *The Pastor Theologian: Resurrecting an Ancient Vision* (Grand Rapids: Zondervan, 2015), and Kevin J. Vanhoozer and Owen Strachan, *The Pastor as Public Theologian: Reclaiming a Lost Vision* (Grand Rapids: Baker Academic, 2015).

[2]Andrew Wilson, "Why Being a Pastor Scholar Is Nearly Impossible," www.christianitytoday .com/ct/2015/september-web-only/why-being-pastor-scholar-is-nearly-impossible.html; Mark Jones, "Pastor Scholar? Not Likely," www.reformation21.org/blog/2015/09/pastorscholar -impossible.php.

While the critiques in these essays are valid, both miss the mark with respect to the vision of the Center for Pastor Theologians. ⌐We are not suggesting that pastors should write academic scholarship. Rather, we are suggesting that pastors are uniquely positioned to make ecclesially focused contributions to contemporary theological discourse. In other words, we envision (some) pastors writing what we call *ecclesial* theology—a distinct cousin of both *academic* theology and *popular* theology.⌐

We made an initial attempt in our book *The Pastor Theologian* to distinguish between academic and ecclesial theology.[3] However, since contemporary theological scholarship is now almost exclusively academic, the popular imagination has a difficult time conceiving of any other kind of theological scholarship than academic scholarship; the terms *academic* and *scholarly* have become virtual synonyms. Given this difficulty, I aim in this essay to clarify further the differences between academic and ecclesial theology, with a view to clarifying the role of the ecclesial theologian.

Toward this end, I invite you to consider four basic spheres of theological scholarship: research, systemization, ecclesial significance articulation and ecclesial implementation. These four spheres represent the fields of research that every theological project must engage if it is to be meaningful for the church. In what follows I attempt to classify these four spheres, and show how academic theologians and pastor theologians are each uniquely positioned to operate in complementary yet distinct spheres. Since I intend to build on what we have already written, I will begin by summarizing the main lines of our book. From there I will move to an articulation of the four spheres and show how these spheres inform our understanding of ecclesial theology and the work of the pastor theologian.

SUMMARY OF *THE PASTOR THEOLOGIAN*

We take it as a starting premise in our book that the pastor theologian has fallen on hard times. ⌐By this we mean that the pastoral community is no longer—in the main—considered to be, by its own self-understanding or the understanding of the academy, the theological center of gravity in the church⌐ It is difficult to prove empirically the truthfulness of this claim, but

---

[3]Hiestand and Wilson, *Pastor Theologian*, 88-101.

anecdotal evidence is abundant. Recently, I was invited to give an address to the student theological society of a Christian Bible college. This group of motivated theology students meets once a week to discuss the latest issues in theology. Most weeks they invite a guest theologian to speak about a specific issue. After I gave my presentation, the student president said to me, "You are the first pastor that we've invited to the group in the two years I've been doing this."

That should give us all a moment of pause. At a theological college that is training men and women for ministry in the church, the student theological society had been conditioned to look away from the pastoral community for theological leadership. That's not an indictment against any particular college; the orientation of the students was, I believe, reflective of the sort of "pastor vs. theologian" bifurcation that can be seen across the breadth of contemporary evangelicalism.[4] Of course, it is possible to find shining exceptions to this rather dark rule, but I suspect most of us concerned about such things will agree that the pastoral vocation is no longer sufficiently conceived of in distinctly theological terms.[5]

Evangelicalism's current lack of attention to the inherent theological nature of pastoral ministry has led, we believe, to twin problems: the theological anemia of the church and the ecclesial anemia of theology. With the migration of our theologians from the pulpit to the lectern, our churches have become bereft of crucial theological leadership. Likewise, much of contemporary theological discourse has lost its ecclesial orientation, too often being subordinated to academic methodologies and agendas that do not lend themselves to ecclesially useful projects.

Our solution to these twin problems is the resurrection of the pastor theologian. Toward this end, we have conceived of the pastor theologian along a threefold taxonomy: the pastor theologian as *local theologian*, the pastor theologian as *popular theologian*, and the pastor theologian as

---

[4]Such has not always been the case, however. For a detailed analysis of the pastor theologian in church history, see Hiestand and Wilson, *Pastor Theologian*, 21-41, 133-72; also Kevin J. Vanhoozer and Owen Strachan, *The Pastor as Public Theologian: Reclaiming a Lost Vision* (Grand Rapids: Baker Academic, 2015), 69-93.

[5]This is especially the case for those traditions that trace their heritage to the Second Great Awakening. See Nathan Hatch, *The Democratization of American Christianity* (New Haven, CT: Yale University Press, 1989), 27-30.

ecclesial theologian.[6] The "local theologian" is a pastor theologian who brings theological leadership to a local congregation. Here, the primary mechanism for doing theological work is the sermon. This theological leadership is also extended through education classes, a church newsletter or perhaps individual counseling situations. The key here is that the principal audience of the local theologian is the laity of the local congregation. This is probably the most common understanding of the pastor theologian in contemporary parlance.[7]

The "popular theologian" is a pastor theologian who has embraced the calling of the local theologian but has extended his or her theological reach through a writing ministry. This might take the form of a blog, but more often it takes the form of books that address theological topics at a popular level. The idea here is of a pastor theologian who reads theological scholarship and then serves as a translator of theology for the uninitiated. The popular theologian sorts through the salient scholarship, determines what is relevant to the church and then repackages it in ways that can be communicated to laypeople. Like the local theologian, the principal audience for the popular theologian is the laity, spread out over a number of congregations.

Both of the above identities are vital to the health of the church, but they do not exhaust the full range of possibilities for the pastor theologian. At the Center for Pastor Theologians we affirm both of the above models while pressing toward a third kind of pastor theologian—the pastor theologian as "ecclesial theologian." What we have in mind here is a pastor who embodies the best of the local theologian, does some of the work of a popular theologian and then, beyond this, is doing theological work for other theologians and pastors. Ecclesial theologians draw on the ecclesial

---

[6]Another articulation of our taxonomy, slightly edited for use here, can be found in Gerald Hiestand, "Theological Vocation and the Church," in *Journal of Markets and Morality* 18, no. 2 (Fall 2015): 423-24. For our full treatment, see Hiestand and Wilson, *Pastor Theologian*, 79-87.
[7]See Vanhoozer and Strachan, *Public Theologian*; Vanhoozer, *The Drama of Doctrine: A Canonical Linguistic Approach to Christian Doctrine* (Louisville, KY: Westminster John Knox, 2005), 454-55; the twin essays by John Piper and D. A. Carson in *The Pastor as Scholar and the Scholar as Pastor: Reflections on Life and Ministry*, ed. Owen Strachan and David Mathis (Wheaton, IL: Crossway, 2011); and Al Mohler Jr., *He Is Not Silent: Preaching in a Postmodern World* (Chicago: Moody, 2008), 105-14. For a similar vision of the pastor theologian in the mainline tradition, see Wallace M. Alston and Cynthia A. Jarvis, eds., *The Power to Comprehend With All the Saints: The Formation and Practice of a Pastor-Theologian* (Grand Rapids: Eerdmans, 2009); and Michael Welker and Cynthia A. Jarvis, eds., *Loving God With Our Minds: The Pastor as Theologian* (Grand Rapids: Eerdmans, 2004).

social location of their pastoral vocation; from this vantage point, they construct theology that is particularly sensitive to ecclesial concerns and questions. The key identifying mark of the ecclesial theologian is audience; the ecclesial theologian is not primarily writing to laypeople but to other theologians and scholars.

The resurgence of all three "species" of pastor theologians is vital for the health of the church. Local theologians embody the doctrines of the church, teaching not just bare doctrinal truths but even more importantly modeling the way of wisdom. Popular theologians help translate the difficult yet life-giving content of Christian doctrine into language that is accessible to the average believer. Ecclesial theologians help preserve the ecclesial orientation ←
of contemporary theological scholarship, ensuring that the church's theo-logical discourse stays centered on issues relevant to the life of the church without getting hijacked by the academy.

The boundary between these three categorizations is porous; many ec-clesial theologians write popular theology, some popular theologians may occasionally write scholarly works and hopefully both are effective local theologians. Our aim is not to insist that every pastor must be neatly catego-rized according to our taxonomy, but rather to open up multiple and com-plementary ways of envisioning the identity of the pastor theologian.

At this point I must clarify the nature of the ecclesial theologian in re-lation to the academic theologian. If the ecclesial theologian is a pastor who writes theological scholarship for other theologians, isn't he really just an academic theologian in disguise? This is not our vision. Rather, the ecclesial theologian is a pastor who writes ecclesial theology—not academic theology. To explain the difference, it will be helpful to lay out the four spheres of theological scholarship.

THE FOUR SPHERES OF THEOLOGICAL SCHOLARSHIP

Any theological project useful for the church must necessarily operate within four overlapping spheres of theological scholarship. These spheres can be categorized as follows: research, systemization, ecclesial significance articulation and ecclesial implementation (fig. 1). After describing the four spheres below, I will suggest how academic theologians and ecclesial theo-logians are each uniquely positioned, via their respective social locations, to partner together across all four spheres. But before providing a brief sketch of each sphere, I need to make three points of clarification.

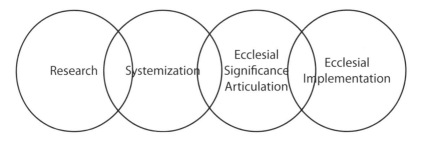

Figure 1. The four spheres of theological scholarship

First, I will not be suggesting that scholars work only in a single sphere, as though some scholars do research and others do systemization. These are spheres of theological scholar*ship*, not *scholars*. Nearly all scholars will operate meaningfully in multiple spheres.

Second, by the term *ecclesial significance articulation* I am not referring to the latent meaning that each scholar brings with him or her to the scholarly task; this permeates all four spheres of scholarship. I am instead referring to the act of articulating, in writing, the ecclesial significance that one finds in a particular project for the Christian community.

Third, all four spheres of scholarship are on the theory side of the theory/praxis spectrum. Thus the ecclesial implementation sphere is not the sphere where one applies scholarship; rather, it is the sphere of scholarship where one does research about how best to implement a given paradigm (for example, scholarship about preaching vs. the act of preaching).

Research. I am here referring to research as that task of theological scholarship wherein the scholar sets about to locate the basic data relevant to a given project. One example might be a medieval scholar working on notions of divine impassibility in the twelfth century; part of this project may involve the translation of a previously unpublished Latin text housed in the Vatican Library. Another scholar may be writing on Barth's view of gender in his *Church Dogmatics*; foundational to this task will be the work of reading the *Church Dogmatics* and identifying and gathering together the relevant passages. Or again, one might think of a scholar writing a book on Gnostic cosmology; a foundational aspect of the project will be the task of simply reading Gnostic writings and identifying the relevant content that speaks to the focus of the project.

I am not here suggesting that research is a value-neutral task conducted by disinterested scholars; this is an Enlightenment ideal that postmodernity has rightly chastised. My claim is not epistemological. Rather, I am making the more modest, and obvious, observation that one cannot write a book on a topic for which one has no data. For our purposes, research is simply the task of locating and gathering data. According to this narrow definition of research, raw research is not often published independent of the next sphere of theological scholarship—systemization.

Systemization. Systemization is the sphere of theological scholarship that seeks to identify patterns (or the lack thereof) within a given data set with a view to presenting a coherent picture of the data. In actual practice, research cannot be done independent of systemization, since some level of systemization necessarily takes place as research is being conducted. Yet the task of systematizing data and then presenting it in a coherent way to a particular audience is distinct from the task of locating data. Here we might think of Colin Gunton's *The Triune Creator: A Historical and Systematic Study.*[8] In his work, Gunton presents his research on the doctrine of creation in a way that offers a coherent systemization of the doctrine throughout the history of the church. Another example is Alister McGrath's *Iustitia Dei: A History of the Christian Doctrine of Justification.*[9] McGrath's research on the doctrine of justification is arranged chronologically and seeks to identify the key themes and issues surrounding this doctrine throughout church history.

While research and systemization necessarily go together, scholars often tend more readily toward one or the other. (No doubt every doctoral supervisor knows what it is like to have a student enthusiastically begin systematizing a field of knowledge that they have not yet mastered—or conversely, a student who seems unable to arrange and present their research in a systematized and coherent manner.) Again, we need not overly complicate the issue. I simply wish to observe that for a theological project to be useful for

---

[8]Colin Gunton, *The Triune Creation: A Historical and Systematic Study* (Grand Rapids: Eerdmans, 1998).
[9]Alister McGrath, *Iustitia Dei: A History of the Doctrine of Justification* (Cambridge: Cambridge University Press, 2005).

the church, data must be collected (research), and having thus been collected, must be arranged and presented in an organized way (systemization).

Ecclesial significance articulation. Ecclesial significance articulation is
the sphere of theological scholarship wherein the scholar makes explicit the
significance that the systematized data has for the Christian community.
Here I do not have in mind the subjective "Gadamerian"[10] meaning that a
scholar brings to his or her research (that is, one's personal prejudices and
first thoughts). Instead, I am more objectively referring to the actual *act* of
articulating, in writing (or speech), the significance that a scholar's research
has (in the estimation of the scholar) for the Christian community. Thus, in
this sphere of theological scholarship, we are looking for the scholar to make
explicit moral assertions and admonitions directed to the Christian community. Or again, we are looking for the scholar to make his or her *private*
agenda a *public* agenda.

It is in this sphere of theological scholarship that our above Gnostic cosmology scholar will argue that pastors must be diligent to eradicate the
persistent strains of Gnostic cosmology and anthropology that still cling to
contemporary expressions of evangelical preaching. Or perhaps a scholar
working on the doctrine of justification will assert that Athanasius's doctrine
of sin should be embraced as a helpful corrective for combating the under-
realized eschatology of contemporary Reformed soteriology. Or perhaps a
theologian might argue that Augustine's *ordo salutis* is more biblical and
better suited to evangelistic preaching than Calvin's (or vice versa). In each
instance, the ecclesial relevance of an idea or concept is foregrounded, and
the theologian asserts a moral or doctrinal judgment on behalf of the contemporary Christian community. Thus ecclesial significance articulation
entails a clear call as to how the systematized research should modify,
confirm or otherwise transform the Christian community.

Ecclesial implementation. Ecclesial implementation is the sphere of
theological scholarship that seeks to clarify and prescribe how an idea or
concept should be implemented in the Christian ministry or within the
Christian community. As noted above, this sphere of theological scholarship
is still on the theory side of the theory/praxis spectrum. Thus I am not

---

[10]Hans-Georg Gadamer, *Truth and Method* (New York: Continuum, 2011).

referring to the actual implementation of a theological concept (praxis); I am referring to scholarship about implementation. Ecclesial implementation moves beyond saying that an idea has relevance and meaning (the domain of ecclesial significance articulation) and offers practical suggestions about how an idea might be brought to bear in specific ministry contexts. These suggestions are grounded in a deep working knowledge of the context where one's data is to be applied.

By way of example, one might think of a manual on preaching, based on a close reading of the Pastoral Epistles, with suggestions about the most effective preaching methods for preachers with different personality types. Or perhaps a field manual for counselors that draws upon Luther's law/gospel distinction and then uses this distinction to inform counseling theory. Or again the sphere of ecclesial implementation might include suggestions, based on an Augustinian account of the will, about the most effective corporate church evangelism strategies in a wealthy urban context. The key here is that tangible, field tested advice is being given, coupled with theological research, about how to apply a given idea or principle in a particular ecclesial context.

Our brief account of these four spheres can be summarized as follows: If *x* represents an idea, then the research sphere is an effort to determine *that x is*; the systemization sphere is an attempt to understand *what x is*; the ecclesial significance articulation sphere is an attempt to say *what the meaning of x is* for the Christian community; and the ecclesial implementation sphere is an attempt to say *how x should be applied* in a particular Christian context. Deep work in all four spheres is necessary if the church is to be served by theological scholarship.

ACADEMIC THEOLOGIANS, ECCLESIAL THEOLOGIANS AND THE FOUR SPHERES OF SCHOLARSHIP

My aim in delineating these four spheres is to show how academic theologians and ecclesial theologians can work together to make meaningful contributions across all four spheres. My primary claim is that academic theologians are maximized, by nature of their vocation, to make significant contributions in the first two spheres of theological scholarship. Ecclesial theologians, on the other hand, are maximized to make significant contributions in the last two spheres. This is not to say that academic theologians and ecclesial theologians

are incapable of working outside the strengths of their respective social locations; they can and do. Rather, I am saying that each vocational social location—the academy and the church—has a unique vantage point from which
to engage in theological scholarship.

The vocational strengths and weaknesses of the academy. The modern
research university is a product of the Enlightenment.[11] The Enlightenment
has now become the favorite whipping boy of our more epistemically sophisticated age (and often for good reasons), yet it must be hailed nonetheless as a remarkable achievement. Modern medicine and science—two
fields of study for which humanity must be eminently grateful—are the legitimate children of the Enlightenment's obsession with objectivity and research.[12] And though the Enlightenment's valorization of neutrality was
excessive, its emphasis on objectivity and specialization resulted in enormous
gains in knowledge and precision. These gains were not only realized in
science and medicine, but in all fields of learning—anthropology, sociology,
history, theology and so on. Our primary texts are more precise, our research methods more careful and our analysis is more exact than at any
other time in human history.

Given the modern university's genesis in the Enlightenment, it should
not surprise us that the post-Enlightenment research university has most
effectively operated in the first two spheres of theological scholarship: research and systemization. Insofar as academic theologians are vocationally
situated in the academy, they are especially well-positioned to engage in
research and systemization. The library resources, the exacting guild standards, the institutional and financial support for primary level research, the
opportunity for research leave, the potential for grant funding—all of these

---

[11]Michael C. Legaspi tells this story well in his *The Death of Scripture and the Rise of Biblical Studies*
(Oxford: Oxford University Press, 2010). For more, see Edward Farley, *Theologia: The Fragmentation
and Unity of Theological Education* (Eugene, OR: Wipf and Stock, 1994), 39-48, and Hiestand and
Wilson, *Pastor Theologian*, 43-46.

[12]But lest we concede too much to the Enlightenment, it must be noted that much of the triumph
often associated with the Enlightenment finds its origins in Christian pre-Enlightenment thought.
The achievements of Galileo, Johannes Kepler, Francis Bacon and other Christian thinkers, cul-
minating with Isaac Newton, laid the foundation for the scientific advances that would come to
mark the Enlightenment. In short, religious thought, far from obstructing advances in science,
actually paved the way for the modern age of science. For more on this, see Amos Funkenstein,
Theology and the Scientific Imagination from the Middle Ages to the Seventeenth Century (Princeton,
NJ: Princeton University Press, 1986).

things give a distinct advantage to academic theologians as compared with ecclesial theologians. Indeed, if a project requires spending a summer in Rome translating a twelfth-century Latin text housed in the Vatican Library, the most likely candidate for such a project is an academic scholar. Of course, this is not the only kind of work academic theologians do, but it's the sort of work that they are especially well-positioned for.

But with all the strengths of the post-Enlightenment university, the academy has consistently been a no-show with respect to the third and fourth spheres of theological scholarship: ecclesial significance articulation and ecclesial implementation.[13] Within the wider academic world, attempts at ecclesial significance articulation are often viewed as improper to the scholarly task. McGrath's work on justification illustrates the point. In his discussion regarding Lutheranism's later modification of Luther's theology, McGrath writes, "It would be improper to inquire as to whether this . . . modification was justified; it is however right and proper to note that it took place."[14] Saying what the church *used* to believe is permissible; saying what it *should* believe is out of bounds according to the reigning academic guild standards. There are, I believe, two primary reasons why academic theology struggles when it comes to ecclesial significance articulation.

First, the modern research university, to the extent that it is an heir of the Enlightenment, has adopted the Enlightenment's ideal of disinterested objectivity. While there is a certain (qualified) appropriateness to objectivity in research and systemization, ecclesial significance articulation is too often sacrificed on the altar of neutrality and objectivity. This sort of methodological agnosticism is seen especially in historical studies (where the fear of anachronism reigns supreme) and also in biblical studies, which, following the German schools, has become little more than another version of historical

---

[13]I am aware that the term *academy* does not apply equally to the various institutions that employ Christian scholars: Cambridge University is not Wheaton College, which is not Trinity Evangelical Divinity School. While granting that all of these academic institutions will not equally fall prey to my critique, David Wells has rightly pointed out that the larger university context sets the research agenda and guild standards for those Christian academic institutions that wish to operate in the larger university world. See David F. Wells, *No Place for Truth: Or Whatever Happened to Evangelical Theology?* (Grand Rapids: Eerdmans, 1994), 127. To the degree that they wish to be a member in good standing within the larger academic fraternity, the methodology and orientation of the larger university shapes the agenda of Christian universities, colleges and even divinity schools.

[14]McGrath, *Iustitia Dei*, 219. See also page 395 for his concluding comments, which reflect a similar sentiment.

studies. The doctoral student in biblical studies is allowed to make a claim about what Paul believed, but she is not allowed to make the claim that Paul should be believed. The latter claim is in the domain of ecclesial significance articulation. Insofar as the university valorizes objectivity and neutrality, the guild constraints of the modern university do not encourage academic scholars to explicitly state the relevance of their work for the church.[15]

The second, and less sinister, reason is that academic theology is simply not constructed in the environment that theology is primarily meant to serve—the church. This is not a critique as much as it is a fact. The academy is its own legitimate social location with its own questions, concerns, priorities and audience, but these are often distinct from or tangential to the concerns on the ground in the church. As such, academic theology is not always in touch with many of the questions that most need to be asked on behalf of the Christian community.

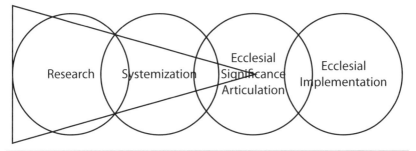

Figure 2. Academic theology and the four spheres of theological scholarship

In the main, academic theology tends to move from the research sphere toward systemization (see fig. 2). Very frequently it stalls out before it makes any meaningful progress into the sphere of ecclesial significance articulation, and it makes even fewer forays into ecclesial implementation. This has, I believe, led to the much-lamented "gap" between the academy and the church. Rightly, those on the ecclesial side recognize that academic scholarship doesn't generally get the whole job done. Wrongly, this has led many of them to conclude that the work of academic theologians is irrelevant. But academic scholarship is not irrelevant; indeed, the research and systemization done in

---

[15]For more see Hiestand and Wilson, *Pastor Theologian*, 65-78, and George Marsden, *The Outrageous Idea of Christian Scholarship* (Oxford: Oxford University Press, 1997).

the academic context is often the foundation upon which the entire scholarly edifice is based. Yet this scholarship is insufficient to the extent that it fails to meaningfully cover all four spheres.]

The proposed solution to this deficit has generally been to call academic scholars to do more work in the last two spheres. But this is an unrealistic burden to place on academic theologians. It is nearly impossible for a single scholar to work equally well across all four spheres, and the social location of the academy does not lend itself to deep, sustained work in the last two spheres. This is not to say that academic scholars are incapable of working in the last two spheres; they can and sometimes do. But in the main, the university context does not reward work in these spheres in the same way it rewards work in the first two spheres. The answer, then, is not to ask academic scholars to work outside their social location but to ask a different guild of theologians to do the work not generally being done by academic theologians and scholars.

Ecclesial theologians and the last two spheres. Ecclesial theologians are, by nature of their vocation, uniquely positioned to operate in the last two spheres of theological scholarship. Pastors are not beholden to academic guilds, with their emphasis on neutrality and objectivity. We have the vocational space to engage in sustained reflection about the meaning our research has for the Christian community and the vocational freedom to make this meaning explicit in our work. As pastors, we cannot be satisfied with simply saying what is; we are called to say what must be in light of the gospel. We are called to exhort, to cast a vision for how the gospel should shape the people and mission of God.

Likewise, our social location inevitably pushes us up against the pressing questions of the church. The concerns of plumbers, mothers, grandparents, doctors, teens and children all shape the questions that we bring to the theological task. We are compelled, by nature of our vocation, to know firsthand the trials, concerns, joys and hardships of average Christians. And we are expected to speak into these experiences with the wisdom of God's Word, God's Spirit and God's church.

Academic theology may tell us with precision that Luther and his heirs had different views of justification, but it does not always tell us with prophetic urgency the significance of this difference for the church today or which view should be preferred over the other. Even then, once a determination has been made, the hard intellectual work remains of figuring out how this conclusion should be applied in various Christian ministry settings.

This is not to say that ecclesial theologians cannot make contributions in the first two spheres. We can and do, just like academic theologians can and do make contributions in the last two spheres. But ecclesial theologians will fill the gap in theological scholarship to the degree that we become effective in making contributions in the last two spheres. The ecclesial theologian relies on the good research and systematizing work of academic theologians, then builds on and deepens this work as he or she launches into the last two spheres of scholarship. Though ecclesial theologians may not be best positioned to write a history of the doctrine of justification, they are best positioned to draw on that history and say what it means for the church today. What's more, ecclesial theologians are best positioned to know which aspects of that history are most relevant and worthy of deeper exploration. The situation on the ground provides the initial way into the study, thus focusing the work of ecclesial theologians and enabling them to draw insights out of that study that academic theologians may not be as sensitive to. Ecclesial significance articulation and ecclesial implementation are not mere appendices to scholarship. Indeed, these last two spheres are the consummation of the whole scholarly enterprise.

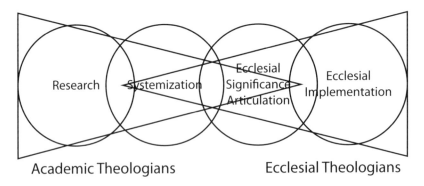

Figure 3. Academic theologians, ecclesial theologians and the four spheres of theological scholarship

In sum, I envision academic theologians moving from research toward systemization and ecclesial theologians moving from ecclesial implementation toward ecclesial significance articulation (fig. 3). They will meet in the middle and at times cross into each other's domains. Working in tandem, ecclesially sensitive academic theologians and academically sensitive ecclesial theologians will span the breadth of the scholarly enterprise, seeking together the advance of Christ's kingdom and the good of God's people.

CONCLUSION

There can be no turning back the clock. With the birth of the modern research university, the fields of knowledge have become too specialized for a single scholar to work equally well across all four spheres. But there is more to theological scholarship than research and systemization. This, I believe, is at least part of the answer to Wilson's and Jones's critiques.

If we conceive of theological scholarship solely as research and systemization, then Wilson and Jones are correct that being a pastor scholar is difficult (even if perhaps not as impossible as their essays might suggest). But when we broaden out our understanding of the scholarly enterprise, we recognize not only that pastors can make valuable scholarly contributions but, indeed, pastors are vocationally the best situated to make these contributions. Not every pastor needs to be an ecclesial theologian, but some of us need to do the hard work of ecclesial significance articulation and ecclesial implementation. Before God, and according to his Word, the theological integrity of the church is the burden of the pastoral community; may we rise to embrace this responsibility.

5

The Pastor Theologian
as Cruciform Theologian

TODD WILSON

I WANT TO SET UP THIS CHAPTER BY IDENTIFYING one of the key claims
Gerald Hiestand and I make about the pastor theologian; then I would like
to make an honest confession about this claim. First the key claim: One of the
leading insights for us at the Center for Pastor Theologians has been the influence of *social location* on theological reflection. In the high tide of postmod-
ernism, it's almost cliché to make this point, but for pastor theologians it's still
a point worth emphasizing. Pastors inhabit a different vocational space or
social location than, say, academics. Theirs is an *ecclesial* location, and this
shapes their theological reflection—for the better, we believe.[1]

Now the honest confession: While we've rightly insisted on the importance
of the pastor's social location for doing theology, we've not yet articulated
precisely *how* or *in what way* this unique social location shapes theological
reflection. We've asserted that this is the case, but we've not tried to elaborate
how or in what way.

This chapter, then, is a modest attempt at such an elaboration. I want to
address the questions, What is it about the pastoral calling, or pastoral
social location, that influences theological reflection in unique and helpful
ways? What is true of the pastoral calling, different from other callings, that
influences the doing of theology? Or what is it about that pastor's social and

---

[1] See Gerald Hiestand and Todd Wilson, *The Pastor Theologian: Resurrecting an Ancient Vision* (Grand Rapids: Zondervan, 2015).

ecclesial location that shapes the kind of theological reflection he or she offers the church? I will address the important theme of the pastor theologian as a *pastor*, which means I will try to articulate what it is about the pastor's calling or life that contributes to the work of being a pastor *theologian*.

THE ECCLESIAL LOCATION ENTAILS CRUCIFORM VOCATION

The more I read the New Testament, read biographies of pastors of old, and reflect on my own experience, the more I arrive at the conclusion that the pastor's ecclesial location entails a *cruciform vocation*. Cruciformity is literally conformity to the cross of Christ; in Pauline idiom, it is being *crucified with Christ so that I no longer live but Christ lives in me* (Gal 2:20). While we may slip into the bad habit of thinking of this as an abstract concept, there was nothing abstract about it for Paul; he bore on his body the brand marks of Christ (Gal 6:17). Cruciformity means real, concrete suffering—not splinters but self-sacrifice. Cruciformity is suffering, big and small, in Jesus' name for the good of others.

This kind of suffering is part and parcel of the pastoral calling. You can't be a pastor without embracing a large helping of heartache and heartbreak—your own and that of the people you serve. What God hardwired into the apostle Paul's calling he has hardwired into every pastor's calling: "I will show him how much he must suffer for the sake of my name" (Acts 9:16).[2] And while the divine necessity is perhaps not the same, the stubborn and uncomfortable fact of suffering certainly is.

The apostle's suffering was dramatic, much more so than anything you or I are likely to experience. Over the years, I have found one or two rubber chickens in my mailbox and quite a few not-so-nice-emails in my inbox on a Monday morning. Yet I've not—not yet, at least—been thrown into prison or beaten or suffered forty lashes minus one or been in danger from robbers or shipwrecked or nearly stoned to death or even gone without food or sleep for a single night.

But for Paul these intense examples of suffering don't top his list of painful experiences as a pastor. Instead, as he says at the climax of his famous catalogue of suffering, "Apart from other things, there is the *daily pressure on me of my anxiety for all the churches*. Who is weak, and I am not weak? Who is

---

[2]Unless otherwise indicated, Scripture quotations in this chapter are from the English Standard Version.

made to fall, and I am not indignant?" (2 Cor 11:28-29, emphasis added). And so Paul the pastor speaks for all pastors when he says,

> We are afflicted in every way, but not crushed; perplexed, but not driven to despair; persecuted, but not forsaken; struck down, but not destroyed; *always carrying in the body the death of Jesus, so that the life of Jesus may also be manifested in our bodies.* For we who live are always being given over to death for Jesus' sake, so that the life of Jesus also may be manifested in our mortal flesh. So death is at work in us, but life in you. (2 Cor 4:8-12, emphasis added)

So the pastor's ecclesial location *with people* means cruciform vocation *for people*: death at work in the pastor, so that life might be at work in the pastor's flock. Like the prophet Jeremiah, a pastor theologian *as pastor* is yoked to people and thus yoked to suffering with and for people.

This Is Where Theology Is Born

But this dual aspect to the calling of the pastor theologian as a pastor—their ecclesial location and thus cruciform vocation—isn't a hindrance to theology but a help. It is even the generative source of theology, the place where it is born.

Nicholas Wolterstorff is one of America's leading Christian philosophers. He taught for many years at Calvin College and Yale University and was responsible, with Alvin Plantinga, for the movement known as "Reformed epistemology." A number of years ago, he lost his twenty-five-year-old son in a tragic climbing accident. As a result of this painful experience, he wrote in his 1987 book *Lament for a Son* that when he meets people and they ask him, "Tell me a little bit about yourself," he feels compelled to answer, "I am one who lost a son." He says this because "that loss *determines my identity*; not all of my identity, but much of it. It belongs with my story."[3]

Pastors are specialists in loss. As I was writing this essay, the angel of death visited our congregation, and we lost three of our own. Two were senior saints, and one was a young woman in her late twenties who died the day after her son's third birthday, leaving behind a dismayed little boy and a shattered husband. While this was an especially intense week in the life of one congregation, as every pastor knows this is neither unusual nor unprecedented. Even if we may not have faced the loss of our own child, as Wolterstorff has, the fact

---

[3]Nicholas Wolterstorff, *Lament for a Son* (Grand Rapids: Eerdmans, 1987), 6.

is that pastors specialize in loss, in hurt, in pain, in trauma, in suffering, in soul anguish of one kind or another. The loss *determines our identity*—not all of our identity, but much of it. It belongs to our story. And it shapes our entire outlook on life and ministry and the church and God and, yes, even our theology. Cruciformity is not a hindrance to doing theology; indeed, it is the place where theology is born.

Jürgen Moltmann, one of the twentieth century's leading German theologians, describes the trauma he experienced living through the horrific events of World War II. In his *Experiences in Theology*, he describes how traumatizing it was in July of 1943 to watch the destruction of his hometown of Hamburg, in a bombing attack the British Royal Air Force called "Operation Gomorrah." Some 40,000 people died, literally burned to death. Moltmann nearly lost his own life, and watched his friend be, as he says, "blown to pieces" while he was standing next to him.[4]

We might think this kind of horrific experience would destroy any prospect of doing theology. But listen to Moltmann, who sounds remarkably Pauline at this point: "My experiences of death at the end of the war, the depression into which the guilt of my people plunged me, and the inner perils of utter resignation behind barbed wire: *these were the places where my theology was born.*"[5]

For pastor theologians as pastors, in their ecclesial location and thus cruciform vocation, this is where theology is born. Indeed, this is where it is nursed and nurtured and, by the grace of God, reaches its full maturity—in the cauldron of the church, the crucible of suffering.

CRUCIFORMITY'S INFLUENCE ON THE PASTOR'S THEOLOGY

In what *specific ways* does cruciformity shape a pastor's theology? Let me distill it down to four essentials. I should hasten to say, though, that these aren't the only ways in which theology is formed, nor do these things happen *only* or *exclusively* to pastor theologians as opposed to academic theologians. Hopefully every theologian, pastor or otherwise, will embrace the salutary effects of suffering. But for pastor theologians, cruciformity is essential to their calling in a way it isn't for other callings.

---

[4]Jürgen Moltmann, *Experiences in Theology: Ways and Forms of Christian Theology*, trans. Margaret Kohl (Minneapolis: Fortress, 2000), 3-4.
[5]Moltmann, *Experiences in Theology*, 4.

First, cruciformity helps you *see*, theologically. It corrects for epistemic nearsightedness or blindness. There is, in other words, proven hermeneutical value in suffering for the sake of others, not least in one's reading of the Bible. I wouldn't, for example, have been able to recognize the "person who stirs up division" (Tit 3:10) if I had not collided with some of these prickly characters in my own church. I would've never caught the force of Paul's charge to Timothy not to let the Ephesian church despise him for his youth (1 Tim 4:12) if I had not received a hostile thirty-two-page missive in my inbox that referred to me as "Young Todd" no fewer than fourteen times. I would've never grasped the beauty of Scripture's declaration that "male and female he created them" (Gen 1:27) if I'd not walked alongside a man in our church who wakes up most mornings wishing he was a woman. Perhaps this is what Job meant when he confessed at the end of his journey with suffering, "I had heard of you by the hearing of the ear, but now my eye *sees* you" (Job 42:5-6, emphasis added). Suffering has a salutary hermeneutical effect; it helps you see.

Second, it helps you *sift* your theological priorities. According to Isaiah Berlin's twofold classification of intellectuals, you could say that cruciformity turns pastor theologians into hedgehogs, not foxes. Berlin says that foxes "pursue many ends, often unrelated and even contradictory, connected, if at all, only in some de facto way, for some psychological or physiological cause, related to no moral or aesthetic principle."[6] If they were fired from a shotgun, they'd be scattered like bird- or buckshot, not fired straight like a slug. Hedgehogs, on the other hand, "relate everything to a single central vision, one system, less or more coherent or articulate, in terms of which they understand, think and feel—a single, universal, organizing principle in terms of which alone all that they are and say has significance."[7]

Hedgehogs don't have intellectual ADHD; they have a singularity of theological vision that imitates the apostle Paul's. It's cruciformity that got them there, because *there's nothing like suffering for others to help focus the mind*. It helps you see, and then it helps you sift, so you learn to reckon with what really counts. John Calvin had this singularity of vision; as his biographer T. H. L. Parker puts it, "He was not unfamiliar with the sound of the mob

---

[6]Isaiah Berlin, *The Hedgehog and the Fox: An Essay on Tolstoy's View of History*, 2nd ed. (Princeton: Princeton University Press, 2013), 2.
[7]Berlin, *The Hedgehog and the Fox*, 2.

outside his house threatening to throw him in the river and firing their muskets."[8] Perhaps this explains the elegance and profundity of Calvin's *Institutes*, for Parker adds, "The *Institutes* was not written in an ivory tower, but against the background of teething troubles."[9]

Third, cruciformity *cultivates* the virtues—not just moral but intellectual. The kind of serious theological reflection that pastor theologians are called to do depends on what the philosophers refer to as "excellent epistemic functioning"—that is, well-cultivated habits of mind that are conducive to this kind of reflection, what are known as the intellectual virtues.[10]

Here I'm tapping into a philosophical tradition known as virtue epistemology. No one will deny that cruciformity has a way of cultivating moral virtues in our lives, but I want to suggest that cruciformity also cultivates intellectual virtues, like wisdom, prudence, discernment, the love of truth, firmness and generosity. At the same time, cruciformity has a way of *purging* from us things like folly, gullibility, dishonesty, obtuseness and naiveté—various intellectual vices. Listen to virtue epistemologist Jay Wood: "Sometimes knowledge gives way to dogmatism, understanding grows clouded, and intellectual agility and acuity become calcified and unyielding."[11] Perhaps countering this very thing is what Paul has in mind when he urges us "to present your bodies as a living sacrifice" and thus not to be "conformed to this world, but be transformed by the renewal of your mind" (Rom 12:1-2).

Fourth, cruciformity drives us back, again and again, to that first of theological acts: *prayer*. In 1963, the famed Swiss theologian Karl Barth arrived for the first time in America to give a series of lectures in Princeton and Chicago. Those talks are now gathered under the title *Evangelical Theology: An Introduction*. In that volume, Barth identifies the work of prayer as *chief* among all that the theologian does. His reasoning is simple: "All theological work can be undertaken and accomplished only amid great distress, which assails it on all sides." Thus, he insists, "The first and basic act of theological

---

[8]T. H. L. Parker, *Portrait of Calvin,* reprint ed. (Minneapolis: Desiring God, 2008), 41.

[9]Parker, *Portrait of Calvin,* 80.

[10]See Robert C. Roberts and W. Jay Wood, *Intellectual Virtues: An Essay in Regulative Epistemology* (Oxford: Oxford University Press, 2010).

[11]W. Jay Wood, *Epistemology: Becoming Intellectually Virtuous* (Downers Grove, IL: IVP Academic, 1998), 21.

work is *prayer*."[12] Of course, prayer isn't the pastor theologian's *only* task, but it is the most basic:

> Undoubtedly, from the very beginning and without intermission, theological work is also *study*; in every respect it is also *service*; and finally it would certainly be in vain were it not also an act of love. But theological work does not merely begin with prayer and is not merely accompanied by it; in its totality it is peculiar and characteristic of theology that it can be performed only in the act of prayer.[13]

Theological reflection, if it is to be fruitful, must have not only windows to the outside world but also skylights to the heavens above. There must be a *vertical* dimension, so the theologian doesn't fall prey to the conceit that he operates independently from God, a kind of intellectual Pelagianism. Besides, as Barth says, all theological work is but an act of listening, adoration and discovery, since the object of theological reflection isn't some *thing*—but some *One*.[14]

It is cruciformity, like nothing else, that leads pastor theologians into the wilderness of affliction, where they learn not only how to suffer but how to theologize. No wonder one of our best-known American pastor theologians, Eugene Peterson, distills the pastor theologian's role down to this: to teach his congregation to pray.[15]

A Closing Plea to Professors, Pastors, Lay Leaders and Students

Luther was right when he said about what actually makes a theologian, "Living, even dying and being damned, make a theologian, not understanding, reading or speculating."[16] Not a PhD, or a big church, or the vain pleasure at being called "Doctor," but cruciformity in the service of Christ. In closing, let me offer a few words of encouragement to the different kinds of folks reading this chapter.

First, to the *professors*, may I gently encourage you to embrace the suffering God brings into your life. Don't begrudge it as though it were merely

---

[12]Karl Barth, *Evangelical Theology: An Introduction* (Grand Rapids: Eerdmans, 1992), 159.
[13]Barth, *Evangelical Theology*, 160; emphasis original.
[14]Barth, *Evangelical Theology*, 163.
[15]Eugene Peterson, *The Contemplative Pastor: Returning to the Art of Spiritual Direction* (Grand Rapids: Eerdmans, 1993), 89.
[16]Cited in Alister McGrath, *The Passionate Intellect: Christian Faith and the Discipleship of the Mind* (Downers Grove, IL: InterVarsity Press, 2014), 59.

a distraction from the business of doing theology, but lean into it as a possible generative source for your best theological reflection. When we embrace the suffering God sends into our lives, it deepens and sweetens our souls, and thus all our thinking and speaking as well. Embracing suffering, in other words, will turn you into the priest in Victor Hugo's *Les Misérables*, whose wife paid him the highest of all compliments a minister or theologian could ever be paid: "He did not study God; he was dazzled by Him."[17] Don't underestimate the power of suffering to engender theological wonder and insight.

Second, to *pastors*, understand that cruciformity is essential to your calling in ways it simply isn't to other callings. Because of this, though, recognize that it is not a *hindrance* to your ministry but a *help*. If you will lay hold of it by faith as a gift, you will find it does not only amazing things to your character but to your theologizing and your preaching. You'll find your preaching will look like the kind of preaching Marilynne Robinson defines as "parsing the broken heart of humankind and praising the loving heart of Christ."[18]

As you embrace the salutary effects of suffering, you'll also be equipped to destroy the operative theological outlook of most ordinary Americans— what sociologist Christian Smith has termed "Moralistic Therapeutic Deism" (MTD). He defines MTD this way:

> This is not a religion of repentance from sin, of keeping the Sabbath, of living as a servant of a sovereign divine, of steadfastly saying one's prayers, of faithfully observing high holy days, of *building character through suffering*, of basking in God's love and grace, of spending oneself in gratitude and love for the cause of social justice, etc. Rather, what appears to be the actual dominant religion among U.S. teenagers [and, I would add, Americans in general] is centrally about feeling good, happy, secure, at peace.[19]

It's a huge idol, but cruciformity equips you to tear it down with the potent sledgehammer of suffering-inspired and refined pastoral theology.

To *lay leaders*, let me encourage you to lay hold of the fact that cruciformity is part and parcel of your pastors' calling. So do your best not to add to their burdens but to pray for them, to encourage them and to strengthen

---

[17]Victor Hugo, *Les Misérables*, trans. Isabel F. Hapgood (New York: Crowell, 1887), 52.

[18]Marilynne Robinson, *Home: A Novel* (New York: Picador, 2009), 50.

[19]Christian Smith, *Soul Searching: The Religious and Spiritual Lives of American Teenagers* (Oxford: Oxford University Press, 2009), 155 (emphasis added).

them in ministry. And sit under their preaching ministry, Sunday by Sunday, with bated breath, hungry for something theologically substantive—a parsing and praising. And when you hear it—or better yet, when you see it—then tell them so. They'll thank you for it and be stronger because of it.

Finally, to *students* training for ministry, I recognize that from a marketing standpoint the vision cast in this chapter isn't the best recruiting tool for the calling of the pastor theologian! I'm doing what Sir Ernest Shackleton did when he was looking for a crew of folks to join him on a ridiculously dangerous attempt to cross the whole of Antarctica. It was 1914, and he put an ad in the *London Times* selling the trip this way: "Men wanted for Hazardous journey. Small wages, bitter cold, long months of complete darkness, constant danger, safe return doubtful. Honor and recognition in case of success."[20] In his book on leadership and inspiration, *Start with Why*, Simon Sinek adds, "The only people who applied for the job were those who read the ad and thought it sounded great. They loved insurmountable odds. The only people who applied for the job were survivors. Shackleton hired only people who believed what he believed."[21]

Students, if you don't want to live in the cauldron of the church and thus the crucible of suffering, then the pastoral calling may not be your thing. The calling of the pastor theologian *certainly* won't be your thing. But if this all still sounds enticing to you, then by all means say your prayers—and go for it!

Besides, what greater soul-satisfying endeavor can there be than to embrace cruciformity in the cause of Christ for the good of others? Every parent reading this knows this to be true. "What man and woman," asks the Christian novelist Frederick Buechner, "if they gave serious thought to what children inevitably involve, would ever have them? Yet what man and woman, once having had them and loved them, would ever want it otherwise?"[22] What Buechner rightly says of parents in their suffering love I want to say of pastor theologians *as pastors*: "To suffer in love for another's suffering is to live life not only at its fullest but at its holiest."[23]

---

[20]Quoted in Simon Sinek, *Start with Why: How Great Leaders Inspire Everyone to Take Action* (New York: Portfolio, 2009), 92.

[21]Ibid.

[22]Frederick Buechner, *Listening to Your Life: Daily Meditations with Frederick Buechner* (HarperOne, 1992), 239.

[23]Ibid.

Part Two

The PASTOR THEOLOGIAN
in HISTORICAL PERSPECTIVE

6

Pastoral and Theological Leadership in Calvin's Geneva

SCOTT M. MANETSCH

SHORTLY BEFORE HIS DEATH IN 1564, John Calvin recalled the desperate condition of Geneva's church when he first visited the city twenty-eight years earlier: "When I first arrived in this church there was almost nothing. They were preaching and that's all. They were good at seeking out idols and burning them, but there was no Reformation. Everything was in turmoil."[1] Calvin's memory of this desperate situation was on the whole accurate. The departure of most of the Catholic clergy from the city by the summer of 1536 created a vacuum in leadership and a crisis in pastoral care. There was no church constitution; no program to recruit new ministers; no plan to instruct the children. The Catholic mass had been abolished, but no liturgical forms had been created to replace it. The relationship between church and city magistrates had yet to be defined. Calvin and the other Protestant ministers of Geneva quickly discovered that it was one thing to demolish the existing religious order and quite another to construct a new one in its place.

Over the next five years, Calvin and his pastoral colleagues worked tirelessly to construct a new religious order in Geneva that was faithful to scriptural teaching and attentive to their unique historical context. In 1541, Calvin

---

[1]"Discours d'adieu aux ministres," in John Calvin, *Ioannis Calvini opera omnia quae supersunt,* ed. G. Baum, E. Cunitz and E. Reuss (Brunsvigae: C. A. Schwetschke, 1863–1900), 9:891-94. Hereafter abbreviated as *CO.* This essay contains material adapted from my book *Calvin's Company of Pastors: Pastoral Care and the Emerging Reformed Church, 1536–1609* (New York: Oxford University Press, 2013).

drafted a church constitution entitled the *Ecclesiastical Ordinances* that articulated the primary elements of what would become Calvin's distinctive ecclesiology, including the fourfold division of church offices; the priority of preaching *lectio continua* in each parish; the practice of church discipline through an institution known as the Consistory; and the commitment to unadorned Word-centered public worship.

In this essay I will briefly describe Calvin's conception and construction of the pastoral office, focusing particularly on the priority that he gave to rigorous theological conversation and leadership. Though Calvin recognized that different members of Geneva's Company of Pastors would play different theological roles within the church, he expected that *all* of the city's ministers would be "pastor theologians" of a sort—that is, they would all be engaged in careful biblical and theological reflection for the purpose of enriching their pulpit ministries, guiding and nourishing their spiritual flocks, and protecting the larger church from doctrinal error.

THE STRUCTURE OF THE PASTORAL OFFICE IN GENEVA

The *Ecclesiastical Ordinances* organized Genevan church leadership into four offices: pastor, doctor, elder and deacon.[2] Calvin believed that this fourfold division reflected the practice of the apostolic church and was faithful to the pattern prescribed in Paul's epistles. The pastors or ministers were responsible for preaching the Word of God and administering the sacraments. But the ministry of the Word required more than the public exposition of Scripture; it also entailed the declaration and application of God's Word to individuals through the sacraments, liturgy, corrective discipline, catechetical instruction, household visitations and spiritual counsel and consolation. As Calvin noted, "The office of a true and faithful minister is not only to teach the people in public, which he is appointed to do as pastor, but also, as much as he is able, to admonish, exhort, warn, and console each person individually."[3] For Calvin, Christian ministers were expected to provide intensive, personal, spiritual support that would

---

[2]Calvin was the primary author of the *Ecclesiastical Ordinances*. The best edition of this document is found in Jean-François Bergier, ed., *Registres de la Compagnie des Pasteurs de Genève* (Geneva: Droz, 1964), 1:4. Hereafter cited as RCP.
[3]Calvin, "De La Visitation des Malades," in *La forme des prières et chantz ecclésiastiques* (Geneva: n.p., 1542), M3v-M4.

nurture their parishioners' Christian understanding and spirituality over the course of a lifetime, from cradle to grave.

As the chief human architect of the Genevan church, Calvin created a variety of institutions that were intended to supervise the ministers and assist them as pastors and church leaders. The *Company of Pastors* had primary responsibility for overseeing the day-to-day ministry of Geneva's churches.[4] With Calvin serving as its moderator, the Company consisted of the city's ministers and theological professors (usually around 18-20 men in all) who met for several hours every Friday morning. The Company was built on the conviction that all Christian ministers possess equal authority by virtue of their common vocation to proclaim the Word of God and administer the sacraments. Consequently, in their deliberations Geneva's ministers were equal gospel partners, with each pastor possessing a single vote. The pastoral company supervised every aspect of church life: it assured that right doctrine was taught from the city's pulpits; it recruited and examined ministerial candidates; it offered godly advice and correction to the city's magistrates; it oversaw the work of deacons and public benevolence. Over time, this collaborative body of Geneva's ministers and professors also emerged as a kind of nerve center for international Calvinism as foreign Reformed churches looked to it for theological advice, pastoral candidates and financial and political support.

A second church institution founded by Calvin was the *Congrégation*.[5] Patterned after Huldrych Zwingli's *Prophezei* in Zurich, the *Congrégation* was a weekly conference in which ministers, professors, theological students and interested laypeople studied the Scripture for several hours together. According to the 1561 version of the *Ecclesiastical Ordinances*, the primary purpose of the *Congrégation* was to preserve the purity and unity of doctrine within the church and to ensure that all Geneva's ministers were diligent in study and capable expositors of God's Word.[6] Accordingly, every

---

[4]The domestic and international role of Calvin's Company of Pastors has been explored in a variety of monographs and articles. See, for example, Robert Kingdon, *Geneva and the Coming of the Wars of Religion in France, 1555–1563* (Geneva: Droz, 1956); David Foxgrover, ed., *Calvin and the Company of Pastors*, Papers Presented at the 14th Colloquium of the Calvin Studies Society (Grand Rapids: CRC Product Services, 2004); Manetsch, *Calvin's Company of Pastors*.

[5]For more on Geneva's *Congrégation*, see Erik De Boer, *The Genevan School of the Prophets: The Congrégation of the Company of Pastors and their Influence in Sixteenth-Century Europe* (Geneva: Droz, 2012).

[6]*Ecclesiastical Ordinances* (1561), CO 10.1:96.

Friday morning, Geneva's pastors took turns leading the *Congrégation*. They provided detailed commentary and discussion of the biblical text of the day, after which those in attendance would offer feedback and discuss various theological and practical entailments of the passage. For Calvin, this collegial approach to Scripture study and interpretation was essential for the competence of the pastoral office and the well-being of Christ's church. "The fewer discussions of doctrine we have together, the greater the danger of pernicious opinions," Calvin once observed. Indeed, "solitude leads to great abuse."[7]

Of all the institutions established by Calvin, the *Consistory* remains the best known and the most controversial.[8] For Calvin, church discipline was essential for a healthy church: "All who desire to remove discipline or to hinder its restoration," he stated, "are surely contributing to the ultimate dissolution of the church."[9] When properly administered by pastors and elders, Calvin believed, church discipline served as spiritual medicine that God used to hasten the repentance of the sinner, protect the congregation from wicked examples and preserve the moral and doctrinal purity of Christ's church. During Calvin's lifetime, the Genevan Consistory, which consisted of the city's pastors and twelve lay elders, met every Thursday at noon to address a sizeable caseload of moral infractions that included quarrels, fornication, gambling, swearing, blasphemy, heresy, popular religion, Catholic behavior and drunkenness. Occasionally, Geneva's ministers themselves were called as defendants before the Consistory and reprimanded, or even suspended from the Lord's Supper, for such sins as fornication, fighting, dereliction of duty, rebellion and scandalous behavior. Clearly, woven into the DNA of Geneva's Reformed church was Calvin's conviction that ministers of the gospel stand beneath the authority of Christ and his Word, and that ministers must be accountable to the collective judgment of their colleagues.

---

[7]Calvin to Wolfgang Musculus, October 22, 1549, *CO* 13:434.
[8]For more on Calvin's Consistory, see William Monter, "The Consistory of Geneva, 1559–1569," *Bibliothèque d'Humanisme et Renaissance* 38 (1976): 467-84; Robert Kingdon, "The Geneva Consistory in the Time of Calvin," in *Calvinism in Europe, 1540–1620*, ed. Andrew Pettegree, Alastair Duke and Gillian Lewis (Cambridge: Cambridge University Press, 1996), 21-34; Kingdon, *Adultery and Divorce in Calvin's Geneva* (Cambridge, MA: Harvard University Press, 1995); Manetsch, *Calvin's Company of Pastors*, 182-220.
[9]Calvin, *Institutes of the Christian Religion*, ed. J. T. McNeill, trans. F. L. Battles (Philadelphia: Westminster, 1960), 1230.

A final clerical institution Calvin established was the *Quarterly Censure*.[10] Once every three months—shortly before Geneva's quarterly celebration of the Lord's Supper—all of Geneva's pastors met behind closed doors for a time of communal examination and fraternal correction. This was an opportunity for the ministers to air their grievances against one another and offer reproofs on matters of doctrine and personal conduct. At the end of the examination, the pastors shared a meal of soup as a visible sign of their unity in Christ. In the Quarterly Censure, Calvin and his colleagues confronted a variety of sinful actions and attitudes: ministerial colleagues were censured for arrogance, slander, negligence of study and harboring resentment toward their colleagues. The company also sometimes raised questions about the theological content or potential impact of a fellow minister's sermon or book. Though conflicts, disagreement and moral failings were inevitable, the Quarterly Censure was one important way in which Geneva's ministers sought to preserve the unity, moral integrity and theological purity of the pastoral office.

THEOLOGICAL LEADERSHIP IN CALVIN'S GENEVA

The myth that presents John Calvin as the "pope" or "dictator" of Geneva has been decisively put to rest by recent historical scholarship. To be sure, owing to his strong personality, his brilliance as a theologian and exegete, and his sizeable international reputation, Calvin exercised significant *moral* authority within Geneva's church and society. Yet, at the same time, Calvin was only one member of a company of city ministers. Like his colleagues, he received his salary from the city council, which could dismiss him on forty-eight-hours' notice (which happened in 1538). Moreover—and this is the central argument of this essay—the way that Calvin constructed the pastoral office, and the actual day-to-day practice of church ministry in Geneva, placed responsibility for theological leadership on all of Geneva's ministers. Not just Calvin but each of the city's ministers was expected to be a pastor theologian. Here I will briefly explore three levels of theological leadership that can be identified among the ministers who belonged to the Company of Pastors.

Professors of theology. As we have seen, in his *Ecclesiastical Ordinances* Calvin made a clear distinction between the offices of pastor and professor

---

[10]For more on the Quarterly Censure (also known as the Ordinary Censure), see Manetsch, *Calvin's Company of Pastors*, 127-28.

(or doctor). Theological professors, like pastors, were charged to interpret the Scriptures and teach sound doctrine. However, their mandate extended beyond the local congregation to the larger church; it was the professors' responsibility to teach future pastors *and* protect the broader church from doctrinal error. As Calvin noted:

> Pastors, to my mind, are those to whom is committed the charge of a particular flock. I have no objection to their receiving the name of "doctors," if we realize that there is another kind of doctor, who superintends both the education of pastors and the instruction of the whole church. Sometimes he can be a pastor who is also a doctor, but the duties are different.[11]

The office of professor or "doctor" took institutional shape in 1559 with the founding of the Genevan Academy, which consisted of a lower-level Latin school (*schola privata*) for schoolboys, and an upper-level "seminary" (*schola publica*) for young men preparing for Christian ministry, law and medicine.[12] During Calvin's lifetime and in the generations that followed, a handful of Geneva's ministers—including Calvin, Theodore Beza, Lambert Daneau, Antoine de La Faye, Jean Diodati and Theodore Tronchin—were elected by the Company of Pastors to joint appointments whereby they served as both parish ministers and as professors of Bible or theology. In addition to their parish responsibilities and their teaching duties at the Academy, most of these theological "professionals" undertook extensive writing ministries in the service of Protestant and Reformed Christianity throughout Europe. Calvin, for example, published nearly one hundred theological and exegetical works during his tenure in Geneva. During the 1550s, the Reformer's literary output ranged from 100,000 words per year to an eye-popping 250,000 words per year.[13] Similarly, Calvin's colleague and successor Theodore Beza published more than seventy-five works, including theological tracts, Bible translations, commentaries, sermon collections, ethical treatises, historical works and poetry collections.[14]

---

[11]Calvin, commentary on Eph 4:11, *CO* 51:198.

[12]For more on the history and structure of Geneva's Academy, see Karin Maag, *Seminary or University? The Genevan Academy and Reformed Higher Education, 1560–1620* (Aldershot: Ashgate, 1995).

[13]Jean-François Gilmont, *John Calvin and the Printed Book*, trans. Karin Maag (Kirksville, MO: Truman State University, 2005), 284-85.

[14]For the definitive bibliography of Beza's writings, see Frédéric Gardy, *Bibliographie des oeuvres théologiques, littéraires, historiques et juridiques de Théodore de Bèze* (Geneva: Droz, 1960).

A sizeable number of these books written by Geneva's theological professors had a distinctive apologetic purpose, as they defended Reformed churches from the attacks of Anti-Trinitarians, Roman Catholics and Lutheran opponents. To be a doctor of the church, therefore, was a strategic role—but it could also be an exhausting one. In a rare moment of self-disclosure, Calvin admitted: "I get so tired from that endless writing that at times I have a loathing for it and actually hate writing."[15] But true religion needed to be defended in print as well as from the pulpit, and Calvin felt the weight of this responsibility. "I would be a real coward if I saw God's truth being attacked and remained quiet without a sound."[16]

Table 1. Number of titles produced by Genevan ministers during their pastoral tenure, 1536–1609

Subject Area	Number of Titles [Calvin]	Percentage of Total
Bibles and Exegetical Aids	14	4%
Commentaries on Scripture	34 [26]	10%
Commentaries on Patristic/Classical Texts	6	2%
Correspondence	3 [1]	1%
Devotional Writings	20	6%
Ethics	17 [7]	5%
Geography	1	—
History/Biography	29 [1]	8%
Natural Sciences	3	1%
Poetry and Music	9 [1]	3%
Politics	5	1%
Sermon Collections	28 [21]	8%
Theology and Polemics	130 [42]	37%
Translations and Editions	51	15%
Total	**350 [99]**	**100%**

Producers of theology. Theological professors were not the only authors who produced religious literature in sixteenth-century Geneva. During Calvin's lifetime and in the half-century that followed, around one in six of all of Geneva's ministers wrote books in the service of Christ's church. As

---

[15]Calvin to Heinrich Bullinger, March 13, 1551, *CO* 14:51.
[16]Calvin to the Queen of Navarre, April, 28, 1545, *CO* 12:67.

is evident from table 1, the literature produced by Geneva's ministers between 1536 and 1609 was substantial and surprisingly eclectic.

The Genevan minister Simon Goulart (1543–1628) is a good example of
a pastor theologian who never occupied an academic post but nevertheless
employed his pen in the service of Protestant Christianity in Europe. Goulart
was recognized by his contemporaries as an outstanding preacher and
Christian statesman; he was also "one of the most indefatigable writers" of
his age, producing no fewer than sixty-five separate works over the course
of his fifty-year tenure in the pastoral office.[17] The catalogue of his writings
includes such diverse literary genres as works of poetry and music; historical
chronicles; biographies; martyrologies; theological, political, and medical
treatises; moral essays; and devotional works.

The focus and thrust of Goulart's writing ministry was slightly different
from that of Calvin or Beza. For one, Goulart's literary corpus contains few
original works of systematic or polemical theology; instead, he devoted his
energies to translating, publishing and promoting the theological work of
other prominent Reformed leaders, including Beza, Antoine de Chandieu,
William Perkins, Peter Martyr Vermigli, Zacharias Ursinus and Jerome
Zanchi. Second, as a theologian, Goulart prioritized the *application* of Reformed theology to the everyday concerns and needs of the Christian life.
With rich insight and raw emotional honesty, Goulart's books probe such
topics as doubt and Christian assurance, spiritual consolation, personal
sanctification, wealth and poverty, suffering, spiritual warfare and the art of
dying well.[18] At the risk of anachronism, Goulart might be described as a
practical or *pastoral* theologian, applying Reformed theology to the pressing
daily concerns of the Christian men and women.

Practitioners of theology. Though theological leadership in Geneva was
entrusted to a small group of the city's ministers and professors, nevertheless
every member of the Company of Pastors was required to participate in
regular, sustained theological reflection and discussion. In a very real sense,

[17]The quotation reflects the assessment of Pierre Bayle, in his *Dictionnaire historique et critique*,
    3rd ed., vol. 2 (Rotterdam: Fabri et Barrilot, 1715), 272-73. The best biography of Simon Goulart
    remains Leonard Chester Jones, *Simon Goulart, 1543-1628: Étude biographie et bibliographique*
    (Geneva: Georg & Cie., 1917).
[18]For more on this dimension of Goulart's writing ministry, see Manetsch, "Simon Goulart
    (1543–1628) and the Consolation of Troubled Souls," *Calvin Theological Journal* 49 (2014): 201-20.

all of Geneva's ministers were expected to be pastor theologians. Candidates for pastoral office in Geneva underwent rigorous examinations to determine their command of Scripture, their knowledge of Christian theology, their ability to preach and the quality of their moral character. Once installed, Geneva's ministers were subject to formal guidelines requiring them to mature as students of the Word. Those ministers who neglected personal study of God's Word, who treated Scripture in a scandalous fashion or who taught doctrines that were contrary to Geneva's Confession of Faith were subject to formal rebuke and, if repentance was not forthcoming, dismissal from the pastoral office.[19] Calvin and his colleagues believed that it was imperative for God's Word to be taught with "knowledge and edification."[20]

Moreover, as noted earlier, Calvin established church institutions such as the *Congrégation* and the Quarterly Censure to insure that Geneva's ministers continued to mature as competent exegetes and theologians. So too, as members of the Consistory, city ministers routinely applied their theology of repentance, sanctification and sacraments to the never-ending caseload of broken relationships, wrong belief and sinful behavior. Finally, weekly meetings of the Company of Pastors provided a particularly important venue for substantial theological conversation and doctrinal formulation. During the year 1572, for example, the Company of Pastors deliberated and offered its judgment on these significant theological and practical questions:

- Is it permissible for Reformed Christians who live in Lutheran territories to subscribe to the Augsburg Confession?

- What is the value of the Jewish Talmud for Christian readers?

- How should Reformed Christians in France respond to proposals calling for the introduction of congregational church government?

- Does the Bible allow a man to marry the sister of his deceased wife?

- What theological method should be adopted in the curriculum at the Genevan Academy?

- Is it permissible for Geneva's municipal bank to charge interest rates above 5 percent?

---

[19] *Ecclesiastical Ordinances* (1541), RCP 1:4.
[20] RCP 5:37-38.

- Does witchcraft constitute biblical grounds for divorce?
- How should the church restore beleaguered Protestants who had abjured their faith during times of Catholic persecution?[21]

Customarily, the ministers' collective judgment on these theological and practical concerns was recorded in the register of the Company of Pastors or in its official correspondence.

It is clear that all of Geneva's ministers were expected to be students of God's Word who were growing in theological discernment, competent to exercise theological leadership within their parishes and over Christ's church. This vision for pastoral leadership presupposed rigorous personal study as well as substantial, consistent participation in a theological community. Only a handful of Geneva's ministers were "professional" theologians who wrote books and instructed future pastors at the Academy. But in Calvin's Geneva, every member of the pastoral company was a theological practitioner, called to be a pastor theologian.

CONCLUSION

I close this chapter with three brief remarks by way of contemporary application.

First, Calvin saw the value of creating religious institutions to ensure clerical accountability and promote theological awareness—and so should we. Although our situation is vastly different from that of Calvin's, the need to formalize pastoral collaboration and substantial theological reflection has not changed. Pastoral institutions, whether constructed within local churches or between area clergy, have the potential to mitigate pastoral isolation and promote ministerial wisdom and gospel faithfulness.

Second, Calvin reminds us that faithful theological reflection is best done collaboratively, in the context of Christian community. Calvin was right: "The fewer discussions of doctrine we have, the greater the danger of pernicious opinions, [for] solitude leads to great abuse."

Finally, the example of Calvin's Geneva suggests that the strategic task of Christian theology belongs not only to academic theologians but to pastor theologians in local churches who are well-equipped to formulate, translate and apply God's truth to the particular concerns and needs of the people in

[21]RCP 3:36-98.

their congregations. In one of his earliest writings, Calvin articulated this *pastoral* vision for theology in a most memorable fashion: "I require only this, that faithful people be allowed to hear their God speaking and to learn from his teaching."[22] May this central concern be ours as well.

---

[22]Calvin, "Preface to Pierre Olivétan's French Bible," in *CO* 9:788.

7

Thomas Boston as Pastor Theologian

PHILIP GRAHAM RYKEN

I T WAS AN INAUSPICIOUS BEGINNING. In the autumn of 1699 Thomas Boston (1676–1732) arrived at Simprin to pastor the smallest church in the smallest parish in Scotland. There were fewer than one hundred adults in the entire parish, and only seven came to church to hear the new minister.

Though the congregation was small, Boston preached as if his life depended upon it. He expounded a passage that recently had been on his mind: "My people are destroyed for lack of knowledge" (Hos 4:6).[1] The new minister began by preaching to himself, arguing that "the Ignorance of a people living under a Christian name, occasioned by the carelessness of their teachers, will be laid to the teachers charge as well as to their own." In other words, preachers must answer to God for the spiritual condition of their congregations. Indeed, "Ministers by carelessness become the murderers of the souls of their people."[2]

Thomas Boston was determined not to be a careless minister. Nor would he allow his congregation to remain mired in spiritual ignorance for long. He embarked on a yearlong series of sermons on the sinfulness and misery of "man's natural estate" and on "Christ the remedy for man's misery."[3] For Boston, the depravity of humanity and the grace of God in Christ were the

---

[1]Unless otherwise indicated, Scripture quotations in this chapter are from the King James Version.
[2]"MSS of Thomas Boston of Ettrick," Aberdeen University Library, MS.3245/2, 157 (hereafter "Aberdeen MS").
[3]Thomas Boston, *The Complete Works of the Late Rev. Thomas Boston of Ettrick*, ed. Samuel M'Millan, 12 vols. (London, 1853; repr., Wheaton, IL: Richard Owen Roberts, 1980), 12:153.

fundamentals of true religion, and therefore practically and theologically critical for his congregation to understand.

The doctrines of sin and grace occupied Boston's attention throughout his early years in ministry. When he was called to the parish of Ettrick in 1707 he began with the basics once again. This time, however, he organized his preaching on sin and grace into four parts: Innocence, Nature, Grace and Eternity. Boston traced the history of humanity from created perfection, to the fall into sin, through redemption in Christ, to the eternal realities of heaven and hell. The sermons went through a series of revisions until finally they were published as *Human Nature in its Fourfold State* (1720).[4]

The *Fourfold State*, as it was called, became the most popular Scottish book of the eighteenth century. Because it was a bestseller during the Great Awakening (1725–1760), it became a foundational document for evangelical theology. Jonathan Edwards (1703–1758) liked it "exceeding well" and considered Boston "a truly great divine."[5] George Whitefield (1714–1770) found it "of much service" to his soul.[6] John Wesley (1703–1791) went so far as to publish an abridgment of the *Fourfold State* in his Puritan library.[7]

Thomas Boston never aspired to international acclaim, nor did he expect it. Only after his death did his writings gain wide exposure. During his lifetime his pastoral influence largely was confined to the borders of his own parish, so much so that he sometimes felt "staked down" in Ettrick. These humble surroundings—rather than his posthumous success—make Boston a valuable model for pastor theologians. He did not found his own organization or start his own movement. He was not the head of a megachurch. He was simply the pastor of a small local church.

It was in this context that Thomas Boston exemplified the ideals of a pastor theologian that I will set forth in this chapter: reverence for the triune God, confidence in the Bible, theological simplicity, respect for the sacraments and love for the church, with equal passion for its peace and purity.

---

[4] The most readily available edition is Thomas Boston, *Human Nature in its Fourfold State* (Edinburgh: Banner of Truth, 1964; repr. 1989).
[5] Jonathan Edwards, *The Works of Jonathan Edwards*, ed. John E. Smith (New Haven, CT: Yale University Press, 1957–), 2:489.
[6] George Whitefield, in Donald Fraser, *The Life and Diary of the Reverend Ralph Erskine* (Edinburgh: William Oliphant & Son, 1834), 317.
[7] Thomas Boston, *The Doctrine of Original Sin*, ed. John Wesley (London: n.p., 1774).

"None Other God but One"

Like most Presbyterians in the Puritan tradition, Thomas Boston was impressed with the weightiness of God. In the words of the apostle, he knew "that there is none other God but one" (1 Cor 8:4), and thus his overarching purpose was to magnify the sovereignty and majesty of Almighty God. His preaching was suffused with a sense of the divine presence. He had a surpassing awareness of the Godness of God.

Today many preachers seem preoccupied with meeting felt needs, with immersing themselves in popular culture—or worse, with making people laugh. An older and better style of preaching valued reverence over relevance. Pastor theologians in this tradition were concerned primarily to glorify God the Father, Son and Holy Ghost. They gave precedence to the vertical dimension of preaching (God to humanity) over the horizontal (person to person). Like Jeremiah (Jer 9:23-24) and Paul (1 Cor 1:31), their boast was in the Lord.

Thomas Boston commended this kind of reverent ministry in a sermon entitled "A Heart Exercised unto Godliness, Necessary to Make a Good Minister." The sermon was delivered, as one might expect, at an ordination to gospel ministry. In it Boston preached what he practiced: "If the fear of the Lord be not on our spirits, to counterbalance the fear of men, we cannot avoid being ensnared in unfaithfulness. But a heart exercised to godliness, will lead us on to act, as in the sight of God, whether in public or in private, that no souls perish through our default."[8] Boston's point was that a faithful minister conducts every pastoral duty in the presence of God.

Practicing the presence of God is necessary for all Christians, not just for clergy. Boston thus concluded a sermon series, "Of God and His Perfections," with this exhortation:

> Thus we have given you a short description of what God is. Imperfect it is, and imperfect it must be, seeing he is incomprehensible. Do ye study to believe what is taught you of God, and apply to him, through the Son of his love, for further discoveries of his glorious perfections and excellencies; and at length ye shall see him as he is, having a more enlarged and extensive knowledge of him, his nature and ways; though even then ye will not be able to comprehend

---

[8]Boston, *Works*, 4:79.

him. For it was a wise and judicious answer of one that was asked, What God is? that if he knew that fully, he should be a God himself. And indeed that being which we can comprehend, cannot be God, because he is infinite. O study God and ye will increase in the knowledge of him.[9]

These words capture both a humility about how well God can be known and a hunger to know him as well as possible.

"The Book of the Lord"

The one true God makes himself known through his Word. For this reason, Thomas Boston was deeply committed to teaching the Scriptures as the Word of God. The Bible is, as he termed it, "The Book of the Lord."[10]

Boston's love for God's Word led to a lifetime of careful study. Since Hebrew was not then part of the divinity curriculum at Edinburgh, he assembled a library of grammars and concordances to teach himself how to read the Old Testament in the original. Eventually he became a skillful enough Hebraist to publish a learned Latin treatise on the accentuation of the Hebrew text.[11]

Boston held to the inerrancy of the Bible in its original autographs. This defining doctrine of evangelical orthodoxy was held (almost) universally until the nineteenth century. As Boston asked rhetorically in his exposition of 1 Peter 1:20-21, "If all scripture was given by inspiration, if no scripture be of private interpretation, nor came by the will of man, but holy men spake as they were moved by the Holy Ghost, how can there be any error in any passage of scripture?"[12]

The inerrancy of Scripture was more than simply a theory for Boston; it was a matter of practice as well as faith. God's Word was given so that God's people might become godly:

What then remains . . . but, that we diligently read the holy scriptures as being the word of God, and the rule which he hath given to direct us both as to faith and practice; and that we fervently pray to God, that he may give us his holy Spirit to enlighten our minds in the saving knowledge of the

[9]Boston, *Works*, 1:130.
[10]Boston, *Works*, 1:56.
[11]Thomas Boston, *Tractatus Stigmologicus, Hebraeo-Biblicus* (Amsterdam: n.p., 1738).
[12]Boston, *Works*, 1:30.

word, without which we will remain in the dark, and the word will be but a dead letter to us?[13]

In answer to Boston's question, the only thing that remained was to preach the Word of God. Thus Bible exposition was at the center of his ministry. Worship services included prayers, of course, and singing psalms, but mainly they consisted of reading and preaching the Bible. In addition to preaching the main sermon, Boston regularly lectured on a Scripture reading.

Once Boston mounted the steps of his pulpit he preached in the Puritan style.[14] He took a single verse for his text, or sometimes only a phrase from a verse. He began by making several exegetical observations about the text. Next he stated its central doctrine in propositional form. After explaining and expounding this preaching proposition, he concluded with the "use" of the doctrine.

The "use" referred to the usefulness of the doctrine for practical Christian living. This often took as much as half the sermon. The Word was not simply to be heard or preached; it was carefully to be applied: "If we would be good Christians, or good ministers, we must study this, not simply as a book of knowledge, that we may speak of the truths contained in it; but as a book of saving knowledge, that we may feel the power of the truths of it on our hearts."[15] Boston never tired of reminding his congregation (or himself) that "religion is not a matter of mere speculations to satisfy men's curiosity, but a matter of practice."[16]

PLAIN AND SIMPLE

Boston's belief in the utility of God's Word led him to strive in his preaching for practical and theological simplicity. He was wary of "vain ostentation" in the pulpit, preferring to "stoop to the understanding of the meanest, and not to give the people a comment darker than the text."[17] As Boston observed, simplicity was characteristic of the teaching ministry of Jesus Christ, who taught "plainly and perspicuously" in the Gospels. In the same way that Jesus

---

[13]Boston, *Works*, 1:37.

[14]See Perry Miller, *The New England Mind: The Seventeenth Century* (New York: Macmillan, 1939), 332-3.

[15]Boston, *Works*, 4:76.

[16]Boston, *Works*, 2:649.

[17]Boston, *Works*, 1:420.

used words and images adapted "to the low and dull capacities of men," so "he would have his ministers to preach."[18]

Despite his breadth of reading, Boston rarely quoted from learned divines or repeated anecdotes from classical sources. Partly he was afraid of anything that would distract from the biblical message. Early in his ministry he wrote, "I have been helped to speak to the people by similitudes; but exacting an account of the sermon from the people, several of them told me the earthly part, but quite forgot the heavenly part; which was very wounding to me; so that I know not how to preach so as they may be profited."[19] This shows the value of soliciting sermon critiques: Boston did not simply assume that his message was getting through; he checked to be sure. It also poses a perennial homiletical conundrum: parishioners remember the illustrations but forget what they illustrate!

Boston's decision to eschew anecdotes did not lead to dull or uninspiring sermons; his preaching retained two sources of imaginative appeal. The first was biblical imagery. Boston gravitated toward the metaphors and narratives of Scripture. Often he used a single image to organize an entire sermon. A particularly vivid example is his exposition of Song of Solomon 2:3 ("I sat down under his shadow with great delight, and his fruit was sweet to my taste"), which he titled "Suitable Improvement of Christ the Apple Tree."[20]

Second, Boston derived analogies from the common experiences of life on the farm. The daily tasks of a rural community afforded a rich field for illustrating the truths of Scripture. In one of his first sermons, Boston exhorted his people to learn how to read "the book of creation." "When you Dight [prepare] it, sow it, plough, harrow, [etc.] ye may learn much."[21] Or, as he asserted on another occasion, "Every pile of grass is a preacher of the loving-kindness of the Lord."[22] As a pastor theologian, Boston used general revelation to illustrate special revelation.

The *Fourfold State* exemplifies many of the virtues of Boston's preaching. To begin with, the book has a simple structure. Its organizing principle comes from Augustine's *Treatise On Rebuke and Grace*, in which Augustine

---

[18]Boston, *Works*, 1:419.
[19]Boston, *Works*, 12:99.
[20]Boston, *Works*, 3:165-79.
[21]Boston, Aberdeen MS, 175.
[22]Boston, *Works*, 1:203.

(354–430) distinguishes between the grace God gave Adam to be able not to sin (*posse non peccare*) and the grace he will give the saints in heaven not to be able to sin (*non posse peccare*).[23] The great medieval systematician Peter Lombard (c. 1095–1169) later took this idea and expanded it into four states or conditions of humanity: innocence, fallen nature, grace and glory.[24]

Boston's innovation was to preach through these four states. He wanted his people to know their origins (creation) and their destiny (eternity). He especially wanted them to recognize their sin (fall) and come to Christ for salvation (grace). The basic structure of the *Fourfold State* provides a simple, systematic, memorable framework for understanding Christian life and doctrine.

The *Fourfold State* makes frequent use of the stories and similes of Scripture. Its treatment of the doctrine of union with Christ is a good example.[25] Boston took John 15:5 for his text: "I am the vine, ye are the branches." Then he used this simple metaphor to show how justification, sanctification, adoption, glorification and all the other benefits of salvation flow from Christ to the Christian. This organic metaphor was doubly appropriate for parishioners in Ettrick: it was agricultural as well as biblical.

One other feature of Boston's preaching seems worthy of mention: his sermons were short. Some Puritans preached two hours or longer, but not Thomas Boston. He carried an hourglass with him into the pulpit; when half an hour was up, he stopped. Later, he would mark an "x" in his manuscript to remind himself where to begin the following Lord's Day.

Boston kept things simple. He did not try to entertain his congregation. He was not a people-pleaser. Yet he did strive to preach so people could understand and apply the Word of God. His gift for simplicity was greatly admired by his ministerial colleagues, who lauded his "peculiar talent for going deep into the mysteries of the gospel, and at the same time for making them plain."[26]

---

[23] Augustine, *De Correptione et Gratia*, ed. J. P. Migne, Patrologiae Cursus Completus, Series Latina, 44 (Paris, 1863), cols. 915-46 (X. 28).

[24] Peter Lombard, *Sententiae in IV Libris Distinctae*, 3rd ed., Spicilegium Bonaventurianum 4–5 (Grottaferrata: Editiones Collegii S. Bonaventurae ad Claras Aquas, 1971), II.25.2. The history of the fourfold state is traced in Philip Graham Ryken, *Thomas Boston as Preacher of the Fourfold State*, Rutherford Studies in Historical Theology (Carlisle, UK: Paternoster, 1999).

[25] Boston, *Works*, 8:177-231.

[26] Messrs. Calder, Wilson and Davidson, "Sketch of the Author's Character," in Boston, *Works*, 12:451.

Simplicity was one key to Boston's success as a pastor theologian. His published works were not for pastors or theologians, primarily, but for Christians of the common sort. One nineteenth-century historian aptly described the *Fourfold State* as the "gospel of the peasantry."[27] Its unexpected popularity was due in no small measure to Boston's frequent prayer that the Holy Spirit would give him "plainness in treating of gospel-mysteries."[28]

HOLY FAIRS

Thomas Boston was a minister of sacrament as well as Word. Here we encounter a paradox: the Lord's Supper was celebrated rarely in eighteenth-century Scotland, yet it remained at the center of church life. This seeming contradiction arose from the practice of "communion seasons." Instead of observing weekly communion, many congregations hosted annual Eucharistic services. One church historian described them like this:

> Sacramental occasions in Scotland were great festivals, an engaging combination of holy day and holiday. They were, as one divine said, "fair-days of the gospel," festal events in a Reformed calendar otherwise dominated by the week-to-week observance of the Sabbath. In them religion and culture, communion and community, piety and sociability commingled. Regularly times of renewal and revival, they were the high days of the year.[29]

Once the date for the Lord's Supper was set, preparations began in earnest. Other ministers were invited to participate, as were their congregations. Church members opened their homes as guests from other parishes began to arrive.

Services generally were held out of doors—sometimes under tents or pavilions—and followed a conventional pattern. Thursday was a fast day. On Friday communicants were examined by their elders. This was a primary means of church discipline in the Scottish church. In order to receive the sacrament, communicants were required to present a communion token from their elders. The token certified that the holder was a confessing sinner

---

[27]Henry Grey Graham, *The Social Life of Scotland in the Eighteenth Century*, 2 vols. (London: Black, 1900), 2:80.

[28]Boston, *Works*, 12:262.

[29]Leigh Eric Schmidt, *Holy Fairs: Scottish Communions and American Revivals in the Early Modern Period* (Princeton, NJ: Princeton University Press, 1989), 3.

and a professing Christian. A preparation service was held on Saturday, at which congregants were challenged to confess their sins before receiving the body and the blood of Christ. The Lord's Supper finally was celebrated on Sunday morning. Communicants came in groups to sit around a common table. This practice helped symbolize the Lord's Supper as a covenant meal. The communion service was followed by services of thanksgiving on Sunday evening and again on Monday. Communicants celebrated their salvation in Christ and pledged to live in new obedience to Christ. Given the pattern of repentance, faith and new commitment, it is not hard to recognize the roots of American revivalism in these "holy fairs."

Thomas Boston regularly participated in communion seasons throughout southern Scotland. He took the sacrament seriously, only coming to the Lord's Table after careful self-examination. One early diary entry gives a glimpse of the way he prepared himself. After citing a variety of Bible verses describing the heart desires of a true Christian, Boston reasoned:

> 1. I am content to part with all sin, and take Christ to follow him . . . 2. I desire union and communion with Christ . . . 3. I desire a whole Christ, and would as fain have sin subdued and mortified, as guilt taken away. 4. I esteem Christ above all; give me Christ, and take from me what thou wilt. 5. Sin is a burden to me, especially my predominant lust. 6. I endeavour, in some measure, to seek after Christ; Lord, thou knowest. Therefore I have true faith.[30]

While there are obvious disadvantages to infrequent communion, this shows one advantage: the communion season was an important time to examine one's spiritual life.

As his reputation grew, Boston often was asked to preach at communion seasons in nearby parishes. Many of the sermons in his published works were first preached during a "holy fair." On one such occasion he was deeply affected by the spiritual realities represented in the sacrament:

> The elements after consecration being declared to be no more common bread and wine, but sacred symbols of the body and blood of Christ, I felt in my spirit a sensible change accordingly; I discerned the sacramental union of the signs and the thing signified, and was thereby let into a view of the mystical union. I saw it, I believed it, and I do believe it to this day. I do not remember

---

[30]Boston, *Works*, 12:40.

myself ever to have been so distinct in the view and faith of this glorious mystery; and that with application, for I do believe that Christ dwells in me by his Spirit, and I in him by faith.[31]

Boston's last communion season at Ettrick must have been a grand occasion. Wave upon wave of communicants approached the Lord's Table—in all, some 777 tokens were presented.[32] The presiding minister had come a long way from his first service at Simprin, when only seven parishioners came to hear him preach.

BAPTIZED INTO THE DEATH OF CHRIST

"The sacraments," Boston taught, "are external means of spiritual washing, and are made effectual by the Spirit, being received by faith." He believed this to be true of baptism as well as communion. Baptism is a sign and a seal of union with Christ and all his benefits: remission of sins by the blood of Christ, adoption into the family of God, regeneration by the Holy Spirit and resurrection unto life eternal. It is also a sign and seal of "our engagement to be the Lord's, to be his only, wholly and for ever."[33]

As a devout Presbyterian, Boston believed in the efficacy of infant baptism. Yet he was careful to point out that baptism, in and of itself, does not save. It was partly for this reason that Boston refused to conduct private baptisms, even when a newborn seemed to be dying. He was convinced that sacraments belong in the public worship of God. To ride out from the manse every time a baby was ill would only encourage a superstitious view of the efficacy of baptism. This was not merely a theoretical issue; the infant mortality rate was high in those days, and a minister buried children nearly as often as he baptized them. Boston himself was deeply scarred by personal tragedy: six of his ten children died in infancy.

The death of one son was especially tragic. Boston had already lost a son named Ebenezer, meaning "Hitherto hath the LORD helped us" (1 Sam 7:12). When his wife delivered another son he considered naming the child Ebenezer as well. In effect, the boy would be a second pillar of faith set up in praise to God. Yet Boston was troubled by the thought, "What if he die too?"

---

[31]Boston, *Works*, 12:262.
[32]Boston, *Works*, 12:435.
[33]Boston, *Works*, 2:476-77.

That would be a blow almost too bitter to bear. It was only "after no small struggle" that he decided to name the boy Ebenezer.

It was an act of courageous faith. Nevertheless, the boy was sickly, and Boston describes going out to the barn to intercede for his newborn son: "There I renewed my covenant with God, and did solemnly and explicitly covenant for Ebenezer, and in his name accept of the covenant, and of Christ offered in the gospel; and gave him away to the Lord, before angels, and the stones of that house as witnesses. I cried also for his life, that Ebenezer might live before him, if it were his will."[34] Alas, Ebenezer never recovered. As Boston gently put it, "It pleased the Lord, that he also was removed from me."[35]

Only a grieving parent could tell the agonies Boston endured at the death of his second Ebenezer. Yet he did not despair. Instead, he entered into deeper and fuller intimacy with God, as his description of his son's burial reveals:

> When the child was laid in the coffin, his mother kissed his dust. I only lifted the cloth off his face, looked on it, and covered it again, in confidence of seeing that body rise a glorious body. . . . I see most plainly, that sovereignty challenges a latitude, to which I must stoop, and be content to follow the Lord in an untrodden path; and this made me with more ease to bury my second Ebenezer than I could do the first. . . . I learned not to cry, How will the loss be made up? but being now in that matter as a weaned child, desired the loss to be made up by the presence of the Lord.[36]

These painful events taught Boston something of what it means to be baptized into the death of Christ Jesus (Rom 6:3-4). Since the man cannot be separated from the ministry, they also were woven into the tapestry of his pastorate. He entered deeply into the kind of ministry the apostle Paul desired, knowing both the power of Christ's resurrection and the fellowship of sharing in his sufferings (Phil 3:10). To put it another way, he carried out his life and ministry in union with Christ.

The Shepherd of Ettrick

Thomas Boston was a compassionate minister, deeply devoted to the flock under his care. In addition to ministering to the sick and bereaved, he

---

[34]Boston, *Works*, 12:206.
[35]Boston, *Works*, 12:205.
[36]Boston, *Works*, 12:207.

maintained an ambitious schedule of pastoral visitation. Traveling by horseback and ranging over territory covering some 100 square miles, he visited every home in his parish twice annually.

The purpose of these visits was to promote the spiritual welfare of every member of the congregation. Boston prayed, read Scripture, catechized children and generally inquired how each household was growing in its love and knowledge of Jesus Christ. By doing so, he was following the directives of the General Assembly of the Church of Scotland, which instructed ministers to "be painful [careful] in catechising, frequent in visiting of families, and in private personal conference with those of their charge about the state of their souls."[37]

Recognizing that they were living in ungodly times, members of the Assembly also reminded elders and pastors of the necessity of church discipline. They recommended "the vigorous, impartial, and yet prudent exercise of Church discipline against all immorality, especially drunkenness and filthiness, cursing and swearing, and profaning the Lord's Day."[38] Since discipline begins in the pulpit, Boston often preached against these and other sins. Where necessary, flagrant sinners were reproved individually, as his session minutes reveal.[39]

Although Thomas Boston was not afraid to reprove sin, he greatly preferred to promote righteousness. One way he did so was by starting a small group shortly after arriving in Simprin. Notes from the group's first meetings have survived, and their title explains their purpose: "Cases of Conscience discoursed on at the weekly meeting for prayer and Christian fellowship."[40]

These meetings for prayer and fellowship began with a question about the Christian life, such as "What may be the marks of true and saving faith?" or, "How is prayer to be gone about so as it may be accepted of God?" Finding answers to such questions made for the most inductive of Bible studies. Members of the group gave answers and suggested relevant passages for Scripture study. Boston carefully wrote down each answer, as well as references to any Bible passages the group consulted.

---

[37] *Acts of the General Assembly of the Church of Scotland, 1638–1842* (Edinburgh: Edinburgh Printing & Publishing Co., 1843), 280.
[38] *Acts of the General Assembly*, 280.
[39] "Simprin Kirk Session Minutes—1699–1714," Scottish Record Office, CH 2/346/1.
[40] Boston, "Aberdeen MS," 77-82.

Small groups and home Bible studies are sometimes considered a recent phenomenon. Ultimately, of course, they go back at least as far as the house churches of the New Testament. Yet small group Bible studies have more immediate antecedents among the Puritans. Then, as now, Christians practiced the communion of the saints by meeting in one another's homes for prayer and Bible study.

HOW TO MINISTER DURING A CRISIS

Sooner or later, every minister faces a crisis—maybe more than one. Thomas Boston faced multiple challenges in the Scottish church of the early eighteenth century. By all accounts, ungodliness was epidemic. As a young minister Boston lamented the "great ignorance prevailing" in the parish of Simprin.[41] Later he drew a comparison between Ettrick and Corinth "in her three grand evils, self-conceit, a divisive temper, and sins of uncleanness."[42] His estimation of the spiritual condition of the nation was, if possible, even lower: "The land is defiled with idolatry, superstition, sinful swearing, Sabbath breaking, unfaithfulness in all relations, murders, uncleanness, dishonesty and fraud, lying, and covetousness."[43]

In addition to the problem of general ungodliness, there were particular controversies within the church. Heterodoxy was gaining its first foothold in the Scottish universities. This was most evident in the prolonged heresy trials of John Simson (1667–1740), who was Professor of Divinity at the University of Glasgow. Simson was accused of a number of theological errors, the most egregious of which concerned the person of Jesus Christ. Another controversy—known as the Marrow Controversy (1718–1723)—showed that the Scottish church was in danger of losing its grip on the gospel. The controversy arose from a book Boston himself discovered: *The Marrow of Modern Divinity*. *The Marrow*, as it was called, was a short summary of Reformation theology written in 1645. Boston found it helpful on a number of topics, especially in its opposition to legalism, emphasis on the assurance of faith and insistence on the free offer of the gospel.

---

[41] Boston, *Works*, 12:103.
[42] Boston, *Works*, 12:459.
[43] Thomas Boston, *A Collection of Sermons, Shewing the Grounds of the Lord's Controversy with this Church and Land* (Edinburgh: John Gray, 1772), 16.

Eventually *The Marrow* was condemned by the General Assembly, but the controversy helped make Scottish preaching more explicitly evangelistic.

Other crises that Boston faced during his ministry included a series of droughts that caused widespread famine. There was also war in Scotland and England between Protestants and Catholics, especially during the Jacobite Rebellion of 1715. But what is perhaps more important than the crises themselves is the way that Boston handled them.

When the crisis was outside the church—such as war or famine—he called his people to public prayer and fasting. Fasting has become a neglected spiritual discipline. Thankfully, in addition to fasting himself and calling his congregation to fast, Boston wrote one of the church's finest works on the subject: "A Memorial Concerning Personal and Family Fasting and Humiliation."[44] In the memorial Boston defined fasting as "a religious exercise, wherein a particular person, having set apart some time from his ordinary business in the world, spends it in some secret place by himself, in acts of devotion tending to his humiliation and reformation, and particularly in prayer, with fasting."[45]

When the crisis was inside the church, Boston was a reluctant but active participant. During the Simson affair he pleaded with the General Assembly to defend the deity of Jesus Christ by removing Simson from the ministry. He was also a central figure in the Marrow Controversy, writing documents, testifying before committees, speaking on the floor of the Assembly and even publishing a carefully annotated edition of *The Marrow* itself (1726).

In all these disputes Boston distinguished himself by behaving honorably and peaceably. Then, as now, Presbyterian ministers vowed before God and their presbytery to maintain the peace and purity of the church. These virtues often appear to be diametrically opposed. On the one hand, doctrinal purity has a way of disturbing the peace. Theological rigor often leads to disputes and divisions in the church. On the other hand, peace can come at the expense of purity. Naive tolerance of doctrinal error means the death of theological truth.

It is a rare pastor theologian who has equal concern for both the peace and the purity of the church. Boston's colleagues considered him such a rarity. Shortly after his death, they praised his

---

[44]Boston, *Works*, 11:341-93.
[45]Boston, *Works*, 11:349.

joint concern for purity and peace in the church; no man more zealous for the former and at the same time more studious of the latter; having observed and felt so much of the mischief of division and separation, [he] was exceedingly cautious and scrupulous of any thing new or unprecedented, until he was thoroughly satisfied of its necessity and ground. It was his settled mind, that solidly and strongly to establish the truth, was in many cases, the best, the shortest, and most effectual way to confute error, without irritating and in-flaming the passions of men, to their own, and to the truth's prejudice; on all which accounts, he was much respected and regarded, by not only his brethren that differed from him, but generally by all sorts of men.[46]

This is a remarkable epitaph for a remarkable minister. The pastor theologian who received it was deeply impressed by Paul's commendation of King David: "David served God's purpose in his own generation" (Acts 13:36). Thomas Boston used this verse to define "generation work" as the particular call of God to every Christian in every generation. His words serve as a call to action for the pastor theologian, and indeed for every Christian:

Our generation-work . . . is the work we have to do for God and the generation in which we live, that we may be useful not for ourselves only, but for our God and fellow-creatures . . . There are, by the wise dispensation of God, several generations of men in the world, one after another; one goes off the stage, and another succeeds. Each generation has its work assigned it by the sovereign Lord; and each person in the generation has his also. And now is our time of plying of ours. We could not be useful in the generation that went before us; for then we were not: nor can we personally in that which shall come after us; for then we shall be off the stage. Now is our time; let us ply it, and not neglect usefulness in our generation.[47]

---

[46]Messrs. Calder, Wilson and Davidson, "Sketch of the Author's Character," in Boston, *Works*, 12:452.
[47]Boston, *Works*, 5:254.

8

The Pastor Theologian as Mentor

The Legacy of John Henry Newman

CHRIS CASTALDO

IF YOU WERE TO SEE MY COPY OF GERALD HIESTAND and Todd Wilson's *The Pastor Theologian*, you would find the letter Q in the margin of many pages, indicating quotable strokes of genius. Only once did I pause and think, "They missed it." This did not refer to an error so much as an omission. On page 40, speaking of Calvin's life as a "clerical" theologian, they write, "Yet after three years in Strasbourg (where Calvin hoped to once again settle into the quiet life of a scholar), Calvin was recalled to Geneva by the council. He returned and this time stayed for the remainder of his life."[1] The omission is Martin Bucer's mentoring of Calvin in Strasbourg. As Randall Zachman writes, "Above any other in his life, Martin Bucer was the one from whom Calvin learned the most about the office of [pastoral] ministry."[2] To be sure, Hiestand and Wilson's omitting this period in Calvin's development was innocent and minor. Nevertheless, it left me feeling shortchanged. Like a child who learns of Dorothy's arrival in Oz without hearing about the yellow brick road, the reader unaware of how Calvin *became* Calvin the pastor theologian knows only half the story.

Thus I originally planned this chapter to deal with Bucer's legacy as mentor of pastor theologians. I eventually recognized, however, that while

---

[1]Gerald Hiestand and Todd Wilson, *The Pastor Theologian: Resurrecting an Ancient Vision* (Grand Rapids: Zondervan, 2015), 40.
[2]Randall C. Zachman, *John Calvin as Teacher, Pastor, and Theologian: The Shape of His Writings and Thought* (Grand Rapids: Baker, 2006), 22.

providing many inspiring anecdotes, Bucer's example offered less in the way of theological rationale: explicit principles by which he accomplished this work. Therefore, I decided to shift focus to a different mentor—John Henry Newman—whose legacy not only inspires but also provides more detailed principles for engaging in such ministry.

But first I must point out that the historical moment in which we live poses challenges to mentoring. While the last decade or two has seen increased religious formation in seminaries and many local churches developing residency programs, still there are cultural forces that militate against this work. I will mention three.

First, we live in a time when persons are constantly degraded. The more abhorrent examples include the abortion merchants of Planned Parenthood and Boko Haram enslaving girls in Nigeria, but how about subtle cases? Is it possible that even evangelical leaders, applying the methods and techniques of corporate America to grow churches and produce measurable results, unwittingly abuse the fundamental sanctity of each person? Because it is through persons that God reveals himself, and because the persons whom we serve are unrepeatable, irreducible and eternal, we must take a genuinely personal approach and not push men and women through a spiritual assembly line.

Second, evangelicals in the United States also find themselves vulnerable to the sterility of individualism. Social life inside and outside of the church must never be reduced to the defense of autonomous freedom and the protection of personal interests, even pastoral interests. As Paul declares in Galatians 5:13, "Do not use your freedom as an opportunity for the flesh [that is, to advance our religious agenda, Mosaic or otherwise] but through love serve one another" (ESV). Let's face it: our finest pastoral and missional ideals are always susceptible to corruption by our sinful hearts, causing our best intentions to fall short of the Great Commission because our strategy has unwittingly degenerated into a form of ecclesial narcissism.

Third, we also struggle with utilitarianism, regarding persons as means toward an end. The body of Christ, in which we are saved, provides redemption in solidarity with other persons. It is therefore wrong to marginalize or use others, for in doing so we resemble the teenager who slashes her skin with a blade—an active subject who is also the wounded victim. In

Christ, our identity and mission are personally integrated; as members of the mystical body, we serve and bless one another. Such is our response to divine grace corporate in nature: as living stones constructed as a spiritual house, offering sacrifices acceptable to God through Jesus Christ (1 Pet 2:5).

How can we overcome such obstacles to the Christian service of human persons? For the answer we will look at a bright star in the constellation of pastor theologians: John Henry Newman.

THE SHAPING OF NEWMAN'S PASTORAL THEOLOGY

A renowned English theologian of the nineteenth century, Newman is variously remembered as a Victorian sage, educational theorist, satirist, poet, leader of the Oxford Movement, Catholic convert and forerunner of Vatican II. Library shelves the world over contain his works and volumes dedicated to his life. As a pastor theologian, however, his greatest legacy is perhaps his personal influence on those he mentored. In what follows, I will consider the theological priorities that motivated and guided this ministry.

According to his *Apologia pro vita sua* (Latin for "a defense of his life"), Newman's conversion happened between August and December of 1816, at age fifteen. A few months earlier his father's bank had failed in the aftermath of the Napoleonic wars. Meanwhile, alone at Great Ealing School, Newman became ill.[3] These circumstances led to his spiritual conversion under the influence of his evangelical Calvinist schoolmaster, the Reverend Walter Mayers. In the ensuing months, Mayers served as Newman's guide, mainly through reading assignments that, according to Newman, were "the human means of this beginning of divine faith in me," and "all of the school of Calvin."[4] It is noteworthy that while Newman's religious identity would change during his lifetime, he always looked to his evangelical conversion as the starting point.[5]

Of concern to us is the theological foundation that Mayers laid in Newman's soul. Among the various authors that Mayers recommended, the most

---

[3]This was the first of three serious illnesses that were accompanied by profound spiritual crises. Newman writes, "The first keen, terrible one, when I was a boy of 15, and it made me a Christian—with experiences before and after, awful and known only to God" (Newman, *Autobiographical Writings* [London: Sheed & Ward, 1956], 150).

[4]John Henry Newman, *Apologia pro vita sua: being a history of his religious opinions* (London: Longmans, Green and Co., 1882), 4.

[5]Ibid., 5

significant was Thomas Scott, John Newton's successor as curate of Olney. Newman especially valued Scott's commitment to holiness. Newman writes:

> Besides his unworldliness, what I also admired in Scott was his resolute op-position to antinomianism, and the minutely practical character of his writings. . . . [For] years I used almost as proverbs what I considered to be the scope and issue of his doctrine, "Holiness rather than peace," and "Growth the only evidence of life."[6]

Scott's emphasis on the holiness of the triune God remained with Newman in perpetuity.[7] Indeed, it became Newman's modus operandi to embody and impress upon others the holiness of the triune God. This vision is re-sponsible for feeding Newman's "personalism," or "personation," as he called it.[8] In what follows I will seek to explain Newman's contribution to pastoral theology through his development of this idea that features so prominently in his overall thought. In fact, it was so important that he placed it at the center of his coat of arms: *cor ad cor loquitur* ("heart speaks to heart").

For Newman, the human heart is only satisfied by an encounter with the heart of God—an encounter that is supremely personal. Newman gives ex-pression to the supremacy of this experience through the heroine of his novel *Callista* (1856), who points to the divine heart as the ultimate gift that comes down from above: "There was a higher beauty than that which the order and harmony of the natural world revealed and a deeper peace and calm than that which the exercise whether of the intellect or the purest human affection can supply."[9] In short, to commune with God is the highest and most desirable end, and to impress God's heart upon others was Newman's pastoral calling.

This was Newman's theological vision. How did it find expression through his pastoral ministry? His life of teaching began in 1823, when he was made

---

[6]Ibid.
[7]An especially distilled treatment of Scott's Trinitarian position is found in "The Personality and Deity of the Holy Spirit; with some thoughts on the doctrine of the sacred Trinity" in Thomas Scott, *Essays on the most important subjects in religion*, 4th ed. (London: D. Jaques, Lower Sloan-Street, 1800), 243-60.
[8]Newman used the phrase "method of personation" to capture this emphasis in the second mes-sage of his *University Sermons* entitled "The Influence of Natural and Revealed Religion Respec-tively." We are indebted to John F. Crosby for two excellent treatments of the subject: *The Person-alism of John Henry Newman* (Washington, DC: The Catholic University of America Press, 2014), and *The Personalist Papers* (Washington, DC: The Catholic University of America Press, 2004).
[9]John Henry Newman, *Callista: A Sketch of the Third Century* (New York: D. & J. Sadlier & Co., 1856), 254.

a full fellow at Oriel College, Oxford. Despite opposition from his liberal, anti-Calvinist colleagues, Newman held fast to his evangelical creed and his commitment to serve the church. He took holy orders, and in 1824 he was ordained a deacon and shortly thereafter to the Anglican priesthood. After his appointment as curate of St. Clement's in east Oxford, Newman fully engaged pastoral work while maintaining a routine of research and writing.

At this time Newman experienced a defining moment with far-reaching implications for his vocation as a pastor theologian. He identified a serious flaw in the current system at Oxford, in which academic tutors were mere lecturers who scarcely knew their students. To Newman's personalist convictions, this was unacceptable. Therefore, with the cooperation of likeminded colleagues, Newman revised the tutorship system. In the new scheme, each tutor was responsible for a cohort of pupils who would have first claim on his attention as an instructor and shepherd. Newman made this revision without the involvement of his provost, Edward Hawkins.

Several months passed before Hawkins learned of the change, at which point he expressed his disapproval. Tasked as provost with assigning pupils to the various tutors, Hawkins wished to avoid the political challenges associated with such an invidious role. But Newman could not accept the status quo. Understanding the tutor's role to be "of a pastoral nature," he could not in clear conscience lecture without also attending to the moral and religious needs of his students.[10] A showdown ensued, leading to Hawkins unilaterally overturning Newman's system and the eventual conclusion of Newman's tutorship.

This controversy fed Newman's commitment to mentoring and foreshadowed the trajectory of his life's work. While still at Oxford he had tutored such students as Henry Wilberforce, whom he persuaded to pursue ordination.[11] When Newman withdrew to Littlemore in 1842, he brought with him a band of followers, including William Lockhart (1820–1892), Frederick Oakeley (1802–1880) and Ambrose Saint John (1815–1875). After his conversion to Catholicism, Newman started the Birmingham Oratory of St. Philip Neri, a *Santa Communita* (holy community), as Newman liked to call it, devoted to a vocation of friendship in service of the church. To this day, if you visit Newman's

---

[10]Ian Ker, *John Henry Newman: A Biography* (Oxford: Oxford University Press, 2009), 40.
[11]David Newsome, *The Parting of Friends: The Wilberforces and Henry Manning* (London: John Murray, 1966), 114-15.

room at the Oratory you can see on the wall above the alcove of his altar a great photographic collection of his friends and disciples.

When Newman breathed his last in 1890, *The Times* of London (not exactly a pro-Catholic publication) printed the following words concerning his legacy: "Of one thing we may be sure, that the memory of his pure and noble life, untouched by worldliness, unsoured by any trace of fanaticism, will endure, and that whether Rome canonizes him or not he will be canonized in the thoughts of pious people of many creeds in England."[12] In this brief epitaph, the writer is not remembering the brilliance of Newman's mind or his tightly reasoned arguments or his vast literary output but the sincerity of his faith. This is the legacy of Newman the pastor theologian.

THE APPLICATION OF NEWMAN'S PERSONALIST DOCTRINE

There is much about Newman's personalism from which evangelicals can benefit, even if we do not follow his sacramental and magisterial conclusions. In the remainder of this chapter I will consider how Newman's approach assists pastor theologians in navigating the three challenges to mentoring mentioned above: the degradation of human persons, individualism and utilitarianism.

From degradation to the value of persons. Newman was emphatic that God's self-revelation is fundamentally personal. Of course, our relationship to Christ is not physical in the way it was for the apostles upon the Galilean mountainside, but the incarnation and subsequent pouring forth of the Holy Spirit provides access to the persons of God. For Newman, this gift *exceeds* the impartation of divine grace—think about that for a moment— for the recipient has received an even greater gift: the very presence of God. This notion is elucidated in Newman's famous hymn, "Praise to the Holiest in the Height":

> O wisest love! That flesh and blood
> Which did in Adam fail,
> Should strive afresh against the foe,

---

[12]Quoted by Philip Boyce, in "Newman as Seen by His Contemporaries at the Time of His Death," in Maria K. Strolz and Margarete Binder, eds., *John Henry Newman: Lover of Truth* (Rome: Urbaniana University Press, 1991), 113.

Should strive and should prevail;
And that a higher gift than grace
Should flesh and blood refine,
God's Presence and His very Self,
and Essence all-divine.[13]

Newman applied his doctrine of divine indwelling to the enterprise of mentoring in an Oxford sermon titled "Personal Influence, the Means of Propagating the Truth" (1832). How does God impress his holiness upon the souls of men and women? He does it *personally*. Newman writes that revelation "has been upheld in the world not as a system, not by books, not by arguments, not by temporal powers, but by the personal influence of such [godly men], who are at once the teachers and the patterns of it."[14] He continues, "Men persuade themselves, with little difficulty, to scoff at principles, to ridicule books, to make sport of the names of good men; but they cannot bear their [personal] presence."[15]

Now, we must read Newman's words while recognizing he was a man of letters, a fact to which his mountainous literary output testifies. Furthermore, doctrinal tenets were the foundation of his life. For instance, he wrote of his conversion at age fifteen: "I fell under the influence of a definite Creed and received into my intellect impressions of dogma, which, through God's mercy, have never been effaced or obscured."[16] According to Newman, such formulations are integral to faith, protecting the church from error and leading into all righteousness.

However, while valuing the written word, Newman asserted that mentoring is possible without the use of books. In a paper on university life in Athens during Plato's day, Newman wrote, "I doubt whether Athens had a library till the reign of Hadrian [AD 117–138]. It was what the student gazed on, what he heard, what he caught by the magic of sympathy, not what he read, which was the education furnished by Athens."[17] Such an education

---

[13]John Henry Newman, *Verses on Various Occasions*, new ed. (London: Longmans, Green, and Co., 1893), 363-64.

[14]John Henry Newman, "Personal Influence, the Means of Propagating the Truth," in *Fifteen Sermons Preached before the University of Oxford* (London: Longmans, Green, and Co., 1906), 91-92 (§26).

[15]Ibid., 92 (§27).

[16]Newman, *Apologia pro vita sua*, 4.

[17]John Henry Newman, *Historical Sketches III* (London: Longmans, Green, and Co., 1887), 40.

holds great power because, as Newman explains in his *Grammar of Assent*, "persons influence us, voices melt us, looks subdue us, deeds inflame us."[18]

If this was true in the pagan world, how much more is it so in the Christian community? God reveals nothing less than himself in the person of the incarnate Jesus Christ, not merely theological information. Thus Newman declared:

> As God is one, so the impression which He gives us of Himself is one; it is not a thing of parts; it is not a system. . . . It is the vision of an object. When we pray, we pray, not to an assemblage of notions, or to a creed, but to One Individual Being; and when we speak of Him we speak of a Person.[19]

Because "heart speaks to heart," a personal God to the human heart made in his image, our approach to mentoring must also be supremely personal. Therefore, we ought to ask ourselves a few questions: What are we offering others in the name of "mentoring"? To what degree are we personally present in these relationships? Do we create venues where this can happen? How do our families engage in this work?

From individualism that protects self-interests to serving one another from the heart. Since Newman interpreted the evangelicals of his day as maintaining justification by *mere* imputation, he sought to articulate a doctrine of justification that included the fructifying work of the Spirit, especially in the context of Christian formation.[20] His vision deliberately confronted the overly individualistic (as Newman saw it) approach of evangelicals. His primary bone of contention was not with imputation, strictly speaking, so much as a *reduction* of justification to imputation alone.[21] He observed this problem particularly in the typical exegesis among evangelicals of James concerning the necessity of virtuous works.[22]

Unpacking his doctrine, Newman underscored that believers possess the gift of the Holy Spirit due to the church's union with Christ. This is a gift that,

---

[18]John Henry Newman, *An Essay in Aid of a Grammar of Assent* (New York: The Catholic Publication Society, 1870), 89-90.

[19]John Henry Newman, "The Theory of Developments in Religious Doctrine," Sermon XIV in *Sermons Chiefly on the Theory of Religious Belief* (London: J. G. and F. Rivington, 1843), 331.

[20]John Henry Newman, *Lectures on the Doctrine of Justification*, 3rd ed. (London: Rivingtons, 1874), 63.

[21]Ibid. Newman explains his understanding of imputation at some length in pages 67-78.

[22]Ibid., 291-93.

in his words, "pervades us (if it may be so said) as light pervades a building, or as a sweet perfume the folds of some honourable robe."[23] This fragrance is intended to influence men and women with the beauty of divine holiness. Thus, for Newman, mentoring was an ethical activity that emerged from our union with Christ and the Spirit. In short, because God personally resides in the believer and advances his mission through us, we are compelled to impress his holiness upon others.

What does such a ministry look like in action? Newman offers an eloquent description in his famous sermon "The Parting of Friends," in which he describes the personal affection that characterizes the selfless service of others:

> Orpah kissed Naomi, and went back to the world. There was sorrow in the parting, but Naomi's sorrow was more for Orpah's sake than for her own. Pain there would be, but it was the pain of a wound, not the yearning regret of love. It was the pain we feel when friends disappoint us, and fall in our esteem. That kiss of Orpah was no loving token; it was but the hollow profession of those who use smooth words, that they may part company with us with least trouble and discomfort to themselves. Orpah's tears were but the dregs of affection; she clasped her mother-in-law once for all, that she might not cleave to her. Far different were the tears, far different the embrace, which passed between those two religious friends recorded in the book which follows, who loved each other with a true love unfeigned, but whose lives ran in different courses. If Naomi's grief was great when Orpah kissed her, what was David's when he saw the last of him, whose "soul had from the first been knit with his soul," so that "he loved him as his own soul"? [1 Sam 18:1-3][24]

Not only is this a definition of Christian love; it is the spiritual impulse that animates our ministry when we seek the best interest of others with unfeigned affection and commitment.

Once again, Newman's insight would have us ask some practical questions: How do we express affection to those we mentor? To what degree do we invest ourselves in prayer for them? How do we bless others with unexpected acts of kindness, such as attentive listening over lunch or giving the gift of a book?

---

[23]John Henry Newman, *Parochial and Plain Sermons* (San Francisco: Ignatius, 1997), 368. This sermon was first published in 1835. Hereafter *PPS*.

[24]John Henry Newman, *Sermons Bearing on Subjects of the Day* (London: Rivingtons, 1869), 402.

From utilitarianism to the body of Christ. Thinking with the Eastern tradition, Newman examined the inner Trinitarian relationship of the divine persons to understand how divine life condescends to engage human hearts. He concluded that it is in the Son of God who "came down on earth, and who thus, though graciously taking on Him a new nature, remained in person as He had been from everlasting, the Son of the Father."[25] Accordingly, the Son—precisely because he possesses the same nature as the Father and the Spirit—is never considered in abstract isolation from the members of the Godhead, as popular evangelicalism was susceptible to doing. Rather, the triune deity in personal communion is the starting point for understanding the mission of the incarnate Christ.

Newman's appreciation for the communal intent of Christ's mission was enhanced by the teaching of St. Ignatius of Antioch, which highlighted the Trinitarian activity in salvation such that it "continually invites Christians into a divine community of love."[26] What a beautiful image! Imagine God personally inviting his children into the ongoing interchange of divine affection. For example, in his sermon "The Mystery of Godliness" (1840), Newman asserts:

> [Christ] has taken our nature, and in and through it He sanctifies us. He is our brother by virtue of His incarnation, and, as the text says, "He is not ashamed to call us brethren;" and, having sanctified his nature in Himself, He communicates it to us.[27]

When Newman uses the plural "us" he wishes to stress, by contrast with many of his evangelical contemporaries, the community of God's people in which we live together. Given this corporate identity, membership with one another in Christ's body, it is unconscionable that Christians would use each other for the purpose of selfish gain. What is more, in distinction from the evangelical conception of the real church as invisible, Newman emphasized that the church comprises embodied persons—men and women in whom God dwells.[28]

---

[25]Newman, *PPS*, 1224-25. This sermon was published in 1842.
[26]Dessain, *Spirituality*, 67. Newman explains how the atonement is "continually" being applied to the church in his *Lectures on the Doctrine of Justification*, 202-4.
[27]Newman, *PPS*, 1014.
[28]His sermon, "The Visible Church an Encouragement to Faith," a message published in 1836, makes this point (*PPS*, 633-43). See also Newman's sermon "The Communion of Saints" (ibid., 839-49).

In applying this doctrine to the enterprise of discipleship, Newman regarded the church as a divine gift, extending from Christ himself. Basic to this gift was the sacredness and singularity of other persons. Through such persons God manifests the warmth of his presence, providing comfort, healing and hope. This conviction infused his mentoring, as the following examples illustrate.

A cursory reading of Newman's letters and diary entries reveals a great deal of personal warmth and concern for friends. His standard signature was "Ever Yours Affectionately, JHN," (or variations thereof). At times, Newman also expressed such affection to a third party. Here is a line from a letter he wrote to H. A. Woodgate about their common friend, Hope-Scott: "He is a man I love with my whole heart, and his loss to me is very grievous."[29] Similarly, he wrote to Lady Herbert of Lea regarding another friend: "It is pleasant to hear you talk so warmly of Isy Froude—I love her so much."[30] When Newman felt he had been insensitive to a friend, he did not hesitate to apologize and ask forgiveness. Writing to Henry Wilberforce, one of the more famous pastors that he mentored, he wrote the following: "A fear has come over me lest I should have been severe in my last letter. I dare say I may have worded what I said unkindly and have hurt you; if so, I am very sorry."[31]

What motivated Newman to express such affection and fidelity to those among whom he served? A chief reason was his robust ecclesiology. Newman made this point explicit in a letter to Henry Wilberforce on January 27, 1846. In this letter, Newman, who had recently converted to the Roman Church, is defending himself against a screed written against him in the *Christian Rememberancer.* The anonymous author, whom Newman surmises to be James Mozley, evidently cast aspersions upon Newman's commitment to the Church of England in the preceding years. Among his various lines of defense, Newman concludes with a stout expression of his personalism: "I believe *I* was the *first* writer [among Anglican theologians] who made *life the* mark of a true Church, yet this writer speaks as if I went to books in the first instance not to life. But my *Sermons* are a wholesale refutation of his theory."[32]

---

[29]*Letters and Diaries of John Henry Newman*, ed. Charles Stephen Dessain et al., vols. 11-31 (London: T. Nelson, 1961–1977), 26:193. This letter was written on October 29, 1872.
[30]Ibid., 246. This letter was written on February 7, 1873.
[31]*Letters and Diaries*, 11:216. This letter was written on September 24, 1846.
[32]*Letters and Diaries*, 11:101.

As evidence of the fruit of Newman's ministry among those he influenced, one finds letters of appreciation written to him, such as the following:

> I often think that Christians are remiss in not acknowledging the great debt of gratitude they owe to those who have first planted in them the seeds of that faith, the fruit of which we know is more valuable than the whole world. This, my dear sir, is, I confess, my case as regards you.[33]

The doctrine of the body of Christ requires us to consider how we can make others shine—colleagues, interns, support staff and the flock that we serve. We must also think deeply about how to give others ownership in ministry. A genuinely collaborative approach is essential for equipping the saints for the work of service.

CONCLUSION

On September 25, 1843, Newman delivered his final sermon as an Anglican: "The Parting of Friends." All of the prominent members of the Oxford Movement were in attendance and a multitude of those he had mentored. This was partly because the church of Littlemore was celebrating its anniversary, but mainly because everyone recognized it was Newman's farewell. Capturing the emotion of the moment, Louis Bouyer writes, "Tears rolled down their faces as Newman pronounced those words of final leave-taking, words that told of all he felt he was giving up in leaving the Anglican fold."[34] In these final words of Newman's sermon, we can hear the melody of Newman's personalism, as one heart speaks to another:

> And, O my brethren, O kind and affectionate hearts, O loving friends, should you know any one whose lot it has been, by writing or by word of mouth, in some degree to help you thus to act; if he has ever told you what you knew about yourselves, or what you did not know; has read to you your wants or feelings, and comforted you by the very reading; has made you feel that there was a higher life than this daily one, and a brighter world than that you see; or encouraged you, or sobered you, or opened a way to the inquiring, or soothed the perplexed; if what he has said or done has ever made you take

---

[33]*Letters and Correspondence of John Henry Newman During His Life in the English Church: With a Brief Autobiography*, Anne Mozley, ed., 2 vols. (London: Longmans, Green, 1891), 2:41. This letter is dated May 27, 1834.
[34]Louis Bouyer, *Newman: His Life and Spirituality* (San Francisco: Ignatius, 2011), 251.

interest in him, and feel well inclined towards him; remember such a one in time to come, though you hear him not, and pray for him, that in all things he may know God's will, and at all times he may be ready to fulfill it.[35]

---

[35]Newman, *Sermons Bearing on Subjects of the Day,* 409.

9

The Ecclesial Theology of Dietrich Bonhoeffer

JOEL D. LAWRENCE

THE CHURCH TODAY IS SUFFERING from what Gerald Hiestand and Todd Wilson have called "the Great Divorce," a term they use to describe the chasm that has opened up between the academy and the church.[1] In this situation, the academy is seen as the place where serious theology is done by theologians who are working according to the criteria of the academy, while the church is where pastors are called to guide people in living life, giving them biblical wisdom for tackling the everyday challenges of the real world. The church expects pastors "to be able to preach . . . to know how to lead . . . to be good at solving problems and giving direction." The Great Divorce has created a scenario in which the pastor, rather than being seen as a theological leader within the congregation, much less the wider church, is instead "called to more pedestrian concerns like budgets and buildings, small groups and services, leading meetings and pastoral visitations."[2]

While pastors should certainly be involved in these activities, a danger arises when these activities have come to *define* the pastorate, to be seen as the heart of pastoral work. Hiestand and Wilson argue convincingly that this way of defining the pastoral calling is a mistake that has negative effects on the church in America in the twenty-first century. The failure to conceive of

---

[1]Gerald Hiestand and Todd Wilson, *The Pastor Theologian: Resurrecting an Ancient Vision* (Grand Rapids: Zondervan, 2015), 42-52.
[2]Ibid., 12.

the pastoral ministry as inherently theological is the result of the Great Divorce. This has had detrimental effects on the church's calling to follow Christ and on those who are called to shepherd churches in that mission.[3]

Though the chasm opened up by the Great Divorce is wide indeed, many pastors are questioning the vision of the pastorate that they have inherited from their twentieth-century ecclesial forebears.[4] They are calling for a renewed vision of the pastorate that will lead to the renewal of the church. According to this vision, pastors must once again recapture the biblical notion of what it means to be an under-shepherd of Christ, guiding the congregation to growing maturity through careful attention to both the biblical and theological nature of our mission as God's people. We need pastors who reject the presuppositions of the Great Divorce, recognizing the inadequacy of an academic theology divorced from the church and the inadequacy of a pastoral calling that eliminates theological leadership from the essence of what it means to be a pastor.

To do this, pastors once again need to unapologetically claim the ecclesial location for doing theology. While I agree that "the academy is here to stay,"[5] I also believe it is important for pastor theologians to assert the necessity of doing theology in and for the church and to have confidence in the ecclesial nature of doing theology. In order for us to confidently move forward with our calling as pastor theologians, we must look to pastor theologians who have gone before us and modeled the task of ecclesial theology, a discipline that Hiestand and Wilson describe as "theology that is germinated within the congregation, that presses toward distinctly ecclesial concerns, and that is cultivated by practicing clergy."[6] The great cloud of witnesses contains many whose life and ministry can

---

[3]For more on this, see Thomas Oden, *Pastoral Theology: Essentials of Ministry* (San Francisco: HarperSanFrancisco, 1983). In this work, Oden engages and critiques various models of pastoral ministry that he believes don't line up with the biblical vision and then presents a vision for pastoring that is taken from biblical and theological sources. See also Eugene Peterson, *The Pastor: A Memoir* (San Francisco: HarperOne, 2011), in which Peterson, by telling his own pastoral biography, paints a compelling vision of the pastorate from a biblical and theological foundation that resists the more popular and widespread vision of the pastorate at work in the American church today.
[4]A work that pertains to the questions of theology, the academy, the pastorate and the subject of this essay, Dietrich Bonhoeffer, is Paul House's important book *Bonhoeffer's Seminary Vision: A Case for Costly Discipleship and Life Together* (Wheaton, IL: Crossway, 2015).
[5]Hiestand and Wilson, *Pastor Theologian*, 15.
[6]Ibid., 18.

help us chart a renewed vision of theology done in and for the church; one of these exemplars is Dietrich Bonhoeffer.

APPROACHING BONHOEFFER

The outline of Bonhoeffer's life story is well known. He was a gifted theologian, living in the tumultuous days of the Third Reich, who, though a pacifist committed to Jesus' teaching in the Sermon on the Mount, engaged in a plot to assassinate Hitler.[7] While Bonhoeffer's story fascinates, it also poses an important question: Can we appropriate Bonhoeffer's legacy for today's pastor theologians? Can he be an exemplar for us, given that his life and circumstances are distant from ours and that his actions were lived out *in extremis*, in the midst of one of the most evil regimes in history? Can Bonhoeffer be a guide for pastor theologians in our day?

I believe he can. But for this to happen, we need a different approach to Bonhoeffer than the one that is typical in the American church. As I have traveled around the country speaking on Bonhoeffer, I have noticed that at the core of people's interest in Bonhoeffer is what I call the "Bonhoeffer as case study" approach. Bonhoeffer's involvement in the plot to assassinate Hitler inevitably poses ethical challenges for interpreters of his actions in the conspiracy. They focus on how he could be involved in such a plot and how he could justify being a double agent. This leads people to focus on answering the questions: "Why did he do what he did?" and "Did he do the right thing?"

While these are important and interesting questions, I don't believe they are the ones that will be most helpful in appropriating Bonhoeffer for today's pastor theologians. In this chapter I will focus elsewhere in Bonhoeffer's story, long before he made any decisions about joining the conspiracy against Hitler. I want to move our attention away from "Bonhoeffer the case study" and engage with Bonhoeffer the pastor theologian. Bonhoeffer was an ecclesial theologian whose theology was deeply rooted in the church and whose theology was written in the service of the church. As such, Bonhoeffer's life story and theological commitments contain rich resources for our task of equipping today's pastor theologians for reclaiming the mantle of theological leadership in the church.

---

[7]I commend to anyone looking to reflect more deeply on Bonhoeffer's life and theology Charles Marsh's biography of Bonhoeffer, *Strange Glory: A Life of Dietrich Bonhoeffer* (New York: Vintage, 2014).

BONHOEFFER'S ECCLESIAL THEOLOGICAL METHOD

The ecclesial commitments of Bonhoeffer's theology are evident from Bonhoeffer's theological method. An explication of this method can be found in the series of lectures Bonhoeffer gave in Berlin in the politically volatile summer of 1933, a time in which Hitler, who had risen to power in January of that year, was working to consolidate his power.[8] As this was happening down the street, Bonhoeffer lectured at the University of Berlin, leading students through reflections on the person of Jesus Christ. Bonhoeffer was unable to complete the lectures by the end of the term, a fate that has befallen many a theological lecturer. But what he did leave behind are reflections on Christology that serve as an important foundation for Bonhoeffer's theological method, and that serve as a clear expression of and foundation for Bonhoeffer's ecclesial work as a pastor theologian.

We see from these lectures that Bonhoeffer's theological method is best understood as *Christus praesens*, a thoroughgoing focus on the Christ who is present to the church and who reveals himself as Christ to the church. While this may seem fairly basic, the uniqueness of Bonhoeffer's approach to Christology can be seen in the structure of his lectures, which are divided into three main parts: Part I, "The Present Christ"; Part II, "The Historical Christ"; and Part III, "The Eternal Christ."[9] Most Christologies, and certainly Christologies of the Enlightenment academic tradition—those marked by the Great Divorce—begin with the historical Christ, seeking to establish the reality and meaning of Jesus via history. Bonhoeffer, however, abandons this approach, taking the very different tack of beginning with the *present Christ*. This emphasizes the task of the church to pay attention to the voice of Jesus, who is present as the Resurrected One. He is the ontological center of the church, the community that is, in a quite literal way for Bonhoeffer, the body of Christ, the place where Christ dwells by the Spirit.[10]

In Bonhoeffer's theological method, the way that we have access to Jesus is through the testimony of the present Christ, who encounters us here and

---

[8]The lectures are found in Bonhoeffer, *Berlin: 1932–1933*, Dietrich Bonhoeffer Works vol. 12, ed. Larry L. Rasmussen, trans. Isabel Best and David Higgins (Minneapolis: Fortress, 2009), 299-360.
[9]It is this last section that Bonhoeffer never finished.
[10]Bonhoeffer, *Sanctorum Communio: A Theological Study of the Sociology of the Church,* Dietrich Bonhoeffer Works vol. 1, ed. Clifford Green, trans. Reinhold Krauss and Nancy Lukens (Minneapolis: Fortress, 2009).

now as the Resurrected One. Bonhoeffer is wary of Christologies that begin with the historical Jesus and so are driven by methodologies borrowed from the discipline of history. These methodologies give themselves away by asking such questions as "How can he be both human and divine?" For Bonhoeffer, this approach seeks to categorize Christ through scientific classification. He writes, "All scholarly questions can be reduced to two fundamental questions: First, what is the cause of X? Second, what is the meaning of X?"[11] These questions seek to know objects in relation to one another and therefore are questions of classification. This is the scholarly scheme that had come to dominate Enlightenment universities, including the theology departments of these universities.

Bonhoeffer had put his finger on a significant methodological problem. While these were necessary questions for engagement with immanent things—that is, things that are available to human investigation and rationality—they could not approach the transcendent. For the classification of objects according to the questions of cause and meaning to hold, all objects under investigation must retain a structure of immanent relationship.[12] But what happens if one appears who claims to be transcendent? What happens if Christ, whom Bonhoeffer refers to as "the counter Logos," appears and confronts humanity, "the logos"? The response of classification is to continue to ask the scholarly questions of cause and meaning, which classify objects in relation to other known objects. These questions cannot account for the counter Logos, who "appears, somewhere and at some time in history, as a human being, and as a human being sets itself up as judge over the human logos and says, 'I am the truth.' . . . Here it is no longer possible to fit the Word made flesh into the logos classification system. Here all that remains is the question: Who are you?"[13]

This, according to Bonhoeffer, is a fundamental change in approaching Christ, and so in theological method. The proper Christological question is not a question of classification, not a question of establishing a relation to other known objects, not a question of cause or meaning according to the criteria of the human logos. The proper Christological question is: "Who are you?" When humans are confronted by the counter Logos, we must make a decision:

---

[11]Bonhoeffer, *Berlin: 1932–1933*, 301.
[12]Ibid., 302.
[13]Ibid.

Will we continue to try to classify the counter Logos, to ask questions according to the criteria of immanent knowledge, to stay in the position of judge
of the counter Logos?[14] Or will we recognize that the counter Logos relativizes
our knowledge and puts us in a position of *being* judged? When we do this,
we ask the proper Christological question. According to Bonhoeffer, "This is
the question of horrified, dethroned human reason, and also the question of
faith. Who are you? Are you God's very self? This is the question with which
Christology alone is concerned. Every possibility of classification must fall
short, because the existence of this Logos means the end of my logos."[15]

At the heart of Bonhoeffer's theological method as laid out in these lectures
is the recognition that we must approach Christ with *the question of faith*. This
is the question of the church, whose confession guides our theological reflection. Christology can only be done properly when the question asked of
Christ is the question of the church's faith. The proper Christological question
recognizes the *Christus praesens* and turns our attention to him in faith, no
longer seeking to classify him—that is, to judge him. It recognizes that it is he
who judges us, and so puts us in the place of decision. In making these decla-
rations, Bonhoeffer is resisting the main trends in the academy of his day.
Rather than seeking to find access to Christ and his meaning via the tools and
methodologies of the human logos, Bonhoeffer is proposing that we are given
access to Jesus only when we cease to ask of him the questions of scientific
classification and instead ask the question of faith: "Who are you?"[16]

At this point we must ask, Why did Bonhoeffer adopt this methodology?
Remember that Bonhoeffer was lecturing at the University of Berlin, which
had fully experienced the Great Divorce brought on by the Enlightenment,
in which scientific categories had come to dominate the theological discipline. This is *Adolph von Harnack's* University of Berlin! Harnack was the

---

[14]Bonhoeffer writes that continuing to ask the "how" question "shows how we are chained to our
own authority. It is the *cor curvum in se* [heart turned in upon itself]" (ibid., 303). In other words,
this is more than an intellectual failure—it is a failure of fallen human nature that refuses to
submit to Christ through judgment cloaked as intellectual pursuit.

[15]Ibid.

[16]It is important to underscore here that Bonhoeffer is committed to the historicity of Jesus and
the canonical nature of Scripture, a document written in history. The point is not to deny his
commitment to the historical Christ or the authority of Scripture but to demonstrate that his
theological method of the *Christus praesens* provides a different way of access to the historical
Jesus, the way of access through Jesus himself rather than through the tools of history.

grand old man of German liberalism and the great proponent of theology as history. Harnack's approach to Christianity, and so to Christ, is the approach of the historian.[17] Bonhoeffer learned from Harnack, was Harnack's student assistant, and was asked to give the student oration at Harnack's funeral. And yet here we have Bonhoeffer standing before the students of Berlin offering a very different vision of theology. Why?

BECOMING A PASTOR THEOLOGIAN

Bonhoeffer, though lecturing in the university, presented a Christology normed by the faith of the church rather than scientific criteria. Bonhoeffer spoke not as one who had adopted the criteria of the academy but as one who had adopted the criteria and convictions of the church, and who understood the difference between these approaches.[18] To see how Bonhoeffer came to this place, we must explore two key factors in Bonhoeffer's story that support my proposal that we must engage Bonhoeffer as a pastor theologian. The first is the impact of Karl Barth on Bonhoeffer's theology, and the second is Bonhoeffer's growing sense of his identity as a pastor who belongs to the church.

Barth gave Bonhoeffer a new understanding of the discipline of theology that was rooted not in scientific approaches to theology but in the confession of the church. Barth himself had struggled mightily in the 1920s to find a new approach to theology that would break out of the kind of academic theology exemplified by Harnack.[19] Barth's struggle led him to understand theology as a discipline of the church, a discipline that is to be guided by the commitments of the faith community. Thus it should be held up not to the modern scientific theological criteria of the academy but rather to the criteria inherent in the confession of the church.

The key move in Barth's theological development is found in his *Anselm: Fides Quaerens Intellectum*.[20] In this book, Barth finds the clue to

---

[17]See Adolph von Harnack, *What is Christianity?* (Minneapolis: Fortress, 1986); and *Adolph Von Harnack: Liberal Theology at Its Height*, ed. Martin Rumscheidt (Minneapolis: Fortress, 1991).

[18]See Bonhoeffer, *Berlin: 1932–1933*, 300.

[19]See H. Martin Rumscheidt, *Revelation and Theology: An Analysis of the Barth-Harnack Correspondence of 1923* (Cambridge: Cambridge University Press, 1972).

[20]Karl Barth, *Anselm: Fides Quarens Intellectum: Anselm's Proof of the Existence of God in the Context of His Theological Scheme* (Eugene, OR: Wipf and Stock, 1975).

theological method in recognizing that Anselm's *Proslogion,* in which he describes his teleological argument for the existence of God, is a prayer. As important as Anselm's theological argument is, it is this notion of theology as prayer—and therefore as an expression of faith from within the community of faith—that is the key breakthrough. Instead of writing a *Christian Dogmatics*, Barth instead sets out to work on his *Church Dogmatics.* In making this change, Barth is explicating an approach to theology that is truly the theology of the church and for the church—that is, ecclesial theology. The first line of the *Church Dogmatics* says this: "Dogmatics is a theological discipline. But theology is a function of the Church."[21] Because theology is the task of the church, it is the language of the church in learning to speak the gospel. This speech is normed by the Scripture and the confession of faith that belong within the church.[22] Barth's theological revolution provided Bonhoeffer with categories that could help him reflect on the theological inheritance of the Harnackian tradition and come to express a theological method in a manner that was distinct from his mentor.[23]

The second factor in understanding Bonhoeffer's method as that of a pastor theologian is vocational: When Bonhoeffer was lecturing at the University of Berlin, he was a pastor. His pastoral training ran concurrently with his academic training and early teaching career.[24] In 1925, while working on his dissertation, *Sanctorum Communio,* Bonhoeffer began to teach a Sunday School class for children in Grunewald, a neighborhood in Berlin. Bonhoeffer preached to the children, led them in catechism classes and, by 1927, was leading them in a Thursday evening reading group. Following this experience, in 1928 Bonhoeffer served as an

---

[21]Barth, *Church Dogmatics I.1*, ed. G. W. Bromiley and T. F. Torrance (New York: T&T Clark, 2004), 1.

[22]On this, see my essay "Speak, For Your Servant is Listening: Barth, Prayer, and Theological Method," in *Karl Barth and the Future of Evangelical Theology*, ed. Christian Collins Winn and John L. Drury (Eugene, OR: Cascade Books, 2014), 149-60.

[23]It is important to note here that Bonhoeffer, though he rejected Harnack's theological method, was deeply influenced by Harnack and that appreciation continued to the end of his life. Bonhoeffer should not be seen as having fully repudiated Harnack or his German liberal inheritance, though he did clearly move away from the method at the heart of Harnack's approach to theology. See H. Gaylon Barker, *The Cross of Reality: Theologia Crucis and Bonhoeffer's Christology* (Minneapolis: Fortress, 2015), 50n42.

[24]This follows the narrative of Bonhoeffer's pastoral development found in Eberhard Bethge, *Dietrich Bonhoeffer: A Biography,* ed. Victoria Barnett (Minneapolis: Fortress, 2000), 91-96.

assistant pastor in Barcelona. While his experience in Barcelona was uneven, it gave him further experience in the church and in the pastorate.[25] Following this, Bonhoeffer's experience in New York at Union Theological Seminary, though not as a pastor, was deeply informative for his vision of the church. Here, Bonhoeffer saw the theological limpness of the American liberal tradition in the mainline churches but experienced the passionate preaching of the gospel in the Abyssinian Baptist Church in Harlem, an African-American congregation that gave him a vision of the church that he'd never experienced in Europe.[26]

Upon his return to Berlin, Bonhoeffer once again took up his teaching post in the university, but continued his work as a pastor. He was ordained by Ernst Vits in the Matthiaskirche (Matthew Church) near the Potsdamer Platz on November 15, 1931.[27] He worked as a student chaplain at the technical college in Charlottenburg, led a confirmation class in Wedding, and formed a youth club. These various activities demonstrate a deepening commitment to the church and a deepening sense of calling.

In order to complete our picture of Bonhoeffer the pastor, there is one more important event to note. At some point in the early 1930s, Bonhoeffer experienced some kind of a "conversion." He didn't speak of this experience often, and didn't describe it in depth when he did speak of it. But the clues that he leaves behind are important, and help us to locate Bonhoeffer as a pastor theologian in the summer of 1933. The place where Bonhoeffer speaks most clearly about this event in his life is in a letter to Elizabeth Zinn, to whom Bonhoeffer had been briefly engaged. Writing to her from Finkenwalde in 1936, Bonhoeffer described his conversion experience:

> I plunged into work in a very unchristian way. . . . Then something happened, something that has changed and transformed my life to the present day. For the first time, I discovered the Bible. . . . I had often preached, I had seen a great deal of the church . . . but I had not yet become a Christian. . . . I had never prayed, or prayed only very little. . . . Then the Bible, and in particular the Sermon on the Mount, freed me from that. . . . It was a great liberation. *It became very clear*

---

[25]Marsh, *Strange Glory*, 62-87.

[26]Additionally, Bonhoeffer had further experience with the African-American church through a road trip taken through the United States and Mexico. See Marsh, *Strange Glory*, 101-35.

[27]Bethge, *Bonhoeffer*, 221.

to me that the life of a servant of Jesus Christ must belong to the Church, and step by step it became clear to me how far that must go.[28] (italics added)

Whatever this conversion entailed for Bonhoeffer, it is clear that it created for him a new understanding of his identity. Rather than pursuing a career in the academy, he now saw himself as belonging to the church. And, while we cannot nail down exactly when this experience occurred, it is certain that it happened prior to 1933, and so prior to Bonhoeffer's lecture on Christology that summer.[29]

In light of these two factors of Barth's influence and Bonhoeffer's pastoral development, it is clear that by the time Bonhoeffer stood before his students in the Berlin lecture hall in the summer of 1933, he was a firmly committed pastor. He had come to understand himself and his identity as a member of the church, the body of the resurrected Jesus Christ, and as a pastor within that body. In other words, though he was lecturing in a university hall, Bonhoeffer had made the move from viewing theology as a discipline of the academy to viewing theology as a discipline of the church, of the people of faith who are called to give attention to the present Christ as he speaks his Word to his people. Bonhoeffer's approach to Christology in his Berlin lectures was shaped by the ecclesial commitments that guided his approach to theology. His identity as a theologian was by this time tied to his identity as a pastor who was firmly committed to doing theology within and for the church.

CONCLUSION: BONHOEFFER FOR PASTOR THEOLOGIANS

I believe one of the key tasks for pastor theologians in the twenty-first century will be to unapologetically claim the ecclesial setting of theology. This doesn't mean that there is no place for academic theology, but today's pastor theologians must be clear and confident in our calling to do theology based on criteria not borrowed from or dependent on the academy. Theology that is done in and for the church is confessionally driven, and the criteria for theology done in and for the church are not the same criteria for theology done in and for the academy.

---

[28]Bonhoeffer to Elizabeth Zinn, January 1, 1936, in *A Testament to Freedom*, ed. Geffrey B. Kelly and F. Burton Nelson (San Francisco: HarperSanFrancisco, 1995), 424-25.
[29]We know this because, later in the letter to Zinn, Bonhoeffer speaks of this event happening prior to "the crisis of 1933," that is, prior to Hitler's rise to power.

In this essay, I have demonstrated that Dietrich Bonhoeffer is an exemplar of the pastor theologian engaged in the task of ecclesial theology. Bonhoeffer provides an important model for today's pastor theologians as one who, having been trained in the academy, gave his life to the church. He did this not merely to teach academic theology within the context of the church but to explicate a different kind of theology, a theology that "is germinated within the congregation, that presses toward distinctly ecclesial concerns, and that is cultivated by practicing clergy."[30] By investigating Bonhoeffer's theological method, we have seen that his theology resisted the criteria of the academy because of his commitment to doing theology in and for the church, and also his identity as belonging to the church. I hope that Bonhoeffer will encourage many of us who are seeking to overcome the Great Divorce to take up the high calling of the pastor theologian, to become those who confidently and faithfully enunciate a theology from and for God's holy church.

---

[30]Hiestand and Wilson, *Pastor Theologian*, 18.

The PASTOR THEOLOGIAN *and the* BIBLE

The Pastor Theologian and the Interpretation of Scripture

A Call for Ecclesial Exegesis

EDWARD W. KLINK III

I F IT IS IMPORTANT TO DEFINE THE OFFICE of the pastor theologian, it is also important to give definition to one of its primary tasks: correctly handling the Word of truth (2 Tim 2:15). There is a need to explore how the office of the pastor, or how the social location of the church, in contrast to the social location of the academy, directs and defines the nature of the Bible and the rules by which it is interpreted.

For example, one of the primary resources pastors use when preparing a sermon is the commentary. It is, for all intents and purposes, the guide or tutor for pastors as they perform the interpretation of Scripture. It is standard for the modern commentary to include an introduction to the text to be commented upon, almost always in relation to its historical context. The author, origin and purpose of the document are usually explored and defended with the assumption that such data is significant for the interpretation to follow. No doubt this historical information about the text is vital to understanding correctly its meaning and application, yet it is rare for commentators to defend or even explain this implicit methodological foundation. This is unfortunate for two primary reasons.

First, it minimizes the hermeneutical issues involved in any kind of interpretation. Presumably modern commentators take for granted that

writing a commentary is an overtly historical task, and therefore feel no need
to explain their method and its philosophical/theological underpinnings to
the reader. But this is hardly the case. Not only does the text carry its own
interpretive commands innate to its origin and nature but the act of interpretation forces the interpreter to make a plethora of methodological as-
sumptions regarding the text.

The second reason is even more important: it minimizes that the text in view
is in fact part of the Christian Scriptures. The very reason why there is so much
interest in this particular text is treated as unimportant to the task at hand. By
definition, this text raises the interpretive stakes: Its author is not merely historical but also divine, and its audience is not merely confined to the ancient
world but still exists and receives this text in the modern world. Without denying that this text has an origin and purpose in a time long past, as Scripture
it must also be understood to have a divine origin and eternal purpose that
demands its reception in every generation—even those still to come.

The pastoral office demands a particular definition of the nature of the
Bible and makes particular demands regarding the rules of its interpretation.
Said another way, before we can explain what the Bible *does* we must first
explain what the Bible *is*. This means that exegesis must be appropriately
aligned with the object of study. And since the pastor theologian sits under
the authority of the Bible, its identity, nature and context give direction to
how it is interpreted and to its subject matter. For the pastor theologian,
then, the object of study is not completely defined by the categories of ancient text, literary genre or historical document, for this particular kind of
text demands to be defined according to its identity as Christian Scripture.
Such definitions and practices can be described as an *ecclesial exegesis*—the
manner in which the pastor theologian correctly handles the Word of truth
(2 Tim 2:15).

A DOCTRINE OF SCRIPTURE FOR EXEGESIS

To define any part of the Bible as Christian Scripture is to place it in a much
larger communicative context than the historical context in which it took on
its literary "flesh."[1] By categorizing the Bible as Scripture we are depicting it in

---

[1]The following is adapted from the introduction in Edward W. Klink III, *John*, Zondervan Exegetical
Commentary on the New Testament 4 (Grand Rapids: Zondervan, 2016).

light of its "origin, function, and end in divine self-communication"; yet we are also depicting the manner in which it must be read and the kinds of responses appropriate to its nature: "'Scripture' is a shorthand term for the nature and function of the biblical writings in a set of communicative acts which stretch from God's merciful self-manifestation to the obedient hearing of the community of faith."[2] While such language might not be common in the world of biblical studies and commentaries, it should be, for the object of interpretation demands to be treated according to its true and sacred nature. Not to treat the Bible as Scripture is itself a form of eisegesis, and it is a disobedient hearing of the (canonical) text's own claim and the God by whom it was authored.

The doctrine of Scripture is necessary for the exegetical task in two ways. First, it gives *insight* to the interpretive rules demanded by the object of interpretation. In a sense, Scripture becomes its own kind of genre: "If genre is a function of communal reception and usage as well as of inherent characteristics, then the genre of the biblical texts is that of 'holy Scripture.'"[3] Functionally, then, the doctrine of Scripture explains the (theological) genre of the Bible and the generic conventions to be followed by the faithful reader.

Second, the doctrine of Scripture gives *oversight* to Scripture's constituent parts and unifies their functions. Three are immediately apparent: (1) since the Bible speaks in history, a doctrinal framework is needed to make sure history remains subservient to the God of creation; (2) since the Bible speaks in literary form, a doctrinal framework is needed to make sure words stay subservient to the Word; and (3) since the Bible speaks about the things of God, a doctrinal framework is needed to make sure theology is defined by the person and work of God himself, the true subject matter of the things of God. In short, *the doctrine of Scripture gives oversight to the historical, literary and theological components of the revelation of God, which I will refer to as "creation," "canon" and "creed" in order to match their doctrinal nature.* A brief explanation of each is in order.

Creation. The doctrine of Scripture provides the necessary requirements for understanding the historical content and context of the Bible. If we make

---

[2]John Webster, *Holy Scripture: A Dogmatic Sketch*, Current Issues in Theology 1 (Cambridge: Cambridge University Press, 2003), 5.

[3]Francis Watson, *Text, Church and World: Biblical Interpretation in Theological Perspective* (Edinburgh: T&T Clark, 1994), 227.

interpretive judgments regarding the meaning of the Bible by comparing it to the historical (and social-cultural) setting in which it occurred without allowing the oversight or mediation of the doctrine of Scripture, we conflate the meaning of the text to its historical context. The Bible is not to be read like any other book. If we suppose texts are wholly confined by their immediate circumstances of origin and that as soon as they stray from their appointed time and place they will be misread and misunderstood, we embrace a historical perception of this body of writings that is theologically foreign to them. This is not to say that Scripture is unhistorical or less historical—not at all! It is to say, rather, that it is more; it speaks from a more comprehensive position.

The work of J. Todd Billings is helpful here. He explains that all interpreters implicitly answers two questions when they interpret the Bible:

1. Is revelation grounded in inherent, universal human capacities or in the particularity of God's action with Israel and in Jesus Christ?

2. Is Scripture received from within a deistic hermeneutic or a Trinitarian hermeneutic?[4]

In both cases a doctrinally defined reading of Scripture necessitates the latter option, for an interpretation that is naturalistic and/or deistic is poorly matched to the divine character of Scripture. The interpreter is given dogmatic reasons to believe that God was involved in the entire messy process, from the historical event to the textual expression of the text of Scripture (composition, transmission and reception). This requires a highly theological account of history, not only as a tool of interpretation but also as a philosophical construct.

Murray A. Rae has provided a sophisticated account of a theology of history. He argues that in relation to biblical interpretation, "The very idea of history requires both the biblical doctrine of creation, and a teleology, an account, that is, of the directedness of history towards some goal."[5] Rae argues that in our time theology has been excluded from the consideration of biblical texts, which ironically is itself a dogmatic presupposition.[6] The

---

[4]J. Todd Billings, *The Word of God for the People of God: An Entryway to the Theological Interpretation of Scripture* (Grand Rapids: Eerdmans, 2010), 71-104.
[5]Murray A. Rae, *History and Hermeneutics* (London: T&T Clark, 2005), 2.
[6]Ibid., 19-20.

key for Rae is the logical priority of Scripture: "We simply cannot proceed to investigate the Bible's witness to revelation by assuming that we know apart from revelation what history is. The order of knowing must be reversed."[7] Since all history finds its purpose (telos) in the person and work of God, history only has meaning in the purposes of God. This is why the doctrine of creation is so important (and must be related) to the doctrine of Scripture. Creation implies that the world is invested with a telos. "There is a reason for its being, and history, in consequence, is to be understood as the space and time opened up for the world to become what it is intended to be."[8] History becomes God's own confession, even mission, by which God, under his creative, providential and redemptive purposes, extends himself to the world. The referentiality and meaning of Scripture, therefore, is given definition not only by its placement in the originating (historical) context but also in the fuller context of God's communicative grace.

A doctrine of Scripture allows the biblical narrative, with all of its historical necessity and detail, not to bow the knee to the claims of historical naturalism. According to Webster, "For a Christian theological account of Scripture . . . the problem . . . is not the affirmation that the biblical texts have a 'natural history,' but the denial that texts with a 'natural history' may function within the communicative divine economy, and that such a function is ontologically definitive of the text. It is this denial—rather than any purely methodological questions—which has to form the focus of dogmatic critique."[9]

The history in the Bible, therefore, cannot be understood by rational inquiry without recourse to revelation. Nor can its purpose and meaning be reduced to a set of laws or a comparison to apparent analogous entities; to do so would be naturalistic and deistic. Rather, history, once understood to be framed by the Alpha and Omega (Rev 22:13), becomes a subset of creation—and therefore the Creator—and is embedded with a purpose

---

[7]Rae, *History and Hermeneutics*, 29. See Karl Barth, *Church Dogmatics I/2*, ed. G. W. Bromiley and T. F. Torrance (New York: T&T Clark, 2004), 50: "Revelation is not a predicate of history, but history is a predicate of revelation." Webster, *Holy Scripture*, 6, makes the identical claim: "This order is critically important because, unless their strict subservience to communicative divine activity is stated with some firmness, both text and practices of reading and reception may break loose and become matters for independent or quasi-independent investigation and explanation."
[8]Rae, *History and Hermeneutics*, 51.
[9]Webster, *Holy Scripture*, 19.

that is revealed in the person and work of Jesus Christ, who is both its ground and goal.[10]

Canon. The doctrine of Scripture not only gives definition to the material nature behind the text but also to the literary nature of the text itself. By *canon* I am referring to more than the collection of biblical books; I am referring here primarily to Scripture's *function* and *identity*, both of which have implications for interpreting textual units and books in the Bible.[11] First, according to its *function as canon*, a biblical book cannot be treated as if it were a single unit. Without denying that a biblical book took on literary "flesh" in the context of a particular historical author and audience, as the Word of God it was always intended (doctrinally) to be read as part of a collection. Though an argument could be made that a biblical book was originally created (historically) with this intention from its inception,[12] my argument is more dogmatic than historical. Since a biblical book makes up one of many parts of God's intentional communicative Word, then each book must be viewed as functioning cooperatively. This in no way denies that the book had value and meaning in its particular historical context. Rather, its meaning in its historical context is so tied to its larger canonical context that the latter extends and even explains the former. In the providence of God a biblical book's historical and canonical contexts function symphonically to communicate the intended fullness of the Word of God.

Second, according to its *identity as canon*, a biblical book cannot be treated as if it were a point of access to the Word of God but the very source of the Word of God. That is, the Bible is not a window to that which is inspired but is itself the inspiration. When we speak of Scripture, we are speaking about the source of revelation; we are claiming dogmatically that Scripture is the locus of revelation, not merely a mediator of revelation. This does not deny that the text is referring to real, historical people, places and events, but claims that the revelation, inclusive of real events, is located in

---

[10]Compare Augustine, *Teaching Christianity*, ed. John E. Rotelle, trans. Edmund Hill (Hyde Park, NY: New City Press, 1996), 2.44.152.

[11]See John Webster, *Word and Church: Essays in Christian Dogmatics* (Edinburgh: T&T Clark, 2011), 11-17.

[12]See D. Moody Smith, "When Did the Gospels Become Scripture?" *JBL* 119 (2000): 3-20; compare Edward W. Klink III, *The Sheep of the Fold: The Audience and Origin of the Gospel of John*, SNTSMS 141 (Cambridge: Cambridge University Press, 2007), 252-54.

the inscripturated account: God is giving divine commentary on his own actions in history. This text, as a divinely inspired communicative act, is God's revelation per se (in or by itself).

The Bible cannot be read as just any other book. Its form, function and canonical identity are not ancillary to its interpretation and meaning; they are determinative. Even the reality to which it points cannot be defined without recourse to revelation; nor can its meaning be determined outside of its canonical context. Rather, a biblical book, once understood to be framed by the rest of Scripture, becomes a subset of the canon and embedded with the full significance of the Word of God. Canon is not ultimately a historical account of the biblical collection but "a trinitarian and soteriological account of revelation . . . in which God establishes saving fellowship with humanity and so makes himself known to us."[13] In this way, then, the Bible is addressing not merely the past but the present, and not merely an ancient audience but the contemporary church.

Creed. The doctrine of Scripture not only gives definition to what lies behind the text (creation) and to the text itself (canon) but also guides the reader to the goal of the text, or its true subject matter. In light of God's use of creation in Scripture and the canon of Scripture, the Bible can be described as "Jesus Christ's own self-utterance."[14] Since Scripture is God's communicative act, its message and subject matter is about him—his person and his work.

One of the consequences of the historical-critical approach to the Bible is the loss of connection between the doctrines of the church and the text of Scripture, primarily because Scripture is expected, according to scholarly rules of interpretation, to be grounded historically in its ancient context. This excludes, by methodological necessity, eternal theological truths. The text's "literal sense" refers to subjects driven by and derived from the context of the book's origin, not "figuration or typology [which] was a natural extension of literal interpretation" in earlier eras of biblical interpretation.[15] The doctrines of the creeds, according to this approach, are entirely imposed upon the text of Scripture.

---

[13]Webster, *Word and Church*, 27.
[14]Ibid., 35.
[15]Hans W. Frei, *The Eclipse of Biblical Narrative: A Study in Eighteenth and Nineteenth Century Hermeneutics* (New Haven, CT: Yale University Press, 1974), 2.

Against this understanding, David S. Yeago explains that Scripture speaks not merely with concepts (the use of explicit words/terms) but also judgments. These judgments can use a variety of concepts, but in a manner that speaks beyond them, making a further, implicit referential claim.[16] A text *uses* concepts but *makes* judgments, and "the only way to uncover the judgments made in a text is to pay close attention to what is said and implied, to the specific, contingent ways in which its conceptual resources are deployed."[17] In this way, then, the text may make judgments beyond its use of concepts so that it may (and does!) speak to subjects not contained by any one concept. Ecclesial exegesis, for example, interprets the Gospel of John's depiction of the relation between the Father and the Son as reflective of the Trinitarian identity of God, even if the concept (Trinity) is not used. If God is Trinitarian in nature, then depictions of him, even if partial, are also reflective of the Trinity. In a sense, *without denying the logical priority and authority of Scripture, the subject matter of Scripture functions in a circular manner, not only as the result of a reading of Scripture but also as a guide for further readings.*[18]

The church has deemed the subject matter of Scripture to be clear, and has summarized this in the doctrine called the perspecuity of Scripture. However, it is not clear because the meaning of the text and its subject matter are obvious. Rather, it is clear because of the (doctrinal) conviction "that Scripture has the capacity to address and transform the human being, and to offer a reliable guide to human action."[19] Webster defines it well: "Scripture's clarity is neither an intrinsic element of the text as text nor simply a fruit of exegetical labour; it is that which the text becomes as it functions in the Spirit-governed encounter between the self-presenting saviour and the faithful reader. To read is to be caught up by the truth-bestowing Spirit of God."[20] The doctrine of Scripture guides the reader to look rightly at the text, that is, to look for the self-presentation of God through the work and person of Jesus Christ by the empowering Holy Spirit.

---

[16]David S. Yeago, "The New Testament and the Nicene Dogma: A Contribution to the Recovery of Theological Exegesis," *ProEccl* 3 (1994): 152-64.

[17]Ibid., 162.

[18]Helpful on this point is Carl R. Trueman, *The Creedal Imperative* (Wheaton, IL: Crossway, 2012).

[19]John Yocum, "Scripture, Clarity of," in *Dictionary for Theological Interpretation of the Bible*, gen. ed. Kevin J. Vanhoozer (Grand Rapids: Baker Academic, 2005), 727-30 (727).

[20]Webster, *Holy Scripture*, 95.

POSTURES AND PRINCIPLES OF ECCLESIAL EXEGESIS

So what does an ecclesial exegesis look like? Although certain presuppositions and stances must be adopted from the start, a robust doctrine of Scripture is expressed methodologically not by a rigidly defined procedure but by a posture that is sensitive to the narrative's own movements, pressures and expectations (both explicit and implicit) demanded of an obedient, believing reader. It is an art as much as it is a science.

This posture is especially important when interpreting biblical history. Ecclesial exegesis will begin with certain presuppositions that hold tightly to the necessity and meaning-deriving use of history while at the same time limiting the tenets of historical science by the doctrine of Scripture. But this does not provide a step-by-step procedure, for ecclesial exegesis is directed equally by both the text's historical concepts and context and the text's judgments and theological subject matter. In fact, the art of this kind of interpretation is the ability to allow both the text and its direction for meaning to be cooperatively active and interrelated in the exegetical process. It is an art only because it is a creative balance of two sciences. If there is a foundation, it is God, since by definition Scripture is his spoken Word. Yet this does not distance history but embraces it, since God is the Creator of his creation. And because there is a God, there is a goal (telos) of interpretation: the communicative intention of God, in historical event and written expression.

Ecclesial exegesis might be described as the application to the text of what Webster calls "biblical reasoning," where the text is read and applied by both exegetical and dogmatic reasoning.[21] In this approach the words of the historical authors "are not wholly identical with the divine Word, but they are the subject of a special mission, they are 'sent from God.'" They are an embassy from God in which "Scripture is the textual settlement," extending the prophetic and apostolic speech into the church's present.[22] Ecclesial exegesis, therefore, is an intellectual engagement with the living and gracious communication of God. It is no less than participation in the depths of the life of God by means of his Word to the world.

---

[21]John Webster, "Biblical Reasoning," *AThR* 90 (2008): 733-51.
[22]Ibid., 740.

The posture of ecclesial exegesis might be summarized in ten principles:

General Interpretive Principles

1. It begins with the presupposition that the Bible is living, trustworthy and authoritative.

2. It begins and ends with God—his history, his words, his ordering and intentional communication (Spirit-led, Christ-centered, God-glorifying).

3. Its subject matter is Jesus Christ/the gospel, and its purpose is for the love of God and neighbor.

4. It assumes that the most fitting context for interpreting and hearing the Bible is the church and not the academy, since its message is both content and confession.

5. It is willing to submit to its message: its truths and its commands.

Principles for Interpreting Historical Narrative

6. It is an integration of the historical and doctrinal context.

7. It is an integration of the historical and doctrinal content.

8. It is an interpretation of the text and not the event.

9. It assumes that the details in the text, even the seeming contradictions, are purposeful and intentional in what they intend to communicate.

10. It assumes the text is making canonical connections and not merely historical-author connections.

THE PRACTICE OF ECCLESIAL EXEGESIS: JOHN 3:22 AND 4:2

Here is an example of how ecclesial exegesis plays out with a particular passage: In John 3:22-26, Jesus' ministry became connected to a dispute that took place between the disciples of John the Baptist and an unidentified Jew. The disciples of John (and maybe the unidentified Jew as well) come to him with concerns over Jesus' seemingly parallel ministry, which is becoming more successful. The point of tension between John and Jesus is fueled by a statement in John 3:22, where the narrator informs the reader that Jesus was performing baptisms.

This almost add-on statement has raised more than a few questions—most notably, *why* was Jesus baptizing and *what* did this baptism signify? Even more, just over a dozen verses later, in John 4:2, the narrator explains that Jesus was not baptizing, but only his disciples were. Then why did 3:22 announce so unequivocally that Jesus was baptizing, with the third-person singular verb explicitly connecting the act of baptism to Jesus? That is, why is he named as the author of the baptism (according to 3:22) although he did not physically perform the baptism (according to 4:2)? Hoskyns explains it best: "The dilemma of modern exegesis of the Fourth Gospel is perhaps nowhere more clearly illustrated than in the divergent and opposite handling of this passage."[23]

If these two verses are used to construct an event behind the text, then 4:2 can be used to explain away any confusion or uncertainty regarding 3:22, functionally eclipsing its narrative intention. But interpreted as a text, with both verses assumed to be serving a cooperative purpose, the intention of 3:22 cannot be so easily dismissed (principle 8). In fact, the dissonance created between 3:22 and 4:2 might be exactly the point, directing the reader to see a truth that extends beyond the historical action of an event to a textually mediated theological reality regarding the actions of God (principle 9).

One thing 3:22 clearly does is make a direct connection between Jesus and the baptisms being performed. This connection between baptism and Jesus gives significant direction to the reader. Regarding the larger scene, it is correct to see a similarity between the baptism of John and the baptism Jesus is performing through his disciples. But in another sense, as the following verses make clear, there is also an important difference. In fact, it might be best not to describe Jesus' baptism as being patterned after John's, even if the historical situation made it look that way. For John's baptism was never his own; it was always intended to be (or to become) the baptism of Jesus. And John's baptism was never cleansing in itself; it is no coincidence that John is never even called "the Baptist" in the Fourth Gospel, for he cannot be the true Baptist (see Jn 1:33). As Luther explains, "For now Christ wants to take Baptism over from John, since John had been merely a servant discharging his duties of this office until now."[24]

This verse, therefore, is providing a thematic introduction to the impending scene. While supporters of John (the Baptist) might see a distinction, even

---

[23]Edwyn Clement Hoskyns, *The Fourth Gospel*, 2nd ed., ed. Francis Noel Davey (London: Faber and Faber, 1947), 226.

[24]Martin Luther, *Luther's Works, vol. 22: Sermons on the Gospel of St. John: Chapters 1-4* (St. Louis: Concordia, 1999), 414.

competition, between the two baptisms (John's and Jesus'), there has always
and only been one baptism. It is a baptism from above, involving the Spirit
and performed by Jesus, the true Baptist. In the words of Augustine: "Take
away the water, it is no baptism; take away the Word, it is no baptism."[25]

For this reason it is best to view the comment in John 4:2 not as an attempt to separate Jesus from the act of baptism but as an attempt to show
that the similarity between those who are doing the baptizing, John the
Baptist and the disciples of Jesus, is founded upon Jesus, who is authorizing
true baptism on both accounts.[26] This is why "he was baptizing" in John
3:22 had to be third-person singular, for the same reason that baptism in the
church is always done in the name of Jesus (Acts 10:48; compare Matt 28:19).
It becomes imperative, then, that we not understand the statement "Jesus
was baptizing" to be subsumed under the already existing baptism of John,
as is common when viewing the events from within linear history. While it
is true in one sense that John's baptism came first, in another and more
important sense Jesus/God was already well at work before John—from "the
beginning" (Jn 1:1). And since John's own beginning has already been rooted
in the work of God (see Jn 1:6), it would be entirely inaccurate to view even
the smallest part of John's ministry as conflicting with and not serving under
the ministry of God through Jesus Christ.

In the end, the dissonance created between 3:22 and 4:2 pressures the
reader to see the innate connection between Jesus and the sacrament of
baptism. All baptisms originate and are empowered by the work and person
of Jesus Christ. This doctrinal truth is expressed by the Fourth Gospel not
in propositions but by the dissonance created by two seemingly contrasting
texts in a historical narrative (principles 6 and 7). While historical-critical
exegesis is designed to resolve the conflict, an ecclesial exegesis assumes that
the details in the text, even the seeming contradictions, are purposeful and
intentional in what they intend to communicate (principle 9). A further assumption is that this scene, with all of its historical issues and details, is part
of a greater divine communication that matches the rest of Scripture's

---

[25] Augustine, *Homilies on the Gospel of John, Homilies on the First Epistle of John, Soliloquies*, ed. Philip
Schaff, Nicene and Post-Nicene Fathers, First Series 7 (Peabody, MA: Hendrickson, 1994), 15.4
(p. 100).

[26] Thomas Aquinas, *Commentary on the Gospel of John*, 3 vols., trans. Fabian Larcher and James
A. Weisheipl (Washington, DC: The Catholic University of America Press, 2010), 1:207-8.

depiction of the doctrine of baptism (principle 10). Interestingly, Calvin (against the Anabaptists) and Augustine (against the Donatists) used this text to refute those who denied the validity of a baptism because of a perceived problem with the baptizer.[27] Jesus is, and has always been, the source and substance of Christian baptism.

CONCLUSION: A CALL FOR ECCLESIAL EXEGESIS

For over two centuries the academy has made radical claims regarding the interpretation of the church's book, with professors—not pastors—serving as the interpretive magistrates, defining what the object of interpretation is and, therefore, what interpretation does. The pastoral office requires a different kind of exegesis, just as Scripture is a different kind of text. The exegesis of the pastor theologian includes not only all the categories at home in the social location of the academy but also the categories belonging to the social location of the church. This "ecclesial exegesis," for lack of a better title, is not less than academic but is more than that, for it is concerned with an ancient text that is also the living, authoritative Word of God. The office of the pastor theologian offers its own direction and definition to the nature of the Bible and the rules by which it is interpreted.

---

[27]Compare John Calvin, *The Gospel According to St. John 1-10*, ed. David W. Torrance and Thomas F. Torrance, trans. T. H. L. Parker, Calvin's New Testament Commentaries 4 (Grand Rapids: Eerdmans, 1995), 88: "He calls Christ's Baptism that which He administered by others, to teach us that Baptism is not to be valued from the person of the minister, but that its whole force depends on its author, in whose name and by whose command it is administered."

11

The Pastor Theologian in the Pastoral Epistles

JASON A. NICHOLLS

John Calvin once described a true theologian as someone who "edifies consciences in the fear of God."[1] Gerald Hiestand and Todd Wilson seem to agree with this assessment when they contend that the church needs the kind of theologians who work and write "as those who bear the weight of souls upon their shoulders."[2] They go on to declare that "pastors, not professors, are the theological leaders of the church," and that "the pastoral office retains the burden of the church's theological leadership."[3]

In the Bible, perhaps there is no better place to go to recover an early portrait of a pastor theologian than the Pastoral Epistles.[4] Granted, the apostle Paul stops short of offering us a textbook profile of a pastor theologian, but I hope to offer a few reasons here for why I believe these letters might indeed provide us with the closest biblical portrait of such a role. For starters, the recipients of these letters—Timothy and Titus—were

---

[1]See John Calvin, comment on Titus 1:1 in his *Commentaries on the Epistles to Timothy, Titus and Philemon*, trans. William Pringle (Edinburgh: Calvin Translation Society, 1856; Eugene, OR: Wipf and Stock, 2006), 283. Calvin explains, "And hence we are also informed, that the greater progress any one has made in godliness, he is so much the better disciple of Christ; and that he ought to be reckoned a true theologian who edifies consciences in the fear of God."

[2]Gerald Hiestand and Todd Wilson, *The Pastor Theologian: Resurrecting an Ancient Vision* (Grand Rapids: Zondervan, 2015), 101.

[3]Hiestand and Wilson, *Pastor Theologian*, 57.

[4]Kevin Vanhoozer even refers to the book of Titus as "Paul's epistle on pastoral theology." See Kevin J. Vanhoozer and Owen Strachan, *The Pastor as Public Theologian: Reclaiming A Lost Vision* (Grand Rapids: Baker Academic, 2015), 122.

crucial links between apostolic authority and local overseers. Though
they were not apostles themselves, they were certainly more than local
pastors or overseers.[5] They were commissioned with a special authority
and dispatched to deal with problems that were at root theological. In
many respects, these two men functioned much like pastors. Yet the particular crises they faced, coupled with the distinctively theological nature
of their assignments, should lead us to expand their role. I believe they
are *more* than pastors; they may be our closet scriptural approximation
to the pastor theologian.

The church today might benefit from a fresh look at Paul's portrait of
Timothy and Titus's role in the Pastoral Epistles, not only because it helps
us recover a robust biblical vision for the theologian's task but also because
it highlights some of its oft-neglected *pastoral* aspects. As we look to the
Pastoral Epistles, we are met by five overarching mandates from Paul that
have a bearing on what should be considered the pastor theologian's
overall task. These directives are: (1) a call to guard and protect the gospel;
(2) a call to teach, exhort and pass on; (3) a call to pursue godliness with
exemplary living; (4) a call to share in suffering; and (5) a call to provide
active oversight for the church.

PAUL'S MANDATES IN THE PASTORAL EPISTLES

Before proceeding, it is worth asking to what extent we have warrant to press
this role of the pastor theologian upon the Pastoral Epistles. There is some
debate as to how we should view the recipients of these letters. Thorvald
Madsen, for example, maintains that Timothy and Titus should be seen as
stand-ins between Paul and the local congregations, holding positions that
no longer exist.[6] Philip Towner adds that they should probably be designated
as "apostolic delegates," insofar as they are key leaders dispatched by Paul

---

[5]See Benjamin L. Merkle, "Ecclesiology in the Pastoral Epistles," in *Entrusted with the Gospel: Paul's
Theology in the Pastoral Epistles*, ed. Andreas J. Köstenberger and Terry L. Wilder (Nashville: B&H
Academic, 2010), 196. Gordon Fee describes them as "itinerants on special assignment," sent there
as Paul's "apostolic delegates"; see Gordon Fee, *1 and 2 Timothy and Titus*, New International Bible
Commentary 13 (Peabody, MA: Hendrickson, 1988), 21.
[6]See Thorvald D. Madsen II, "The Ethics of the Pastoral Epistles" in *Entrusted with the Gospel*, 225.
Madsen adds that the Pastoral Epistles "look forward to a time when the tasks of leadership will
fall to others, operating under the authority of these letters and the rest of Scripture."

with more itinerant ministries.[7] Thomas Schreiner, however, points to the overlap between their duties and that of the elders, noting how Paul's admonitions seem to apply equally to both groups. However, given that these men came with the commission and backing of Paul himself, they carried more authority than any one elder would possess.[8] This suggests that there is good warrant for taking Paul's words to these men as paradigmatic for the elders and by extension, I would argue, for the pastor theologian.[9]

Perhaps the best way to make the case that the Pastoral Epistles are a suitable place to give form and shape to the pastor theologian's task is to move into an examination of the five mandates themselves. The first two seem to fit comfortably within the role of a theologian in most any context (academic or ecclesial): guard the gospel, and teach it and pass it on. The latter three mandates, however, are more difficult to accomplish from the social location of the academy. In fact, they appear to require a type of theologian who is fully immersed in a distinctively ecclesial context.[10]

Mandate 1: The call to guard and protect the gospel. From the opening of 1 Timothy, Paul is clear that the reason he had left his protégé in Ephesus was so that he might "charge certain persons not to teach any different doctrine" (1 Tim 1:3).[11] Using vivid military metaphors, he charges Timothy to "wage the good warfare" against the false teachers of Ephesus (1 Tim 1:19). Timothy must assess whether anyone teaches a "different doctrine" (1 Tim 6:3), and be ready to "fight the good fight of the faith" (1 Tim 6:12). Paul's "good deposit," after all, is now being entrusted to Timothy, and he must

---

[7]Philip Towner, *The Letters to Timothy and Titus*, New International Commentary on the New Testament (Grand Rapids: Eerdmans, 2006), 242, 425. Compare Fee, *1 and 2 Timothy and Titus*, 21. Thomas Schreiner believes that while they were certainly leaders, "it is a mistake to conclude that they were pastors." See Schreiner, "Overseeing and Serving the Church in the Pastoral and General Epistles," in *Shepherding God's Flock: Biblical Leadership in the New Testament and Beyond*, ed. Benjamin L. Merkle and Thomas R. Schreiner (Grand Rapids: Kregel, 2014), 90. Philip Ryken, on the other hand, consistently refers to Timothy as a "minister," insofar as he was delegated to lead a local church. See Philip Graham Ryken, *1 Timothy* (Phillipsburg, NJ: P&R, 2007), 3, 7-8.

[8]See Merkle, "Ecclesiology," 197-98.

[9]Schreiner, "Overseeing," 90, 92. Compare 2 Tim 2:2, where Paul urges Timothy to "entrust" to faithful men what he has "heard" from him.

[10]I believe that this strengthens the case made by Hiestand and Wilson—who contend that the task of formulating theology is insufficient if it's not done, at least in part, from the social location of the church. See Hiestand and Wilson, *Pastor Theologian*, 17, 67.

[11]Unless otherwise indicated, Scripture quotations in this chapter are from the English Standard Version.

"guard" its safekeeping (1 Tim 6:20).[12] Several years later, in his second epistle to Timothy, Paul will repeat this charge from his dungeon cell in the infamous Mamertine Prison. He will again compel his spiritual son to "follow the pattern of the sound words" he's heard from him. He is to "guard the good deposit" with which he's been entrusted (2 Tim 1:13-14), wise to the subversive tactics of his wily opponents.[13] Timothy is being called take up a crucial role of guardianship that Paul is relinquishing.[14] In the letter to Titus, this guard/protect motif surfaces once again. Titus may only appoint as elders men who "hold firm to the trustworthy word as taught," so that they can provide instruction and rebuke any contradictors (Tit 1:9).[15] Deceivers and empty talkers must be silenced and rebuked (Titus 1:13), even as Titus avoids all "foolish controversies" (Tit 3:9).

Madsen describes a two-sided teaching ministry here that involves "defense and offense." The overseer is to conserve the gospel entrusted to him (defense), even while directly refuting heresy (offense).[16] What kind of a theologian is best suited to this calling? Certainly the academy has witnessed its fair share of "strange teachings"—and the academic theologian is more than qualified to offer censure there. Yet in his book *Finding Faithful Elders and Deacons*, Thabiti Anyabwile insightfully reminds us that heresies and doctrinal corruptions always and inevitably target the church, and they all "arose while some pastor was on the job." A good pastor, then, must embrace their calling as "the chief theological officer in the church" by guarding and protecting the flock from error.[17] To shuffle this task over to the halls of academia and away from

---

[12]See Towner, *Letters*, 430-31. Alan Tomlinson refers to Timothy as Paul's "apostolic troubleshooter," and notes how the false teachers of 1 Timothy wanted to see themselves as guardians and protectors of the deposit of truth, even while they were misusing the law to champion asceticism. See F. Alan Tomlinson, "The Purpose and Stewardship Theme Within the Pastoral Epistles" in *Entrusted With the Gospel*, 54, 60. Gordon Fee points to Timothy's high level of preparedness because he had been entrusted with previous assignments in Thessalonica, Corinth and Philippi, and had also collaborated with Paul on six of his extant letters. See Fee, *1 and 2 Timothy and Titus*, 2.

[13]Paul likens Timothy's opponents to Jannes and Jambres, men whom Jewish tradition identified as the chief magicians/sorcerers whom Moses had to face in his meetings with Pharaoh (see Ex 7:11). For further discussion see Towner, *Letters*, 563-65. Compare A. Pietersma, *The Apocryphon of Jannes and Jambres the Magicians* (New York: E. J. Brill, 1994), 36-42.

[14]Towner, *Letters*, 478.

[15]As the person commissioned to appoint elders, Titus himself would certainly be expected to embrace and internalize this quality.

[16]Madsen, "Ethics," 226.

[17]Thabiti Anyabwile, *Finding Faithful Elders and Deacons* (Wheaton, IL: Crossway, 2012), 159. Compare Acts 20:28-31.

the church only continues the lamentable pattern of "outsourcing" the entire theological enterprise to the academy.[18] After all, pastors and professors occupy different vocational locations and face different vocational needs, responsibilities and pressures. Pastors, for instance, do not depend for their job security on publishing new and innovative ideas. They are not bound by "guild-specific rules," nor would they endure the frowns of their peers for bringing moral evaluation into their theological beliefs.[19] A faithful pastor recognizes that right theology calls for right living, and wrong thinking leads to foolish living—and that God's people need to be exhorted accordingly. Thus, when Paul advises Titus to "silence" (or literally "muzzle") his theological opponents, we can imagine that this probably wouldn't fly before a tenure committee! Yet within the context of local church discipline, exercised faithfully under the authority of qualified elders, such censure would be quite appropriate. In fact, the integrity and health of God's flock depends on it.

Mandate 2: The call to teach, exhort and pass on. Paul's second mandate connects to the first, since it is clearly Paul's undiluted gospel that Timothy and Titus are to teach and pass on. Timothy in particular is called to "put these things before the brothers" (1 Tim 4:6), to "teach" and "urge" and even "command these things" (1 Tim 4:11; 6:2). Timothy's role, which again is a model for the elders he's appointing, obliges him to devote himself to the public reading of Scripture, "to exhortation, [and] to teaching" (1 Tim 4:13).[20] By the second letter, as Paul nears the conclusion of his earthly ministry and hears how things in Asia are unraveling, he urges Timothy to take his deposit of sound teaching and "entrust [it] to faithful men who will be able to teach others" (2 Tim 2:2). Only Timothy's right handling of the word of truth will enable him to teach and correct his opponents (2 Tim 2:15, 24-25).[21] The exhortations to Titus are similar. He, too, is to "teach what accords with sound

---

[18]Hiestand and Wilson, *Pastor Theologian*, 63.

[19]See the discussion in Hiestand and Wilson, *Pastor Theologian*, 67-74.

[20]For an excellent discussion of how the public reading of Scripture functioned in the believing community, see Philip H. Towner, "The Function of the Public Reading of Scripture in 1 Timothy 4:13 and in the Biblical Tradition," *SBJT* 7/3 (Fall 2003): 44-53. Towner traces the practice of public readings in Judaism and in Greco-Roman society and argues that a balanced and systematic reading of Scripture was needed to curb false teachings and theological speculations.

[21]In his discussion of Timothy's calling to "rightly handle" the word of truth, Philip Towner connects the "irreverent babble" (2 Tim 2:16) with the "godless chatter" (1 Tim 4:7) that Timothy is called to avoid at all costs. All of this "heretical nonsense" that was threatening to bring the teaching of the church "down to the level of base human teaching." See Towner, *Letters*, 523.

doctrine" and "declare," "exhort," and "rebuke with all authority" (Tit 2:1, 15). Crete's unique situation will require a high level of persistence from Titus, which is why he must "insist on these things" (Tit 3:8).

If it is indeed true that the role of the theologian is to make sense of the world, shape beliefs and help us identify our misplaced affections, then the outworking of this second mandate will certainly play a crucial part in it.[22] Each generation of believers needs a fresh deposit of the gospel. As pastors like Zach Eswine remind us, it's naive to assume that just because we preach or say something once, people should "hereafter immediately, always, and forever get it right."[23]

As with the first mandate, we must ask whether the context of academia is completely conducive to this task. (This might be worth asking even for a conservative Christian college or seminary.) Current trends in educational philosophy are witnessing the academy move away from didactic methods to embrace more collaborative approaches to learning that feed off of substantial student input. But if the church is going to continue being the church—called out as different from the world—will she not require a passing on of a faith "that was once for all delivered to the saints" (Jude 3)? And will she not specifically need teachers with a Timothy-like devotion to the public reading, teaching and exhortation of the Scriptures? Timothy Keller is right to remind us that preaching will always have an irreplaceable role as the primary vehicle for how God speaks to and builds up his people. Voices like those of D. Martyn Lloyd-Jones also remind us that there is no substitute for the people of God coming together in a specific place to sit under the expository preaching of the Word.[24]

Yet even the most effective of preachers today will wisely point out that the ministry of the Word is accomplished at several levels and should be *more* than just preaching sermons.[25] The church has an ongoing need for

---

[22]Hiestand and Wilson, *Pastor Theologian,* 55. The theologian occupies a crucial leadership role within the church, for "when beliefs go astray, desires are misplaced, and ethics stumble" (56).

[23]Zach Eswine, *Sensing Jesus: Life and Ministry as a Human Being* (Wheaton, IL: Crossway, 2012), 275.

[24]See D. Martyn Lloyd-Jones, *Preaching and Preachers,* ed. Kevin DeYoung (Grand Rapids: Zondervan, 2011), 51-54.

[25]See Timothy Keller, *Preaching: Communicating Faith in an Age of Skepticism* (New York: Viking, 2015), 2-5, 7. Keller advocates for three levels of "Word ministry," from mutual teaching and informal admonishing to more formal teaching venues, including the authoritative act of preaching. To reduce the ministry of the Word to preaching risks giving the sermon a load that it wasn't meant to bear.

systematic teaching, exhorting and the passing on of the doctrines of the faith. And inasmuch as its pastor enjoys a primary role as the featured weekly speaker, it would seem that a pastor serving as local theologian is indeed the best positioned to fulfill this mandate.

Mandate 3: *The call to pursue godliness and exemplary living.* Paul's third mandate is where the discussion really gets interesting. It's one thing to urge the theologian to guard the integrity of the gospel, even to teach it and pass it on. It's quite another to say, "Put your personal life on display as an example of godliness for all the world to see." Yet that is exactly what Paul calls for. He insists that the theologian's teaching *and life* must be closely watched (1 Tim 4:15-16). Timothy is to train himself for godliness (1 Tim 4:7), setting the believers "an example in speech, in conduct, in love, in faith, in purity" (1 Tim 4:12). His mind must be sharp enough to expose the "foolish, ignorant controversies," and his character sturdy enough to avoid the quarrels that so often accompany them (2 Tim 2:23-24). Titus, too, is commanded to show himself "in all respects to be a model of good works." He must demonstrate such integrity in his teaching and dignity in his interactions that his opponents are left literally speechless for personal attacks (Tit 2:7-8).

This is timely wisdom—not only in today's theological world but also in the wider world. Indeed, when Paul uses the term "sound doctrine," he's contrasting not just ideas but actual practices.[26] Theologians such as Kelly Kapic, in his *Little Book for New Theologians*, warn us about the "theological detachment" that the academy so often cultivates whenever it starts separating theology from spirituality.[27] Instead, he advocates for what he calls an "anthroposensitive" way of doing theology, where the theologian refuses to divorce theological considerations from their practical human application.[28] Most will readily agree that knowing doctrinal content does not equal spiritual growth.

---

[26]Vanhoozer and Strachan, *Pastor as Public Theologian*, 162.

[27]Kelly M. Kapic, *A Little Book for New Theologians: Why and How to Study Theology* (Downers Grove, IL: IVP Academic, 2012), 9. Kapic urges particularly young theologians to remember that "theological reflection is a way of examining our praise, prayers, words and worship with the goal of making sure they conform to God alone" (23). He continues, "One of the great dangers in theology is making our faith something we discuss rather than something that moves us" (64).

[28]Kapic, *Little Book*, 47. Compare Kelly M. Kapic, *Communion With God: The Divine and the Human in the Theology of John Owen* (Grand Rapids: Baker Academic, 2007), 33-34.

Matthew Henry famously warned ministers that if they fail to live what they preach, they risk "pull[ing] down with one hand what they build up with the other."[29] And if it is true that *pastors* are often better at watching their doctrines than their lives, one wonders whether academic theologians fare any better.[30] After all, as Paul knew and warned, heresies often begin with character defects in their proponents.[31] Thus, a faithful theologian will want to model appropriate devotion by embracing and, as Kevin Vanhoozer puts it, even "indwelling" doctrinal truth.[32] Who better to do this than local pastors serving local congregants who know them, walk through life with them, and are able to observe their personal lives in addition to their public ministry?

Mandate 4: The call to share in suffering. This fourth mandate only ups the ante, with Paul demanding even more personal investment. The one who is ordered to "guard the good deposit" (1 Tim 6:20) is also urged to "share in suffering" (2 Tim 1:9; 2:3). Timothy cannot be ashamed of the gospel or where it has landed his mentor. Though comparatively young, prone to illness and reportedly timid by temperament, he was nevertheless called to what John Stott describes as "exacting responsibilities" in the church.[33] He must follow Paul's example and prepare himself for "persecutions and sufferings" (2 Tim 3:11-12), keeping a sober mind as he endures suffering (2 Tim 4:5). Titus, too, should prepare himself for the distinct possibility of being disregarded (Tit 2:15).[34]

Perhaps here is where we can begin to feel, and even affirm, the pain of these men as pastor theologians. We know that Paul's troubles often arose in conflict with anti-gospel forces. Certainly these attacks were also being

---

[29]Matthew Henry, *Matthew Henry's Commentary on the Whole Bible*, 6 vols. (Old Tappan, NJ: Revell, 1983), 6:821.

[30]Anyabwile, *Finding*, 151; Eswine, *Sensing Jesus*, 259, 289. Perhaps this is why the writer to the Hebrews urges us to consider the outcome of our leaders' way of life and to "imitate their faith" (Heb 13:7).

[31]See Madsen, "Ethics," 228.

[32]See Kevin J. Vanhoozer, *The Drama of Doctrine: A Canonical Linguistic Approach to Christian Doctrine* (Louisville, KY: Westminster John Knox, 2005), 21. Vanhoozer explains, "We need to appropriate, embrace, even indwell doctrinal truth. The proper end of the drama of doctrine is wisdom: lived knowledge, a performance of truth."

[33]See John Stott, *The Message of 2 Timothy* (Downers Grove, IL: InterVarsity, 1973), 20. Fee, on the other hand, believes that the timid picture of Timothy "is probably a bit overdrawn." See Fee, *1 and 2 Timothy and Titus*, 2.

[34]Pointing to the well-known (and rather poor) reputation of the Cretan churches, Philip Towner believes that Paul expected further acts of rebellious opposition to Titus's authority. See Towner, *Letters*, 768.

leveled against his apostolic delegates and their newly appointed overseers.[35] Churches were at risk of splitting and leaders were at risk of getting burned out—or worse, run out. And thus, in view of such dire consequences, Paul calls upon these men to endure and stand firm in their responsibility to guard the theological integrity of God's people, whatever the cost.

As with earlier mandates, we must ask whether an academic theological context is the place for this kind of suffering. Hiestand and Wilson point out that academic theology rarely gets "preachy" inasmuch as the academy tends to prioritize "disinterested neutrality." Such careers tend to blossom in the soils of theory and analysis. Pastor theologians, on the other hand, always carry "the preacher's burden" into their scholarship—which is the burden of souls.[36] They find that this burden brings not just shape, but also weight and a sense of measure to all of the truths they want to voice. Pursuing faithful pastoral ministry may be a labor of love, but it is very much a labor. Pointing to Paul's suffering for the gospel, John Piper says that the pastor's job is "to labor so that none of his brothers and sisters is destroyed."[37] Indeed, the pastoral calling itself is a cruciform vocation.[38] And insofar as a pastor is called to proclaim a crucified Christ who calls his followers to die to self, as scholars like Kevin Vanhoozer remind us, "The faithful pastor will always be a countercultural figure."[39]

The disparate demands of the academy and the church as distinct social locations create more tensions for the pastor theologian. For instance, the academy tends to reward specialization, whereas the pastor theologian will want to resist narrow research and try to synthesize more broadly.[40] Instead of moving from simplicity to complexity, as is the trend in academic circles, the pastor theologian will always try to do the reverse.[41] Thus a pastor theologian

---

[35]Madsen, "Ethics," 225-27.

[36]Hiestand and Wilson, *Pastor Theologian*, 92-93. Indeed, Kevin Vanhoozer even notes how so much of what pastors find in scholarly biblical commentaries "is hard, if not impossible, to preach." See Vanhoozer and Strachan, *Pastor as Public Theologian*, 6.

[37]John Piper, *Brothers, We Are Not Professionals: A Plea to Pastors for Radical Ministry* (Nashville, TN: Broadman and Holman, 2002), 107-8.

[38]For a fuller explanation of how the social location of the pastorate gives pastors a cruciform vocation, see chapter 5 of this volume, "The Pastor Theologian as Cruciform Theologian."

[39]Vanhoozer and Strachan, *Pastor as Public Theologian*, 3.

[40]Vanhoozer views the pastor as a "a particular kind of generalist." See "Thesis #10" in Vanhoozer and Strachan, *The Pastor as Public Theologian*, 184.

[41]Hiestand and Wilson, *Pastor Theologian*, 92, 97.

may often feel like one trying to straddle a fence, struggling to keep a foot in two dissimilar fields of discourse. Vanhoozer actually suggests that there are three distinct locations into which the pastor theologian must speak: the academy, the church and the broader society.[42] All of this can easily create a sense of anxiety—pressure that may even lead a pastor theologian to doubt whether pastoral ministry is a viable context for providing theological leadership. The risk is that the angst will be too much and one of these callings will be abandoned.[43] Granted, this kind of "suffering" certainly pales in comparison to a Roman dungeon, but that's not to say that there's no struggle here for the pastor theologian to endure.

Mandate 5: *The call to provide rule/oversight within the church.* This final mandate from Paul is more implied than explicit, but nevertheless it's difficult to miss the call for Timothy and Titus to involve themselves directly in providing church oversight. As Paul sees it, because the church is the "pillar and buttress of the truth," God's people need to know how to conduct themselves in it (1 Tim 3:14-15). Thus at the very center of their mission is this need to establish, or in some cases reestablish, order in the church as God's household.[44]

Stewardship metaphors have been hailed as Paul's "metaphors of choice" for expressing all of the controlling themes in the Pastoral Epistles.[45] Because Paul sees the church as "the household of God" (1 Tim 3:15), he wants his apostolic delegates to teach their churches how to behave accordingly. This will include learning how to pray, how to relate to civil authorities (1 Tim 2:1, 8), and how women should conduct themselves in public worship (1 Tim 2:9-15). Paul also provides qualifications for church overseers (1 Tim 3:2-7), instructions about how to manage older men (1 Tim 5:1-2), guidance regarding widows (1 Tim 5:3-16) and even wisdom on handling elder care (1 Tim 5:17-19). Titus seems to have been dealing with a less-developed ecclesiastical structure, and yet he too was called to lend oversight by providing moral instruction (Tit 3:1-2) and

---

[42]"Pastor-theologians must be trilingual, able to speak the language of all three social locations, or at least speak it well enough to ask directions (and give them)." See Vanhoozer and Strachan, 4-5.
[43]Hiestand and Wilson are sympathetic to the tension faced by pastor theologians, noting how they have traditionally been lured away from their ecclesial contexts, enticed by the patronage, supportive networks and intellectual prestige of the academy (see *Pastor Theologian*, 50-52, 77).
[44]See Tomlinson, "Purpose," 82. Merkle agrees; see "Ecclesiology," 174. Compare R. Kent Hughes and Bryan Chapell, *1 & 2 Timothy and Titus: To Guard the Deposit* (Wheaton, IL: Crossway, 2000), 17.
[45]Tomlinson, "Purpose," 70.

by overseeing church discipline (Tit 3:10). In short, Paul needs Timothy and Titus to be directly involved in all of this multifaceted oversight.

If David Wells is right that theology is "initially and most immediately constructed" for the church,[46] one might argue that providing church oversight is a necessary ingredient in the makeup of any theologian. The pastor theologian, because of his context, is able to witness firsthand just how the drama of doctrine plays out in the tangible structures of real-life, sin-tainted relationships. All of this aligns with what scholars like D. A. Carson have recently argued regarding the importance of pastors providing church oversight: Inasmuch as a comprehensive ministry of the Word "demands" oversight, it should be seen an indispensable part of their role.[47] Thus it's not surprising that these early pastor theologians were commissioned with not just a responsibility to guard and manage doctrine but were also endowed with a critical mission to oversee the workings of local churches.

CONCLUSION

In this essay I have endeavored to argue that the Pastoral Epistles are a suitable and helpful place to go for reclaiming an early portrait of a particular kind of theologian—a pastor theologian. While the original two recipients of these letters held unique roles and served in itinerant ministries, they were nevertheless dispatched to attend to real-life ecclesial crises, facing predicaments that were precipitated by alarming doctrinal aberrations. And so they were charged with the responsibility to teach, correct and refute in the *theological* realm, all for the health and protection of God's flock.

Yet we have also seen that these theologians functioned primarily as *pastors*. Both Timothy and Titus provided active oversight, and in so doing they joined with Paul in suffering for the work of the gospel. Perhaps this— the cruciform nature of pastoral work—is something to which all pastors can attest whenever they face such challenges to stay faithful to their calling.

---

[46]David Wells, "The Theologian's Craft," in *Doing Theology in Today's World: Essays in Honor of Kenneth S. Kantzer*, ed. John D. Woodbridge and Thomas Edward McComiskey (Grand Rapids: Zondervan, 1991), 174.

[47]D. A. Carson, "Some Reflections on Pastoral Leadership," *Themelios* 40.2 (2015): 195-97. Carson goes on to say that if a pastor shows no propensity for godly oversight, then he is not qualified to be a pastor/teacher/overseer—"no matter how good a teacher he may be." And a pastor who tries to delegate it away "fails to grasp that a comprehensive ministry of the Word demands oversight" (197).

Furthermore, we have seen how these men were charged with being living examples of truth—meaning they had to back up all of their corrective theological work with a godly and exemplary life.

These five mandates from Paul, and particularly the latter three, have a distinctly pastoral flavor and would seem to be fulfilled most naturally in an ecclesial context. Thus I believe that the Pastoral Epistles offer us a compelling biblical portrait of a particular kind of theologian who, to return to the words of John Calvin, "edifies consciences in the fear of God"—the pastor theologian.

12

The Female Ecclesial Theologian

LAURIE L. NORRIS

T HE ESSAYS IN THIS BOOK HAVE SHOWN that there is a need to develop and support ecclesial theologians who simultaneously serve
within a local church context and meaningfully contribute to wider biblical-
theological scholarship for the church. But do we have a robust vision for
how *women* fit within this model? If this task is framed largely in terms of
the "pastor theologian," might certain theological convictions regarding the
role of women in church leadership potentially prevent women from participating? I want to explore such questions in hopes of constructing a model
that, both in language and practice, formally includes and encourages the
development of women as competent biblical theologians in service to the
local church.

In doing so, I hope to transcend traditional questions on the role of
women in ministry and encourage us to think creatively about how to include women in this necessary conversation—that is, in this broader vision
of the "pastor theologian" that is being cast both through this book and
through the work of the Center for Pastor Theologians (CPT). I will move
from broader foundations to more particular definitions, and then to some
contextual applications.

THEOLOGY AND THE CHURCH: FOUNDATIONS

Broadly speaking, the work of confessional Christian theology belongs to
the church. As Martin Luther stated, "We are all called theologians, just as

[we are] all [called] Christians."[1] "Whenever we speak about God we are engaged in theology," and these beliefs about God guide every aspect of our lives.[2] Many women in the church, however, do not view themselves as equal participants in theological discourse. Theology is viewed as a male discipline confined to ivory towers. In teaching women in the local church, I have observed in many of them a moment of enlightenment when exposed to the truth—often for the first time—that they, in fact, *are* theologians, reflecting in every conversation and decision their particular understanding of God and his dealings with humanity. Along with all members of the church, women must be encouraged to consciously engage in theological reflection, to strengthen their biblical-theological muscle, and cultivate their theological acumen. Sadly, women all too often feel like they are on the outside, peering through the window as men do the more formal and disciplinary work of theology. Some don't think they are permitted to enter, while others simply have never entertained the idea because they've never been invited. As Christians, women in the church must be encouraged to think theologically—or rather, to think *well* theologically—thinking *Christianly* about all things. In short, if we are asking whether women should think well about God and should be competent readers/interpreters of Scripture, the answer should be a resounding and self-evident "yes."

The focus of the CPT and this book, however, is narrower than that. The purpose of the CPT extends beyond encouraging pastors to think theologically or to display greater theological acumen in their preaching and teaching ministry. Rather, the CPT wants to encourage pastors to *formally play a dual role both as pastors and theologians*—to support vocational pastors who simultaneously are engaged in more formal scholarship as "pastor theologians." In this sense, we are talking about a heightened appropriation of theology as a more formal pursuit. And in this heightened sense, we still must also affirm the need for women doing theology in and for the church.

Women are indispensable voices alongside men in theological reflection on Scripture for the church, even if their experience at times sadly has testified to the contrary. I argue this point on at least two grounds: First, women

---

[1]Martin Luther, "Sermon on Psalm 5," January 17, 1535, quoted in Kelly M. Kapic, *A Little Book for New Theologians: Why and How to Study Theology* (Downers Grove, IL: InterVarsity, 2012), 15.
[2]Kapic, *Little Book,* 15.

must be formally engaged in theological discourse because they reflect "half" the image of God, who is the object of our study. It was not good for man to be alone, so God made a helper suitable to him (Gen 2:18)—that is, one who stood before Adam with perfect correspondence as his equal partner and complement. Together, male and female, in the image of God, he created them (Gen 1:27). Since they are equal image bearers, excluding women from formal contribution in theological discourse (whether overtly or through neglect) concerning the very God whose image they reflect is akin to re-searching a child's genetic history and excluding the mother. On one hand, women are *human* first, and this shared humanity must be recognized beyond our gendered differences, whether prescriptive or descriptive.[3] And yet women also bring their own voice, perspectives and distinctively female life experiences. Women do biblical-theological work from a par-ticular gendered and social location.

Second, we must consider the significance of new creational realities. The "new man" (Greek *anthrōpos*) in Christ (described in Eph 2:15; 4:13, 24; and Col 3:10-11) refers to the new community in Christ's body—a reimaging of God in Christ that has destroyed the enmity of the curse and brought to-gether opposing groups into one, for "he himself is our peace" (Eph 2:14 ESV).[4] As Paul writes in Galatians 3:28, in him there is no Jew or Greek, slave or free, male or female, for we are one in Christ. Christ the "second Adam" was and is the perfect image of God (Jn 1:18; Col 1:15; Heb 1:3). In Christ, God's image is restored among the members of Christ's body. The restoration of that divine image in humanity is reflected, in part, by the unity and di-versity of the church—the "new man" in Christ who is growing in the likeness of its head (Eph 4:15-16). As Paul writes in Colossians 3:9-11 concerning our corporate identity in Christ's body: We "have put off the old self [literally, 'old man'] with its practices" and have put on the new man, "which is *being re-newed in knowledge after the image of its creator*. Here there is not Greek and Jew, circumcised and uncircumcised, barbarian, Scythian, slave, free; but

---

[3]See Dorothy L. Sayers, *Are Women Human? Astute and Witty Essays on the Role of Women in Society* (Grand Rapids: Eerdmans, 2005).
[4]See on this point an illuminating essay by Darrell L. Bock, "'The New Man' as Community in Colossians and Ephesians," in *Integrity of Heart, Skillfulness of Hands: Biblical and Leadership Studies in Honor of Donald K. Campbell*, ed. Charles H. Dyer and Roy B. Zuck (Grand Rapids: Baker, 1994), 157-67.

Christ is all, and in all" (ESV, emphasis added). N. T. Wright observes, with
extended relevance, I believe, to gender as well as race:

> Why does Paul see God being glorified specifically by the joint salvation of
> people of different races? For Paul, as a theologian rooted in the early chapters
> of Genesis, God is glorified when human beings become truly themselves
> through the grace and power of the gospel. God created humans to bear his
> image in the world; and, when that image is restored through the Image
> himself, Jesus Christ, and through the work of the Spirit, the living God is
> glorified as he is reflected into the world.[5]

We observe this oneness lived out in the New Testament and the early
church, even in the most patriarchal of contexts, through a genuine friendship
between men and women in their colaboring for the gospel. Consider those
women with whom Jesus traveled, whom he honored as companions and
members of his inner circle. Consider those women who served as first witnesses to the resurrected Christ, which in itself was radical and countercultural—the *kerygma* of the risen Christ first placed in the mouth of faith-filled
women and entrusted to them for proclamation to the other disciples! Consider Philip's four daughters in Acts 21:9, or those who served as prominent
members of house churches in the Roman Empire like Priscilla, Chloe, Lydia
and the mother of John Mark, or those women who notably colabored with
Paul in the ministry of the gospel like Phoebe and perhaps Junia in Romans
16. Consider those women recorded in the history of the early church, many
whose platform took the form of faithful proclamation through martyrdom,
like Perpetua, Blandina and Thecla (to the extent her story has historical
veracity).[6] Consider the esteemed life and teaching of Macrina, in conversation
with the great Cappadocians,[7] or those female colleagues who, according

---

[5]N. T. Wright, "Paul in Different Perspectives," lecture presented at Auburn Avenue Presbyterian
Church, Monroe, Louisiana, January 3, 2005, http://ntwrightpage.com/Wright_Auburn_Paul.htm.
[6]On Saint Blandina of Lyon, see Eusebius, *Ecclesiastical History* 5.1 and William H. C. Frend, "Blandina
and Perpetua: Two Early Christian Heroines," in *Women in Early Christianity*, Studies in Early Christianity 14, ed. Everett Ferguson, David M. Scholer, and Paul Corby Finney (New York: Garland, 1993),
89. On Perpetua, see also Elizabeth A. Clark, *Women in the Early Church,* Message of the Fathers of
the Church 13 (Collegeville, MN: Liturgical Press, 1983), 18, 21. On Thecla, see "The Acts of Paul and
Thecla" in Clark, *Women in the Early Church*, 37.
[7]For discussion of Macrina, see Saint Gregory of Nyssa's *On the Soul and the Resurrection* in his *As-
cetical Works*, trans. Virginia Woods Callahan; The Fathers of the Church, ed. Roy Joseph Deferrari
(Washington, DC: Catholic University of America, 1967), 266; and Rosemary Radford Ruether,
Women and Redemption: A Theological History, 2nd ed. (Minneapolis: Fortress, 2012), 55-56.

to Clement of Alexandria in the second century, accompanied the apostles on their missionary journeys as fellow ministers, especially to other women. Consider those women who studied with Jerome, or the orders of women (including widows and deaconnesses) in the third century who served sacrificially and performed pastoral duties with respect to other women; these duties included the instruction and baptism of female catechumens, rebuke to the wayward, giving of communion to the sick, prayer, visitation and the laying on of hands.[8]

Particular *roles* in the church aside, we need to pursue genuine friendship and mutual support as men and women engaged in ministry and theological reflection, serving together as colaborers for the sake of the gospel. We need to be doing the work of theology and sharing the ministry load as *brothers and sisters, together—alongside one another*, without competition or suspicion.

So then, as image bearers of God and sharers of his renewed image in Christ as members of one another—brothers and sisters in the family of God, in whom there is no ontological division, but oneness—women must be full and equal participants in theological reflection as colaborers in the gospel.

THEOLOGY FOR THE CHURCH: PRACTICAL ENCOURAGEMENTS

Women increasingly are pursuing formal education in biblical-theological disciplines, seeking to actively engage in theological reflection as part of their vocation. Such study ultimately should be *for* the church. In the pastor theologian model, especially in ecclesial contexts that limit the formal office of pastor to men, we must ask: What vocational outlets exist in the local church for theologically gifted and trained women to steward this knowledge? Are such women relegated to the academy, to parachurch contexts or online platforms disconnected from local church expression? Will they perhaps even be forced into the very dichotomy between the local church and theological scholarship that the CPT and the essays in this book seek to reject? Theologically trained women should be serving in and enriching the church through their scholarship, and women who serve vocationally in the church

---

[8]For a helpful summary of women who served the early church in various capacities, see Catherine Kroeger's article "The Neglected History of Women in the Early Church," *Christian History* 17 (1988), www.christianitytoday.com/history/issues/issue-17/neglected-history-of-women-in-early -church.html.

should be theologically trained. In my mind, this raises two primary issues. The first involves a definition, and the second an application.

Definitions: Formal and informal pastor theologians. Does the designation "pastor theologian" limit our discussion only to those holding positions of pastoral leadership in the church? What do we mean by "pastor"? Depending on one's theological convictions, are women included or excluded in this definition? May women formally serve in a pastor theologian capacity within the church, or must they operate from another platform?

I would argue that many women should (and do) serve the church in a pastoral or shepherding capacity—that is, in the broadest sense of the word *pastoral*, beyond a particular position or office. Also, as mentioned above, some women are gifted and called to engage more formally in biblical-theological scholarship. To the degree that we affirm both of these points—women doing pastoral ministry and women engaging in formal theological reflection—we also affirm the female pastor theologian, or, the female *ecclesial* theologian. To put it another way, if women should be doing theology, based on their creational and Christian identity, and if women are ministering and leading in the church in various contexts and capacities, then the same discussion that applies to men also applies here to women.

At the broadest level of definition, then, we all might give hearty assent to the possibility of female pastor theologians. Such agreement does not, however, yield uniform applications, especially where a more narrow definition of "pastor" is employed. Here, the conversation begins to feel somewhat like a "choose your own adventure" novel, with door one opening a particular set of options and door two leading to a slightly different path relative to one's theological convictions and ecclesial or cultural context. Below I will address both, offering some words of challenge and encouragement.

Applications: Female pastor theologians in practice. First, for those ministering in a context where women may serve as lead pastors in the formal sense, be intentional in your encouragement of women. Refuse to pigeonhole them. Self-reflectively acknowledge your own potential biases concerning a woman's contribution to theology. Remember that holding a theological position that affirms women as pastors does not guarantee a lack of bias in preferring men to women as theological conversation partners, for affirming the principle does not always lead to its practice. In short, elicit and encourage each woman's participation and development in theological discourse as part of her pastoral vocation. As Dorothy Sayers once argued, her voice may or may not reflect *the* or even *a* distinctively *female* perspective, but her voice belongs in the conversation *as a woman*.

Second, for those ministering in a context where certain positions of authority in the church are reserved for men, I challenge you to broaden your vision of "pastoral" ministry. Consider extending this language to include other facets of ministry in the church that involve pastoral responsibilities of shepherding and caring for God's flock—that is, extending pastoral ministry beyond the office of senior pastor. Those who minister to and with women, for example, should be no less theologically robust than their male counterparts.

If the language of "pastor" still precludes women in certain contexts from participating in this vision of the pastor theologian, then we may need to consider an expansion of our *language*. That is, we may need to speak of women as "ecclesial" as opposed to "pastor" theologians—describing their theological work in and for the church more broadly as they serve in various capacities—to ensure that women are not excluded from this vocational calling. Consider creative ways for women to directly or indirectly serve the teaching, preaching and discipleship/spiritual formation ministries of the church through their scholarship. Seek their input in preaching and give voice to their insights. Push them to engage in wider biblical-theological scholarship as you identify women with particular interest and competency in these disciplines. This may involve further education, research and writing for publication, or attendance and presentation at academic conferences. As you think about supporting vocational pastor theologians in the church, consider whether this vision also extends to your women's ministry leader. Is *she* equally encouraged to cultivate or pursue biblical-theological scholarship, if she is so gifted and inclined? Do you encourage women to steward their gifts and invite them to sit at the theological table as equal participants? Recognize that you could be the one to speak a new reality or potentiality into such a woman's life, casting a vision that may not yet exist in her own mind. Even the most conservative of convictions regarding the role of women in biblical-theological *proclamation* should not stifle the active engagement and contribution of women in biblical-theological *reflection*.

Finally, I urge both groups to consciously include women in both leadership and support roles, not just giving lip service or as an afterthought. Guard against a movement of pastor theologians that becomes exclusionary—that inadvertently (at best) communicates to women that theological study and vocation belong exclusively to men. Theological vocation in and for the church should transcend questions of church polity and gender roles. Authority in the church may be positional, but the doing of theology is, to some degree, ontological—that is, an extension of *who we are* as image bearers, both as men and women, and a reflection of our restored image together in Christ.

Beyond a general commitment to women thinking theologically, encourage some women to pursue more formal biblical-theological training. Include women in your theological societies and conferences. Consciously invite women into your theological discourse—including the pronouns that you use. Employ competent women in your church ministries and encourage their biblical-theological scholarship. Within the constraints of your particular context, give women opportunities and platforms to exercise their theological voice and recognize their contribution to theological reflection on God's Word for the church. Consider how their social location contributes to the ecclesial-theological project. For those women who have already found a home for their gifts in academic or parachurch contexts, seek ways to integrate and employ these gifts in service to the local church.

To my fellow women, I implore you to fully pursue God's calling in your life. Walk in faithfulness with him to whom you ultimately shall give account. In whatever platform the Lord gives you—local church, the academy or a parachurch organization—do not withhold your voice from the body of Christ. Engage in biblical scholarship and theological reflection. Faithfully serve the church in ways that align with your biblical convictions and that appropriately reflect your ecclesial/cultural context, your commitment to the unity of Christ's body, and the constraints of your personal conscience. And encourage other women to do likewise.

Sharon Hodde Miller's words offer a poignant summary and challenge:

> No matter where one stands on the issue of women in ministry, I hope we can agree on this: It is the task of the church to steward the gifts of its members. 1 Corinthians 12:7 tells us that each member of the body of Christ

is bestowed with talents for the sake of the common good. The Apostle Paul explains this idea further, emphasizing our profound inter-dependence upon one another. Since we need one another in order to be the whole body of Christ, we must diligently nurture our own gifts and the gifts of those around us. Granted, not every woman is called to *seminary*—no more than every man is called. But if we believe that theological education is an important way to train leaders and guard the integrity of Christian belief, then the skewed gender ratio at evangelical seminaries should give us pause. Are churches intentionally cultivating the gifts of women to the extent that they should? Within our churches, are there systems or programs in place for the stewardship of women's talents? Are church leaders encouraging women who have the gifts of teaching and leading to pursue formal training? ... As the church, we can bury the gifts of women—or simply allow their talents to lie fallow—or we can initiate the cultivation of women (and men!) and their essential gifts, as God commands us to do. For some this will mean going to seminary, and for others it will not, but the agenda is the same. When the church trains and equips its members according to their gifts, the Kingdom only stands to benefit, for the greater glory of God.[9]

Consider, in closing, the analogy of a church choir. Theology often has been like a choir comprised of only tenors, baritones and bass—without sopranos and altos. Something is missing. The choir is incomplete, lacking in richness and full resonance. Without all the parts, we cannot hear the score as it was originally intended. While still enjoyable to the ear, we do not hear the song in its full beauty. Sometimes, of course, the parts are not so easily distinguished. At times we sing in unison. Other times, a tenor and soprano might hit the same note. Some women sing lower, while some men sing higher. The point is not to accentuate the distinctions between parts, but rather to express the *necessity* of all the parts in fully reflecting the musical score of creation and redemption as we do theology *together* and make beautiful gospel music. May we worthily bear God's image together in service to the church.

---

[9]Sharon Hodde Miller, "The Seminary Gap," Her.meneutics, *Christianity Today* (May 23, 2003), www.christianitytoday.com/women/2013/may/seminary-gender-gap.html.

13

The Pastor Theologian as Apologist

JOSH CHATRAW

I N HIS 2014 BOOK *HOW (NOT) TO BE SECULAR*, James K. A. Smith aptly described our faith in the present age:

> We live in the twilight of both gods and idols. But their ghosts have refused to depart, and every once in a while we might be surprised to find ourselves tempted by belief. . . . On the other hand, even as faith endures in our secular age, believing doesn't come easy. Faith is fraught; confession is haunted by an inescapable sense of its contestability. We don't believe instead of doubting; we believe *while* doubting. We're all Thomas now.[1]

When I read this to my students, most of the twentysomethings resonate with it. Even at a university that has the reputation of being quite conservative—though increasingly diverse, oftentimes my students have only been taught to think in two shades—most latch on to Smith's poetic statement about doubt. It expresses a deep feeling that for many had been safely tucked away, that they did not have the vocabulary or courage to express. Smith is drawing on Charles Taylor, the Canadian philosopher who in his acclaimed *A Secular Age* helped us see that we are all now "secular." He points to several different notions of the word, but Taylor's focus is on secularity as "a situation of fundamental contestability when it comes to belief, a sense that rival stories are always at the door offering a very different account of the world."[2]

---

[1] James K. A. Smith, *How (Not) to Be Secular: Reading Charles Taylor* (Grand Rapids: Eerdmans, 2014), 3-4.

[2] Ibid., 10.

It's not, however, just philosophers and theologians (or my students) who are bearing witness to this cultural shift. Sociologists such as Peter Berger have written of how current social conditions have made belief in God no longer inevitable and have argued that Christians now have to be much more intentional about maintaining faith. Modern pluralism and other related cultural shifts have shaped plausibility structures.[3] Today much of life is lived *between* religious certainty and denial. Believers and unbelievers find themselves in the space *between* absolute faith and absolute doubt. Or to come at this from a slightly different angle, as John Stackhouse puts it, "There have always been skeptics, but not on this scale."[4] Looking the other way and wishing for the good ol' days (whatever that means) is no longer an option.

In this complex environment, it is vital for pastors to lead in giving the believer apologetic support and the unbeliever apologetic nudging. After all, who will train Christians—and in particular, who will train those who are in leadership positions—to, as the apostle Paul exhorts, "walk in wisdom toward outsiders, making the best use of the time" so that their speech is always "gracious, seasoned with salt, so that [they] may know how [they] ought to answer each person" (Col 4:5-6)?

In our secular and pluralistic age, we might assume that seminaries would be training up in droves pastor theologians who also identify as apologists, and that the apologetic literature by the pastor theologians of our age would be voluminous. However, while apologetic books are a dime a dozen, by and large they are not written by pastor theologians. I will return to this point momentarily, but first a definition of *pastor theologian as apologist* is in order.

WHAT DO I MEAN BY PASTOR THEOLOGIAN AS APOLOGIST?

I am using this terminology parallel to Todd Wilson and Gerald Hiestand's definition of the ecclesial theologian. They distinguish the ecclesial theologian from the local theologian and popular theologian. The *local theologian* is the pastor who seeks to bring theology to bear on all of life and be the theological leader for their local congregation. This should be the goal of

---

[3]See, for instance, Peter L. Berger and Thomas Luckmann, *The Social Construction of Reality: A Treatise in the Sociology of Knowledge* (Garden City, NY: Doubleday, 1966).
[4]John G. Stackhouse Jr., *Humble Apologetics: Defending the Faith Today* (New York: Oxford University Press, 2002), 37.

every pastor. The *popular theologian*, according to their taxonomy, "is a local theologian, yet with a broader influence."[5] An *ecclesial theologian*, on the other hand, "is a *pastor* who writes theological scholarship in conversation with other theologians, with an eye to the needs of ecclesial community."[6]

In speaking of a pastor theologian as apologist, I'm appropriating Wilson and Hiestand's definition of an ecclesial theologian: pastor theologians are ecclesial apologists who bear shepherding responsibility in ecclesial contexts that their apologetics chiefly serve. They therefore produce their apologetic in conversation with other apologists, theologians and thought leaders with an eye to the needs of their community and its questions and objections. The pastor theologian as apologist, as I am envisioning this role, also writes apologetic works for other Christian (and even non-Christian) thought leaders such as pastors, academics and other writers—though not necessarily technical academic works.

Perhaps two living examples will bring further clarity. Compare the works of Alvin Plantinga and Tim Keller. Both authors have served the Christian community in a variety of important ways, yet most of Plantinga's work has been chiseled out in his native context of the academy. On the other hand, Keller is an example of a pastor theologian as apologist. He has formed his apologetic approach serving as a pastor, first in Hopewell, Virginia and now in Manhattan. He has written popular apologetic books, but has also written books that are aimed more at fellow thought leaders, such as *Preaching* (which at times feels like an apologetics book) and *Walking with God through Pain and Suffering*.[7]

Throughout this chapter, then, I will be working in correspondence with Wilson and Hiestand's vision for the pastor as ecclesial theologian, what we might call the pastor theologian as ecclesial apologist. However, because this label seems a bit cumbersome, I will stick with "pastor theologian as apologist" or simply "pastor apologist."

---

[5]Gerald Hiestand and Todd Wilson, *The Pastor Theologian: Resurrecting an Ancient Vision* (Grand Rapids: Zondervan, 2015), 83.

[6]Ibid., 85.

[7]Tim Keller, *Preaching: Communicating Faith in an Age of Skepticism* (New York: Viking, 2015) and *Walking With God Through Pain and Suffering* (New York: Dutton, 2013). Though these two books no doubt have been beneficial to a wide variety of people, they seem to be aimed at leaders, not simply a lay audience.

Three Observations on the Lack of Pastor Apologists

B. B. Warfield once said, "Apologetics has been treated very much like a step-child in the theological household."[8] Though there might be some signs that the tide is turning, the discipline of apologetics has been met with unease by pastors of varying identities. On the one hand, the pastor whose mantra is "just get it done" might view apologists as ivory tower intellectuals who are not answering the real questions the common congregant is asking. Conversely, the more theologically reflective pastor might not see apologists as real intellectuals at all. Though they likely use some apologetic tools to persuade or as a part of pre-evangelism, most pastors do not gravitate toward sustained reflection on the discipline of apologetics; it is just not primary to their identity. One only has to glance at the list of the degrees and books written by some of the most gifted pastor theologians, the fellows at the Center for Pastor Theologians, to note the lack of PhDs, articles, dissertations or books published in the area of apologetics.[9]

Is this a mere coincidence or an indication of a broader trend among theologically minded pastors? Is there a historical and biblical warrant, as well as a contemporary need, to reclaim the vision for the pastor as apologist? I think there are three main reasons why there are not more pastor theologians who also see being an apologist as part of their primary vocational identity.

First, an "apologist" is identified with philosophers, not exegetes, theologians or historians. It is no surprise that most pastors, and particular those who identify as pastor theologians, are primarily trained in biblical studies or theology. One result is that the "apologist" is an identity that philosophers are left to fill out. And since philosophers most regularly seek posts in the academy rather than within parishes, this means that the concerns and questions being addressed by apologetics are primarily concerns and questions raised by the academic context rather than the broader concerns of the general culture and the ecclesial community. For instance, while both the

---

[8]Benjamin Breckinridge Warfield, *Selected Shorter Writings of Benjamin B. Warfield*, ed. John E. Meeter (Nutley, NJ: Presbyterian and Reformed, 1970), 93.

[9]See www.pastortheologians.com/cpt-fellowships/fellowship-publications. I was, however, glad to see that Kevin Vanhoozer and Owen Strachan included a section on apologetics in their book *The Pastor as Public Theologian: Reclaiming a Lost Vision* (Grand Rapids: Baker Academic, 2015), 174-76; also see the helpful section in the book by Jason B. Hood titled "The Pastor-Theologian as Pulpit Apologist" (180-82).

academy and the church are concerned to answer the questions related to God and suffering, the specific questions are often different. Moreover, the apologetic and undergirding theology of the academic is shaped, to appropriate Wilson and Hiestand's words, "in profound ways by the steady rhythm" of the *Sitz im Leben* of the academy instead of the "grind and press of the pastoral vocation."[10] In contrast, the demands of pastoral care offered in times of pain and heartache cannot help but form the apologetic approach of the pastor to the questions of evil and suffering. Hence, pastor theologians, rather than academic philosophers (as helpful as they are), should be the primary apologists for the church because our apologetic will always be affected and formed out of our particular context.

Second, some see apologetics as antiacademic. Os Guinness describes a conversation during his graduate work at Oxford University. He happened to mention apologetics to his tutor, whom he described as an extraordinarily genial scholar. He "noticeably stiffened. 'Excuse my candor,' he said, 'but I would never use that word again if I were you. *Apologetics* is a dirty word in Oxford.'"[11]

As most of Christianity's best thinkers are trained in the academy, the danger is to imbibe the academy's ethos. In the academy, *apologist* signals either a glibness that ignores complexity in favor of easy answers or a failure to play the part of a disinterested neutral observer—or both. Much of modern scholarship shuns both of these qualities as juvenile, and the culture of the academy cultivates our hearts to want to come of age. On the matter of glibness, unfortunately, they have a point. Even some of the more acclaimed apologists have at times looked rather childish. But on the other hand, in contrast to those who are still clinging to the dream of being a disinterested observer, the pastor apologist is *not* the one who needs to grow up!

The speck (or perhaps plank) in the eye of the apologist is that at times we have failed to sufficiently note the complexity involved in particular issues. This is one reason we need to see apologetics as a team sport; we need people involved from various ecclesial contexts with various academic skills to build apologetic houses on the ground within their ecclesial and local context.

---

[10]Hiestand and Wilson, *Pastor Theologian*, 88.

[11]Os Guinness, *Fool's Talk: Recovering the Art of Christian Persuasion* (Downers Grove, IL: InterVarsity Press, 2015), 213.

As to the modern notion of *neutrality*, the pastor apologist who sits outside of the academic rules of modern scholarship is in an ideal position to name this notion for what it is—a myth—and then move forward, seeking *fairness* rather than neutrality in practicing apologetics in and for the church.

Third, many theologians have problems with how apologetics has been done, and thus they have been reluctant to embrace it as part of their identity. Some of the most notable theologians and pastors have been critical of apologetics. Karl Barth said, "Good dogmatics is always the best and basically the only possible apologetics."[12] Martyn Loyd-Jones stated, "I am not sure that apologetics has not been the curse of evangelicalism for the last twenty to thirty years."[13] Abraham Kuyper, in his oft-cited Stone Foundation Lectures, said, "In this struggle [against Modernism] Apologetics have advanced us not one single step. Apologetics have invariably begun by abandoning the assailed breastwork, in order to entrench themselves cowardly in a ravelin behind it."[14] I probably should stop here before pitting too many theological giants against me.

One response to the collective groans against apologetics could be to cite the wealth of passages in the Bible that function apologetically. Though the list would be long, this would perhaps be missing the point. Simply assuming our contemporary version of apologetics is what the author of 1 Peter means by *apologia* (1 Pet 3:15) or what any other biblical author is doing would be putting the cart before the horse.

Instead, before suggesting that pastor theologians deal with the speck in their eye for neglecting apologetics, apologists have their own pesky planks to acknowledge. For at least part of the issue might be that there are many examples of apologetics done poorly, which have unfortunately loomed large over the entire enterprise. If apologetics means placating the cultural plausibility structures produced by the Enlightenment, sounding like a megalomaniac who is driven by his need to win, or making it a habit to run over anyone who gets in the way, then count me out! However, this is a far cry from the apologetics we see in the Bible. It is certainly not what Peter meant when he uses the term *apologia* in 1 Peter 3:15.

---

[12]Karl Barth, *Church Dogmatics IV/3.2*, ed. G. W. Bromiley and T. F. Torrance (New York: T&T Clark, 2004), 951.

[13]D. Martyn Lloyd-Jones, *Authority* (Chicago: InterVarsity Press, 1958), 14.

[14]Abraham Kuyper, "Calvinism A Life-System," in *Lectures on Calvinism: Six Lectures from the Stone Foundation Lectures Delivered at Princeton University* (Grand Rapids: Eerdmans, 2009).

Most books on apologetics don't go too deep in explaining how the term actually functions in this passage and the wider context of 1 Peter. Instead, the route is to take the word *apologia* and jump very quickly into contemporary questions and approaches. These discussions have their place, but the more foundational question is: How is this famous apologetic proof-text actually functioning in 1 Peter?[15]

The Christian community addressed in 1 Peter was experiencing physical and psychological pressures to conform to the surrounding culture, social antagonism from nonbelievers, temptation from their former lifestyles, tensions within the group itself and their own spiritual doubts. They seemed to have been teetering, on the brink of giving in, weary of the trials. They were being mocked and maligned.

Peter was previously known for his brashness. He wasn't afraid to pick up his sword for the cause, both literally and metaphorically. After his resurrection, Jesus' teachings—which were once confusing and scandalous to Peter—were crystallized and applied in his apostolic teachings:[16]

> To this you were called, because Christ suffered for you, leaving you an example, that you should follow in his steps. "He committed no sin, and no deceit was found in his mouth." When they hurled their insults at him, he did not retaliate; when he suffered, he made no threats. Instead, he entrusted himself to him who judges justly. "He himself bore our sins" in his body on the cross, so that we might die to sins and live for righteousness; "by his wounds you have been healed." (1 Pet 2:21-24 NIV)

With Jesus as the pivotal model in his life, Peter writes this weary community instructing them to rejoice (!) in suffering, trusting in the reward secured by the resurrection of Christ (1 Pet 1:6; 4:12-14). In the midst of trials, Peter reminds them that God has called them out as a *community* (not simply as individuals) to declare to the world the praises of God (1 Pet 2:9). Peter instructs them to live nobly in a way that will give their detractors reason to pause. They were to be characterized by compassion, respect and humility (1 Pet 2:11-12, 15-17; 3:8-9). It is in the context of these instructions that 1 Peter

---

[15]This point emerged out of a conversation I had at one of the Center for Pastor Theologians's fellowship times.

[16]Even if one denies the apostle Peter's authorship of 1 Peter, the basic point in this section still stands.

3:15 commands the believers to be prepared to give an *apologia* for why they have this hope in the midst of suffering. The problem is not that 1 Peter 3:15 is used as a key text for apologetics. The problem is that too often apologists use this verse without the larger context in view. This is just one example, but it serves as an example for how apologetics has at times gotten off track.

In his book *To Change the World,* James Davison Hunter surveys the major approaches to Christian witness, at one point calling out Christians of various stripes for persistently using a "discourse of negation toward outsiders."[17] Hunter does not speak specifically about apologists, but the ethos of negation that he describes is all too often displayed by Christians in debates, both formal and informal, as they interact with unbelievers. Moreover, one of the implications that can be drawn from Hunter's survey is that Christian leaders have too often failed to frame the public defense of the faith within the context of biblical humility and joy. While exceptions can be noted, the dominant approaches to engagement are largely witnesses of negation, too often characterized by hardness and aggression:

> To suffer is one thing; how one bears that suffering is quite another. Among all factions within American Christianity, one can readily find an anger and resentment about what suffering they endure. We know, of course, that bitterness can provide its own consolations. For one, it creates a gratifying sense of being winners and on the right side of history . . . but is the Kingdom of God to be known predominantly by its negations?[18]

Christians confess a crucified Savior, but our posture before outsiders can make our apologetic appeals seem more like power plays scripted by the world's playbook. This is in contrast not only to 1 Peter and Jesus Christ himself, but also the apostle Paul, who combined serious persuasion and great learning with a life committed to a theology—and even an apologetic—of the cross. God has chosen the weak to shame the strong (1 Cor 1:27), and weaknesses are to be boasted in so the "power of Christ" would rest upon us (2 Cor 12:9).

In addition to sometimes sounding like professional spinmeisters and intellectual bullies, other perceptions have loomed large. Narrow approaches,

[17]James Davison Hunter, *To Change the World: The Irony, Tragedy, and Possibility of Christianity in the Late Modern World* (Oxford: Oxford University Press, 2010), 175.
[18]Ibid.

weak ecclesiology, the magisterial role of reason, the decentralization of the cross and the settling for general deistic-sounding arguments have left theologians suspicious of the apologetics enterprise, and too often these suspicions have some merit. In short, if we are going to do apologetics as Christians, it should be *Christian* apologetics.[19]

RESURRECTING ANOTHER ANCIENT VISION:
THE PASTOR THEOLOGIAN AS APOLOGIST

So *what*, or perhaps better, *who* is the way forward? Yet clearly the *who* and the *what* go together. I have already hinted at some of the problems regarding the *what*, and here I can only succinctly state the vision while leaving its full articulation and defense for a later project.[20] The answer to the question "*What* is the way forward?" is that apologetics should be seen through the lens of the cross rather than the lens of (worldly) glory. This means taking people to the cross through word and deed as the church corporately witnesses to Christ and the new creation, humbly submitting to God and humbly engaging with those whom we disagree, both holistically and contextually.

This is in line with what Kevin Vanhoozer has said about the *what* of apologetics: "What is needed today is an enlarged vision of what apologetics involves that integrates logical arguments, the narrative imagination and faithful practices all for the sake of bearing witness in word and deed to the wisdom of God embodied in Jesus Christ."[21] Later he adds, "It is not necessary to choose between propositions, plots, and practices; an enlarged conception of apologetics should include all three. Arguments alone are not enough; we need a biblically informed imagination and biblically informed shape of community life fully to see, and to taste, the wisdom of God in a consistent and compelling manner."[22]

Now, *who*—with their lives and words—will lead in embodying this vision for apologetic witness? Where might we find thought leaders to guide

---

[19]Thanks to my colleague Chad Thornhill, who in a conversation about the integration of theology into various academic disciplines used a similar expression.

[20]Josh Chatraw and Mark Allen, *Apologetics at the Cross* (Grand Rapids: Zondervan), forthcoming.

[21]Kevin J. Vanhoozer, "Theology and Apologetics," in *New Dictionary of Christian Apologetics*, ed. Gavin McGrath, W. C. Campbell-Jack and C. Stephen Evans (Downers Grove, IL: InterVarsity Press, 2006), 42.

[22]Ibid., 43.

Christians—and in particular to lead other Christian thought leaders—in forming a biblical, imaginative, ecclesial and wisdom-oriented apologetic? I suggest that many of the weaknesses in contemporary apologetics could be alleviated if pastor theologians—those who weekly must shepherd their congregation in the Word of God and who bear the burden of responding to the consistent cries of "help my unbelief"—also came to identify themselves and lead as pastor apologists.

Fortunately, just like the vision of the pastor theologian so capably defended by Hiestand and Wilson, the vision of the pastor apologist does not need to be created *ex nihilo*. Instead, the pastor apologist only needs resurrecting. As Avery Dulles points out, "After the first quarter of the second century . . . apologetics became the most characteristic form of Christian writing."[23] In reviewing the notable pastor theologians in the early church, it is hard to find many whose writings did not include major works in the area of apologetics. Irenaeus, bishop of Lyons, used the rule of faith to labor against the Gnostic heresy and is known for his bold defense of the fourfold Gospel. Theophilus, the Syrian bishop of Antioch, defended Christianity by appealing to its ancient roots in the Old Testament. Eusebius, bishop of Caesarea, was best known for his work as a historian but clearly also saw himself as an apologist. Athanasius, bishop of Alexandria, is known for his defense of the full deity of Jesus Christ against Arianism. And certainly not least, who would argue that Augustine did not see himself as an apologist? These were all pastors. These were all theologians. And yes, these were all *apologists*.

It seems that the early church saw apologetics as an imperative in pastoral ministry. It was, to emphasize the point, part of the pastor theologian's identity. It could be that this ancient vision could save the modern church from the perils of both the pragmatic "get 'er done" approach and the "all talk, no action" approach to Christian witness.

In the early church, the highest-caliber pastors of the day used their learning to win the hearts and minds of unbelievers and to answer the doubts of believers.[24] We will do well to learn from their approach. Central in their apologetic was the claim that they, as Christians, suffered and died better than anyone else. The early church saw apologetics entwined with

[23]Avery Dulles, *A History of Apologetics* (New York: Corpus, 1971), 27.
[24]See Michael Green, *Evangelism in the Early Church*, rev. ed. (Grand Rapids: Eerdmans, 2004).

the gospel of the suffering Son, and also saw suffering entwined with apologetics. Shaped by the rhythms of being embedded within the church as the Lord's undershepherd, the pastor theologian is best situated to revive apologetics wedded to the cross of Christ and the cruciform life of the community. This again is getting more into the *what* and even to the *how*, but I pray that God will raise up more of those *who* can lead other Christian thought leaders in answering the questions of *what* and *how* with an enlarged vision for apologetics for a new day.

So I give a wholehearted, "Amen!" to the vision of the pastor as theologian. But while we are in the business of resurrecting ancient visions,[25] I'd like to suggest we pray that the Lord breathe life into another set of dry bones: the pastor theologian as apologist.

---

[25]Here I am drawing upon the subtitle of Hiestand and Wilson's book, *The Pastor Theologian: Resurrecting an Ancient Vision*.

14

The Pastor Theologian
as Giver of Wisdom

I<small>N</small> 2012 J<small>ENNIFER</small> B<small>AKOSKI</small>, <small>A HUMAN RESOURCE MANAGER</small> for the Broward County, Florida, Sheriff's Office, was falsely accused of stealing over one million dollars from her employer by manipulating the payroll system. After illegal seizure of her possessions and termination of her position, the false charges plagued Bakoski for two years. Having been cleared by internal investigations in 2012 and 2013, she filed suit against the sheriff's office.[1]

In a similar event, fifty-nine-year-old National Weather Service employee Sherry Chen was accused of spying for China on the basis of one colleague's report to the Department of Commerce.[2] Chen was suspended without pay and lived with loss of sleep and media news trucks outside of her home until charges were dropped in 2014.

One wonders what might have been the outcomes of these incidents if people in their agencies had acted with wisdom derived from Proverbs 30:10-14:

> Do not slander a servant to his master,
>   lest he curse you, and you be held guilty.

---

[1]Rafael Olmeda, "Former BSO Employee's Lawsuit Alleges Wrongful Firing After False Theft Accusation," *Sun Sentinel*, February 2, 2015, www.sun-sentinel.com/local/broward/fl-bso-wrongful -termination-lawsuit-20150202-story.html.

[2]Angela Fritz, "Falsely Accused of Spying, Weather Service Employee's Life Turned Upside Down," *The Washington Post*, May 12, 2015, www.washingtonpost.com/news/capital-weather-gang/wp/2015 /05/12/falsely-accused-of-spying-weather-service-employees-life-turned-upside-down.

There are those who curse their fathers
  and do not bless their mothers.
There are those who are clean in their own eyes
  but are not washed of their filth.
There are those—how lofty are their eyes,
  how high their eyelids lift!
There are those whose teeth are swords,
  whose fangs are knives,
to devour the poor from off the earth,
  the needy from among mankind.[3]

The writer of these verses understands that the retribution for slandering a servant calls for discernment about the reality of evil people. This set of proverbs contrasts the *observation* of the working of evil with the *perception* or false report of evil.

Hypothetically speaking, had Bakoski's and Chen's employers been believers who were familiar with the wisdom of these verses and other verses like them, they would have had theological resources like patience in judgment and discernment at their disposal. Further, by reading Proverbs 30:10-14 they might have observed four particular things that might have been helpful for discerning criminal activity: some people mistreat their parents, in violation of the fifth commandment (30:11, compare Prov 30:17); some people are hypocritically self-deceived about their own evil (30:12); some people are proud of heart (30:13); and some people speak in such a manner as to keep aid from reaching the needy (30:14).

However, this wisdom text also would caution employers against being hypersensitive, for not every person who is accused of evil is guilty. An employee might *not* be stealing, harassing elderly patients, discriminating against minorities or shaving funds from a cash register. These proverbs teach the believer to give the benefit of the doubt to a customer service representative, store employee, co-worker, subordinate, human resource manager or weather service employee in whom one perceives wrongdoing until evidence is presented to the contrary. It invites the believer to fear the Lord so that the proliferation of evil in society and corresponding conspiracy theories will not turn one into a complete cynic, skeptic or merciless judge

---

[3]Scripture quotations in this chapter are from the English Standard Version.

toward all perceived workers of evil (except oneself). *The potential scorn of an accused employee wisely calls for patience, rather than skepticism, toward perceived evil.* The person in the pew needs such divine wisdom. The pastor theologian is the one called to provide such wisdom through a theological examination of the biblical wisdom corpus.

THE ASSUMPTION OF WISDOM FOR THE PASTOR THEOLOGIAN'S TASK

In *The Pastor Theologian*, Gerald Hiestand and Todd Wilson propose a threefold taxonomy for the pastor theologian related to the spheres of the shepherd's theological engagements. The *local theologian* constructs theology for the local assembly, using the sermon as the primary tool.[4] The *popular theologian* serves pastors and laity beyond the congregation, "[speaking] to issues . . . that tend to be left under- or unaddressed by academic theologians, as well as [translating] academic theology down into the common vernacular of the local church."[5] The *ecclesial theologian* serves other Christian theologians and pastors, acting as theologian for the congregation and as a pastor who interacts scholastically with other theologians, pastoral and academic. Each of these tasks both necessitates the use of wisdom, and provides unique opportunities for giving wisdom as an instrument of the revelation of the knowledge of God.

The pastor theologian's tasks necessitate wisdom, as they assume that wisdom concepts of Scripture are as much theological and gospel-related constructs as ideas like atonement, kenosis, the final state and the new creation. These tasks assume that the relationship between the atoning work of Christ and marriage—"and gave himself up for her" (Eph 5:25)—is significant for believers within their local congregations, the greater church community, and the theological academy.[6] Yet it also assumes that the cruciform foundation of

---

[4]Gerald Hiestand and Todd Wilson, *The Pastor Theologian: Resurrecting An Ancient Vision* (Grand Rapids: Zondervan, 2015), 82.

[5]Hiestand and Wilson, *Pastor Theologian*, 84.

[6]For the greater church community, the sermons that pastors Timothy Keller, John MacArthur and Kent Hughes preached on Ephesians 5 that later became parts of commentaries or popular Christian marriage books are popular theological works related to this passage: see Timothy Keller, *The Meaning of Marriage: Facing the Complexities of Commitment with the Wisdom of God* (New York: Riverhead Books, 2013); John F. MacArthur Jr., *Ephesians*, MacArthur New Testament Commentary (Chicago: Moody, 1986); and R. Kent Hughes, *Ephesians: The Mystery of the Body of Christ* (Wheaton, IL: Crossway, 2013). In the academy, Tom Schreiner is representative of an ecclesial theologian's work on this task; see Thomas R. Schreiner, "Editorial: Marriage and

marriage needs wisdom in order for one to make marital choices that keep
future husbands off the corners of rooftops (Prov 21:9; 25:24) and future wives
from marrying hotheads (Prov 14:17, 29). Couples pronounced man and
wife by the Trinitarian blessing also need Proverbs' wise call to the symbiotic
self-giving and pursuit of mammary intoxication (Prov 5:18-19) in order to
maintain marital fidelity.

Similarly, the pastor theologian who comes to 1 Corinthians 6:1-11 assumes a robust understanding of how justification, progressive sanctification, the mysterious baptizing work of the Spirit and the inheritance of
the kingdom of God influence Christian arbitration policies for a congregation, manuals on church discipline for denominations and broader con-
versations on covenant membership.[7] Those same tasks also assume that
there is an *oudeis sophos* ("one wise"; 1 Cor 6:5)—within every congregation
who can consider the kingdom-cross implications for matters of conflict that
have the potential to turn into formal lawsuits or trials by public media.

THE CASE FOR WISDOM

For all of the calls to recover gospel-centeredness in evangelicalism put forth
within recent publications,[8] very few of them focus on the genre and theology

the Family," *SBJT* (Spring 2002): 2-3. Ronald J. Nydam's "The Messiness of Marriage and the
Knottiness of Divorce: A Call for A Higher Theology and Tougher Ethic," *CTJ* 40 (2005): 211-26,
is representative of an ecclesial theologian's work on marriage, although Nydam now is a professor of pastoral theology rather than a parish pastor.
[7] Although marketed to laity, Jonathan Leeman's *The Church and the Surprising Offense of God's Love:
Reintroducing the Doctrines of Church Membership and Discipline* (Wheaton, IL: Crossway, 2010) is
academic in its thrust. For other works representing ecclesial theologian discussions, see Mark
Dever, "The Practical Issues of Church Membership," in *Those Who Must Give an Account: A Study
of Church Membership and Church Discipline*, ed. John S. Hammett and Benjamin L. Merkle (Nashville: B&H Academic, 2012); Dever, *Polity: Biblical Arguments on How to Conduct Church Life: A
Collection of Historic Baptist Documents* (Washington, DC: Center for Church Reform), 2001;
Dever, "Regaining Meaningful Church Membership" in *Restoring Integrity in Baptist Churches*, ed.
Thomas White, Jason B. Duesing and Malcolm B. Yarnell III (Grand Rapids: Kregel, 2007), 57-60;
and Aaron Mennikof, "The Loving-Kindness of Covenant Membership," *Leadership Journal* (June
2015), www.christianitytoday.com/le/2015/june-web-exclusives/loving-kindness-of-covenant
-membership.html?share=%2fd0TuiSnx3xaSU4i3VDwII8BOAkK1nmW.
[8] A small sampling of recent "gospel-centered" themed books include Jonathan K. Dodson, *Gospel
Centered Discipleship* (Wheaton, IL: Crossway, 2012); D. A. Carson and Timothy Keller, eds., *The
Gospel as Center: Renewing Our Faith and Reforming Our Ministry Practices* (Wheaton, IL: Cross-
way, 2012); Sinclair Ferguson, *In Christ Alone: Living the Gospel-Centered Life* (Lake Mary, FL:
Reformation Trust Publishing, 2007); Michael Horton, *The Gospel-Driven Life: Being Good News
People in a Bad News World* (Grand Rapids: Baker, 2012); Trevin Wax, *Gospel-Centered Teaching*
(Nashville: B&H, 2013); and Jared C. Wilson, *Gospel Wakefulness* (Wheaton, IL: Crossway, 2011).

of wisdom. Yet the written wisdom of God exists to tell individual believers, local congregations and the full people of God how to navigate life in blessing before God.[9] Proverbs, in particular, makes its own case for the need for its wisdom in Proverbs 1–9. It does not do so to the exclusion of the wisdom to be found in Job 28, the wisdom Psalms, Ecclesiastes or the fuller Old Testament. Yet it uniquely gives every verse related to acquiring wisdom for daily living, to making righteous, just, and equitable decisions and to increasing insight into alternative wisdom systems.[10] Proverbs alone puts forth a sense of urgency to gain its truths as a matter of "life" versus "death."[11] A book that holds out the means to obtain a happy life and to avoid disaster and loss of life due to foolish choices is a book that should gain a pole position next to the Gospels and Romans in theological discussions and utility for Christian maturity.

All believers need the Spirit-breathed words of Proverbs. All need its anthill challenges to laziness (Prov 6:6-11), its feet-scorching, vengeful-husband warnings against adultery (Prov 6:28), and its face-of-your-flock admonitions for maintaining a diverse and healthy financial portfolio in preparation for an economic downturn ("know well the condition of your flocks"; Prov 27:23-27).[12] All believers thus would do well to have a shepherd leading them who will use Proverbs and the wisdom literature to teach,

---

Few discuss wisdom and/or Proverbs's place in forming gospel-centeredness. Notable exceptions are Graeme Goldsworthy, *The Goldsworthy Trilogy: Gospel and Kingdom, Gospel and Wisdom, The Gospel in Revelation* (Glasgow: Paternoster, 2001); Goldsworthy, *Gospel-Centered Hermeneutics: Foundations and Principles of Evangelical Interpretation* (Downers Grove, IL: IVP Academic, 2007). To be fair, however, Goldsworthy is developing a biblical theology, whereas other "gospel-centered" texts are using the gospel as a lens by which to shape and/or interpret their subjects. For clarification of the definitional boundaries of the term *gospel-centered*, see Dane Ortlund, "What's All This 'Gospel-Centered' Talk About?," The Gospel Coalition blog, September 16, 2014, www.thegospelcoalition.org/article/whats-all-this-gospel-centered-talk-about. Tim Challies has compiled a list of "gospel-centered" books, "The Gospel-Centered Everything," challies.com, March 7, 2013, www.challies.com/articles/the-gospel-centered-everything.

[9]Proverbs has in focus "the assembly," "people," and "the children of man" within its pages.

[10]See the purpose statements of Prov 1:1-7.

[11]Consider the verses in Proverbs that see physical death as a consequence of unwise choices: Prov 1:19, 32; 2:18, 19; 3:2, 16, 18, 22; 4:10, 13, 22, 23; 5:5, 23; 6:26, 32; 7:23, 27; 8:35, 36; 9:11, 18; 10:2, 21, 27; 11:3, 4, 19; 12:28; 13:3, 13, 14; 14:12, 27, 32; 15:10, 24; 16:14, 17, 18, 25; 17:19; 18:9, 12, 21; 19:9, 16, 18, 23; 20:2; 21:6, 16, 28; 22:4; 23:13; 28:24. Several verses also see Sheol as the natural end for those who live in folly: Prov 1:12; 5:5; 7:27; 9:18; 15:24; 23:14.

[12]"Know well the condition of your flocks and give attention to your herds" literally reads, "Know; you must know the faces of your flock, put your heart to [your] herds." Waltke rightly recognizes that "'faces' . . . reflects the status of their health." Bruce Waltke, *The Book of Proverbs, Chapters 15–31* (Grand Rapids: Eerdmans, 2005), 391.

rebuke, correct and instruct them in righteous living before Christ.[13] The greater body of Christ and the academy need those who will dole out wisdom in a manner that gives us a sense of its immediacy for pleasing God, loving our neighbors and passing the faith to the third and fourth generations of our offspring.

Three Tasks

I would therefore suggest three tasks for the pastor theologian as a giver of wisdom. First, the *local theologian* should encourage members to develop the habits of seeking wisdom. That is, they should model seeking after wisdom with passion, as the Proverbs prescribe, daily reading Proverbs and mining its troves.[14] The thirty-one chapters of Proverbs hold out a natural reading schedule for meditation upon one chapter of Proverbs daily, corresponding to the date of the month. The local theologian should proclaim Proverbs as part of an expositional diet, returning often to the implications of wisdom for all aspects of life and worldview. They also should encourage members to pass on such wisdom to their children and grandchildren by daily discussing their choices in comparison to the words of the Proverbs and other wisdom literature, in the hopes that they will raise them like King Lemuel and the virtuous woman of Proverbs 31—the two final models in Proverbs of lives given fully to wisdom. The local theologian must encourage regular self-examination according to the statutes of Proverbs. This self-examination may take the form of questions such as, *Did I act in wisdom today? Did I judge with prudence? Did I cry out for guidance? Do I embrace wisdom as the chaste maiden with whom I am consummating a union in order to provide life? Did my choices reflect that I fear the Lord, esteeming knowledge and humility while hating evil, pride, arrogance, and the envy of evil people? Or did I pull a dog's ears, kiss a pig with a gold nose ring, or make a she-bear*

---

[13]"Proverbs, read through the lens of Jesus himself, is concerned with becoming wise in everyday life through a relationship with Jesus the Messiah." Jonathan Akin, *Preaching Christ from Proverbs* (Nashville: Rainer, 2014), 19.

[14]Hiestand and Wilson posit, "Insofar as pastors bear the day-to-day burden of teaching and leading God's people, they simply *are* the theological leaders of the church. As goes the pastoral community, so goes the church. . . . The theological integrity of a local church will not rise above that of its pastor. What is true for individual churches is true for the church as a whole" (*The Pastor Theologian*, 57-58). I would suggest that what is true for theology is equally true for wisdom, for people rarely arise above their pastor's spirituality or knowledge of Scripture.

say, "You would have fared better if you had taken my cub"? Ultimately, the local theologian seeks to cultivate a flock that is saturated and saturating itself in wisdom as part of the routine outworking of the gospel. For the local theologian, theology for the people will be faith seeking an understanding according to and demonstrative of the wisdom of Christ.

The *popular theologian*, building upon the work of the local theologian, the historical theology of the church and worship materials, constructs for the church works that demonstrate the importance of wisdom for living *coram Deo* (in the presence of God) and fulfilling the Great Commission.[15] Their works should exhort us to subscribe our thoughts, goals, motives and actions to the sage's life ambition of honoring the name of Christ through acquisition of only two needful things before death: a character of truth and contentment with having our material needs met (Prov 30:7-9).

The church awaits the popular theologians who will fill in gaps in our systematic theologies that would tie wisdom to more than Logos and Gnostic Christologies. Such theologians would manifest that *wisdomology* is significant to theology proper, pneumatology, soteriology and ecclesiology. They would explicate *Christ* as the Wisdom of God, and the *Spirit* as both the Isaianic and Pauline revealer of the Wisdom of God (Is 11:2; Eph 1:17; Col 1:19). Popular theologians will demonstrate that wisdom is necessary for making disciples in a congregation because "the fruit of righteousness is sown in peace" by those making a wise use of their words—words, as James writes, empowered by heaven rather than by the fires of hell (Jas 3:1-18).[16] More than commentaries are needed; a wedding of Proverbs,

[15]One example from historical theology that demonstrates the importance of wisdom is the following quotation from the Westminster Confession: "Neither prayer, nor any other part of religious worship, is now, under the Gospel, either tied unto, or made more acceptable by any place in which it is performed, or towards which it is directed: but God is to be worshipped everywhere, in spirit and truth; as, in private families daily, and in secret, each one by himself; so, more solemnly in the public assemblies, which are not carelessly or willfully to be neglected, or forsaken, when God, by His Word or providence, calls thereunto" (Westminster Confession of Faith 21.6: "Of Religious Worship and the Sabbath"). References for "when God, by his word or providence, calls thereunto" include Prov 1:20-21, 24 and 8:34. For an example of a worship song that demonstrates the importance of wisdom, see Keith Getty and Stuart Townend, "The Perfect Wisdom of God," Thankyou Music and Gettymusic, 2011.

[16]James's wisdom is for those who are heirs of the kingdom God has promised to those who love him (Jas 1:12; 2:5)—those called by the honorable name of Christ (Jas 2:7). James advocates wisdom on the basis of Christ and his kingdom—on the basis of the gospel. Every member needs this wisdom in order to produce fruit in the lives of the students (that is, their disciples).

Ecclesiastes and Job commentaries to be read with a systematic theology text would be beneficial, something akin to John Calvin's commentaries working in conjunction with *The Institutes*.[17]

The *ecclesial theologian*, standing on the work of local and popular theologians, is in position to engage the foolishness of the world and equip the church and its academies to do the same. Ecclesial theologians strive to depict post-gender philosophies as a failure to see the glory of a femininity that fears God rather than as a failure to embrace beauty.[18] They ground the church's academic thinkers in the reality of objective truth as they abominate uneven scales (Prov 11:1; 20:10, 23), level out the rich and poor in the hands of their Maker (Prov 22:2), consider the fugitive nature of a murderer (Prov 28:17), denounce the perversions of justice (Prov 17:15, 26; 18:5; 24:24) and oft repeat the unarguable results of embracing the lips of an adulteress (Prov 2:16; 6:24; 7:5; 22:14; 23:27-28).[19] They keep the church from sliding off the moral cliffs created by those whose foolishness cannot be ground out by mortar and pestle (Prov 27:22).

CONCLUSION

The individual follower of Christ, the church of Christ and the world are in need of wisdom. I would argue that every pastor theologian must be a theological wisdom-giver: Every pastor theologian must see deepening in and

---

[17]Calvin intended that *The Institutes* be read in conjunction with his commentaries: "I shall not feel it necessary, in any Commentaries on Scripture which I may afterwards publish, to enter into long discussions of doctrines or dilate on common places, and will, therefore, always compress them. In this way the pious reader will be saved much trouble and weariness, provided he comes furnished with a knowledge of the present work as an essential prerequisite" (John Calvin, *Institutes of the Christian Religion*, rev. ed., trans. Henry Beveridge [Peabody, MA: Hendrickson, 2007], xiv). It is well known that Calvin did not write a commentary on Proverbs. However, he does often make reference to Proverbs's verses related to the sovereign working of God, such as Prov 16:33 and 21:1, as also does the Heidelberg Catechism after him (see Lord's Day 10). See Amy Plantinga-Pauw, *Proverbs and Ecclesiastes: A Theological Commentary on the Bible* (Louisville: Westminster John Knox, 2015), 89.

[18]Jeremy Egerer, "Miley Cyrus and the Post-Gender Generation," *The American Thinker*, September 3, 2015, www.americanthinker.com/articles/2015/08/miley_cyrus_and_the_postgender_generation .html.

[19]On the significance of the loss of objective truth in postmodern society, see Justin P. McBrayer, "Why Our Children Don't Think There Are Moral Facts," *NYT*, March 2, 2015, http://opinionator .blogs.nytimes.com/2015/03/02/why-our-children-dont-think-there-are-moral-facts, and Peter Pomerantsev, "Russia's Ideology," *New York Times*, December 11, 2014, www.nytimes.com/2014/12/12 /opinion/russias-ideology-there-is-no-truth.html.

faithfully dispersing wisdom as vital to the health and beauty of Christ's church. The pastor theologian, as giver of wisdom, stands at the crossroad of history with a cache of skills that can slow down the slandering of servants and guide believers to do many other things that can change our world.

15

John as Pastor Theologian

2 John as Creative Theological Écriture

DOUGLAS ESTES

I N THE TWENTY-FIRST CENTURY, the pastor theologian must (re-)create a new space for theological development that is fundamentally distinct from the everyday working pastor or the academy-based theologian.[1] Whereas the modern Western social system tends to produce pastors who are ecclesially relevant and academicians who are theologically relevant, the pastor theologian is an individual who must be both ecclesially relevant and theologically relevant. The joining of these two relevancies is of critical importance for the health of the church, and most probably the longevity of academic theological institutions as well.

This space is one that needs definition, as the essays in this book have set out to do. To create this space, we may consider the pastor theologian alongside important possibilities (public theology, political theology, biblical theology), against past identities (Thomas Boston, John Calvin, Dietrich Bonhoeffer) or in light of biblical principles (exegetical, apologetic, gendered). Yet the one thing that ties these things together is *writing*—pastor theologians are primarily known as such from their writing. The possibilities they have to engage will come primarily through their use of the written word. In fact, the only real way we today know pastor theologians from the

---

[1] Gerald Hiestand and Todd Wilson, *The Pastor Theologian: Resurrecting an Ancient Vision* (Grand Rapids: Zondervan, 2015).

past is through their writing. And as Christians we know the importance of writing, with the textual mediation of God's revelation to us through the written word.

That our Scripture comes to us through text is of singular importance for our need to understand how to inhabit a space that is highly relevant both ecclesially and theologically. In fact, if we turn to the Bible we read of people who were both ecclesially and theologically relevant. We would not label all of these "pastor," but there is one in particular that fits the mold of pastor theologian perhaps best: John, the "beloved disciple" and eyewitness to Jesus, who went on to "pastor" a church in Ephesus and who created theology that resounded in his context and continues to resound at the beginning of a third millennium.[2] Of particular interest here are the letters of John, which are texts that speak to their readers from the intersection of ecclesial and theological concern. We Christians consider these texts in-spired and part of that singular importance of the Bible for engagement in our theological and pastoral work. Yet can pastor theologians today get an additional glimpse from these letters of what it means to write in such a way as to make an impact in both our ecclesial and theological contexts? Or, to echo Plato's *Phaedrus*, is there a "recipe" (*pharmakon*) for writing as a pastor theologian?[3]

I believe there is, at least as a starting point. In the three letters of John, the "pastor" John engages in what I call *creative theological* écriture.[4] While this description is not meant to cover every facet of John's writing, each of these three words describes a critical feature of John's writing as it relates to his work as a pastor theologian who uses the written word. Consequently, each of these three words offers a "recipe" for our work as pastor theologians.

---

[2]Based on Hiestand and Wilson's nomenclature, I would identify John as an "ecclesial theologian"; see Hiestand and Wilson, *Pastor Theologian*, esp. 88-101. Whether the author of the letters was John the apostle turned elder or just the elder John is secondary to the author's role as local/regional church leader and ecclesial theologian.

[3]Plato, *Phaedrus* 274e.

[4]The concept of *écriture* has gained wide currency in recent poststructuralist thought (from Barthes to Derrida to Nancy); I do not necessarily follow any one of these thinkers precisely here. Though the simple English translation of the French word *écrit* is "writing," I use the French word to impress upon the reader that this is not "writing in general." Just as *Écriture* in French is not "Writing" but *Scripture*, so too the writing of a pastor theologian must be writing of a certain quality: *écriture*. On the issue of translation see, for example, Antony Hudek and Mary Lydon, translators' notes to Jean-François Lyotard, *Discourse, Figure* (Minneapolis: University of Minneapolis Press, 2011), 428.

Given its brevity and its tendency to be overlooked, I will here focus on the *creative theological* écriture of 2 John as a test case.

CREATIVE

As a pastor theologian, John writes with creativity so as to deepen his engagement with his readers. In the modern world, a creative writer is one who looks past old ideas in order to produce a work that is "new" and "fresh."[5] This is in contrast to the way John would have perceived the creative endeavor—in his world "creativity was achieved through rivalry with, not rejection of, the work of predecessors."[6] Ancient conceptions and expectations of creativity were quite different from our own.[7] From an ancient world perspective, John was a creative thinker who wrote with one eye on the present and one eye on the past.[8]

John opens his second letter with very general language to describe himself ("elder") and his primary addressee ("the elect lady and her children").[9] While most scholars tend to separate these two, often making one a title and the other a metaphor, these descriptions are both allusions with similar strength.[10] John designates himself as "elder" to allude to his role as an overseer of the church, fulfilling that role just as any elder would; and he writes to a real person, calling her "an elect lady," to allude to her role as a key ministry leader in a local congregation. Added to this is "her children," alluding to her helpers and workers, though it is not impossible that a few could be biological offspring or relatives.

Their names are not as important as their commitment to the truth that abides in them both (2 Jn 2). John makes this allusion to demonstrate that both

---

[5]As aptly put by Søren Kierkegaard (1813–1855); see Søren Kierkegaard, *Either/Or*, Part 1, ed. and trans. Howard V. Hong and Edna H. Hong, Kierkegaard's Writings 3 (Princeton: Princeton University Press, 1987), 236.

[6]Thomas Habinek, "Poetry, Patronage, and Roman Politics," in *A Companion to Ancient Aesthetics*, ed. Pierre Destrée and Penelope Murray, Blackwell Companions to the Ancient World (Malden: Wiley-Blackwell, 2015), 76. There are numerous examples of this in practice, but I mention only Clement's creative reworking of Philo; see Annewies Van den Hoek, *Clement of Alexandria and his Use of Philo in the* Stromateis: *An Early Christian Reshaping of a Jewish Model*, Vigiliae Christianae Supplements 3 (Leiden: Brill, 1988), esp. 214-24.

[7]D. A. Russell, *Criticism in Antiquity* (Berkeley: University of California Press, 1981), 100.

[8]Compare C. K. Barrett, *New Testament Essays* (London: SPCK, 1972), 68.

[9]Unless otherwise indicated, Scripture quotations in this chapter are the author's translation.

[10]For an example of this separation, see Robert Kysar, *I, II, III John*, Augsburg Commentary on the New Testament (Minneapolis: Augsburg, 1986), 122-23.

parties are committed to the commandments that they had been given from the beginning (2 Jn 6). This commitment lasts "from here to eternity," as John reuses and recreates a phrase that also describes those who trust in the Lord as being as unmovable as Mount Zion (Ps 125:1). To the psalmist, God's qualities such as lovingkindness (Ps 136), righteousness (Ps 111:3) and covenantal commitment (Ps 111:5, 7) last "from here to eternity," but John chooses to emphasize the quality of God's truth for eternity (2 Jn 2; compare Ps 111:7-8).

The command to love one another is not John writing a new command, though John does recreate the original command by asking the lady and her children to love through their obedience (2 Jn 6; compare Ex 20:6). With echoes of the Old Testament, John creates a "reading whereby one continues to see how an OT text keeps imposing its original sense on" John's work, as he "is creatively developing that original sense beyond what may appear to be the 'surface meaning' of the OT text."[11] Whereas the law suggests that loving God comes alongside obeying God's commands, John synthesizes these two ideas and suggests that loving God *is* obeying God's commands. In fact, we can trace the development of John's theology from obeying God's commands as a condition of loving God (Jn 14:15), to obeying God's commands as the definition of the love God desires (1 Jn 5:3), to love being the action of walking in God's commands (2 Jn 6).[12] Yet this is not a new commandment—John simply recreates the meaning of the original commandment in a new form. It is John's regular, rhetorical redevelopment of the truth about God that creates powerful, written theology.

John does not create text in the modern sense, as something uniquely made, but redevelops and redeploys the truth of Christ for a new audience. His aim is to build on the truth that he has received (2 Jn 5-6). That John can understand the situation and occasion before him and build truth upon it is "of the greatest significance" to his creative work.[13] His work was quickly recreated in the early church by writers such as Polycarp (*To the Philippians* 7.1) and Irenaeus (*Against Heresies* 1.16.3). Thus, the writing objective of a pastor

---

[11]G. K. Beale, *A New Testament Biblical Theology: The Unfolding of the Old Testament in the New* (Grand Rapids: Baker Academic, 2011), 4.

[12]In saying this, I do not necessarily suggest a temporal progression of John's writing; though see also Klaus Wengst, *Der erste, zweite, und dritte Brief des Johannes*, 2nd ed., Ökumenischer Taschenbuchkommentar zum Neuen Testament 16 (Gütersloh: Gerd Mohn, 1990), 230.

[13]Kierkegaard, *Either/Or*, Part 1, 236.

theologian, and probably any thinker of any age, is not to create something new—in the Cartesian sense—but to build on and recreate the best of what has come before.[14] This is because "every generation has to chew it through afresh," which by necessity stresses the importance of theologians' preparation for their readers.[15]

THEOLOGICAL

As a pastor theologian, John theologizes by moving his readers forward in their understanding of the ways of God (2 Jn 9). Of course, any knowledge of God is severely limited and not comprehensible in any quantitative way to us here on Earth (compare Jn 1:18, 6:46).[16] So the task oftentimes is to describe how God acts, or how we as the people of God may "walk" in a hopefully-not-haphazard direction toward the Son (2 Jn 6; compare Jn 6:44-46). As such, John creates his theology with practical and ecclesial concern, so that God's people will not be deceived (2 Jn 7-8) but will obey his commandments and continue to abide in him (2 Jn 6, 9). It is not enough for John to write of history, or ethics, or philosophy (though these may be included); John's task is to reinvigorate his readers' theology in order that they may draw closer to God.

John truly loves his readers, yet makes the point that his readers are beloved not only to John but also to all those who "know the truth" (2 Jn 1). Implicitly, John ties love for each other with the truth about God (2 Jn 3). Here we hear the echo of the people of God living in harmony with each other, drawn together not because they need to be taught the truth any longer but because the truth is already present with them (Jer 31:33-34; 1 Jn 2:27). Since it is impossible to know quantitative truth about God, John substitutes for this the truth about the Son. This is also the same truth that the Spirit teaches (1 Jn 2:27), as this Spirit is, in fact, the Spirit of that truth himself (Jn 14:17). This truth abides in us, and it will be with us forever (2 Jn 2). From this we can understand that one reason that we are to love each

---

[14]Roger Lundin, "Interpreting Orphans: Hermeneutics in the Cartesian Tradition," in *The Promise of Hermeneutics*, ed. Roger Lundin, Clarence Walhout and Anthony C. Thiselton (Cambridge: Paternoster, 1999), 56.

[15]N. T. Wright, in the interview "What Is the Gospel? N. T. Wright," YouTube video, 13:15, posted by RodiAgnusDei, April 27, 2013, www.youtube.com/watch?v=ICHovRHJAYY.

[16]Eberhard Jüngel, *God as the Mystery of the World: On the Foundation of the Theology of the Crucified One in the Dispute between Theism and Atheism*, trans. Darrell L. Guder (London: Bloomsbury, 2014), 3-9.

other is because we who abide in the truth are bound together by that truth (and love) forever.

John explains that to move toward God is to know the truth about the Son, with both positive and negative implications and repercussions. Just as Jesus Christ has come in the flesh, a qualification from the physical realm, so too are John's readers to walk in the truth—also a qualification from the physical realm. It would be easy to spiritualize the act of walking, as popular Christianity often does, but John's intention is likely more practical. Walking is the physical act of living, existing, doing (Rev 21:24). We are to walk in obedience to God's commands (2 Jn 6, echoing Ps 81:13; 119:1, and the problems of Ps 78:10; 89:30). John is excited to find some of the lady's children "walking in truth" and living exactly how the psalmist recommends when he wrote, "Teach me your way, O LORD, that I may walk in your truth" (Ps 86:11 ESV; compare Testament of Judah 24.3). In fact, if we walk in the truth we will become people of truth (Prov 13:20)—and thus much less likely to be deceived.

John also redeploys his thoughts on the relationship between love and obedience (2 Jn 6). From this starting point, he warns his readers of deceivers who are in the world. There is a causal connection (*hoti*) in John's original language between John's call to walk in obedience to God and his warning that there are deceivers. The warning is implicit: his readers must be in obedience, as trouble is coming. The readers do not know where and when these deceivers will try to deceive; they can only know that the deceivers have already gone out into the world.

John's description of these deceivers is monotonic: a deceiver is someone who does not confess that Jesus comes in the flesh (2 Jn 7). John adds that they are not simply deceivers; they are also antichrists. That John focuses on Christology is not surprising. What is surprising, however, is that he limits his Christology to just one quality. Or does he? After all, the nature of deception is that it convinces someone of something that is not true (in a way that is usually quite harmful). These deceivers talk about Jesus but do so in a way that denies his bodily nature. In one fell swoop they have deceived their listeners about the incarnation; Jesus' death, burial, crucifixion, and resurrection; salvation (Col 1:22); eternal life (Jn 6:53); Jesus' patrimony (2 Sam 7:11-16, Rom 1:3); the validity of Old Testament prophecy (Ps 16:9-10; Is 49:1); Second Temple messianic expectations (1QSa II, 19-21, 3 Enoch 48A.10; compare

Psalms of Solomon 17); and even the bodily return of Jesus at the consummation of the ages (Phil 3:21; 1 Cor 15:42-50). These deceivers are *antichristos* because they have hit on perhaps the most potent attack against the person of Jesus and the theology of John.[17]

In many ways, John was the "pioneering theologian" of not only the New Testament but also of his time and place in the world.[18] It would not be unfair to Paul to describe the Gospel and letters of John (who is writing later than Paul) as the "capstone" of New Testament theological development.[19] John understands that these truths are not digestible by his readers as hard facts (if that were even possible when we speak of God), but requires John to create theology in order to make these ideas digestible and palatable to his people. To this end, John does not simply reiterate theological ideas, as a pastor might, but consciously creates new theological expression that can withstand criticism.

ÉCRITURE

As a pastor theologian, John *écrit* so that his communication will stick to the soul of his readers.[20] The concern over the creation of texts—what we simply but simplistically call "writing"—is nothing new; from Plato to Derrida this has been a central concern for the development and continuation of thinking and meaning. John does not simply write in order to write; he is not writing whatever happens to come to mind at the moment. Instead—through the rhetorical development of his thought in proclaiming the kerygma of the Christian faith over the years—he writes with the intent to convey deep meaning to his readers. John *écrit* as a conscious act of creative theology (2 Jn 5-6). It comes from very deep within—his very soul (2 Jn 12).[21] Thus I use the poststructuralist concept of *écriture* to indicate the

---

[17]It is not surprising that Celsus, the first recorded critic of Christianity, follows this line of argument in his attempt at refutation; see Celsus, *On the True Doctrine: A Discourse Against the Christians*, trans. R. Joseph Hoffman (Oxford: Oxford University Press, 1987), 81, 86, and esp. 104-5. According to John, Celsus was an *antichristos*.

[18]Udo Schnelle, *Theology of the New Testament*, trans. M. Eugene Boring (Grand Rapids: Baker Academic, 2009), 749; compare Wolfhart Pannenberg, *Systematic Theology*, trans. G. W. Bromiley (London: T&T Clark, 2004), 1:2.

[19]D. Moody Smith, *First, Second, and Third John*, Interpretation (Louisville: John Knox, 1991), 7.

[20]On the use of the untranslated French *écrit* see footnote 4 above.

[21]Compare Plato, *Phaedrus* 276a.

significance of John's communication as more than words on a page; it is "thicker" than everyday writing and can "stick" to the soul of the individual.[22] John writes theology not simply as a means of conveying information, as an academic might, but consciously creates theological communication that impacts (and continues to impact) local churches for the relevant truth of the gospel. To paraphrase Jacques Derrida, "Each time we write something out about Christ, it leaves our hand, unable to return, we live our life in Christ in our writing."[23] By the significance of John's writing, he continues to live his life in Christ.

It is not enough to "know" the truth of Jesus—to read and remember facts from a page—it is truth that must be walked and abided in (2 Jn 6, 9). Even though John's readers have heard these commands from the beginning, there is still a need to remind them of the direction in which they must head (2 Jn 6). This raises the question: What is it about writing that does or does not stick? Why are commands given and then forgotten? Socrates suggests it is because writing discourages our ability to retain truth over time—if we hear and experience truth in life, we keep it; but if we read something, we too quickly put the book on the shelf and only remember it in passing.[24] We may contrast Socrates' view with John's emphasis on the actions of obedience. John encourages his readers to walk in the truth, and applauds those who *are* walking in the truth. He exhorts his readers to abide in the teaching of Christ—not simply to hear it but to live and act through it. By walking and abiding in the truth, John tries to imitate (*mimēsis*) in his words the human action (*praxis*) to which he calls his readers.[25] John, in sharp contrast to Socrates's concerns, tries to creatively transform writing about theological truth into a truth that is lived for and within his readers. For pastor theologians, the "recipe" for writing to grow in Christ is to build our encouragements around kinetic knowledge.

For these reasons, John's readers—even though they may be in the practice of imitating the truth in their actions—must watch out that they do not lose what they have worked for, so that they may receive a rich reward

---

[22]Compare Lyotard, *Discourse, Figure*, 9; and in response, 2 Jn 12; 3 Jn 13.

[23]Jacques Derrida, *Learning to Live Finally: The Last Interview*, trans. Pascale-Anne Brault and Michael Naas (New York: Palgrave Macmillan, 2007), 32-33.

[24]Plato, *Phaedrus* 274e-275a.

[25]Russell, *Criticism in Antiquity*, 106-7; compare Aristotle, *Poetics* 1448b4-19, and 3 Jn 11.

(2 Jn 8). Again John calls his readers to a thoughtful action, a posture that privileges a thickness to life that transcends any simple act. For the one walking in truth, the need to watch does not ever disappear in this life; walkers-in-truth must be alert as long as they are in this world into which deceivers are released. They also cannot "go ahead" of where they are in Christ (2 Jn 9), because if they lose the teaching of Christ in their life they do not have God. Only the reader who remains "stuck" to the teaching of Christ has the Father and the Son. This, then, is the challenge of writing the truth of God to others: pastor theologians must write with words and composition that help the teaching of Christ to stick to their readers' souls.[26]

The critical importance of the truth about Christ is such that John instructs his readers to not welcome people who do not carry the teaching of Christ. Implicit in John's remarks are that these people are deceivers, antichrists and people who do not walk in truth. While hospitality is a virtue, welcoming deceivers imitates the wrong action for those who are trying to walk in the truth. It is a movement in the wrong direction.[27] It is also to share in their deception, because welcoming deceivers does not permit one to walk in the truth (2 Jn 11).

John concludes his letter with the admission that he cannot write sufficiently on everything that he wants to tell his readers. Like Socrates, John understands the limits to the written word (though like Plato, John still writes). John hopes to visit his readers so that he can give living voice to his encouragements (2 Jn 12). In his conclusion, John sends the greetings of the "sister" to the "elect lady" (2 Jn 13).

Following John, the pastor theologian must be creative and write afresh for each generation, all the while remembering that writing goes stale over time, especially in a literate culture.[28] One of the inherent weaknesses of writing is that there will be future readers whom the writer may never imagine as readers.[29] This complicates the writing process and compounds its importance for those of us who write to encourage the people of God to abide in the truth. At the same time, the pastor theologian must write

---

[26]Even the aesthetic quality of the composition is critical; Longinus, *On the Sublime* 39.3.

[27]Reflecting John's guidance, similar expectations for teachers and prophets are expressed in Didache 11.

[28]Plato, *Phaedrus* 274e-275a.

[29]Plato, *Phaedrus* 275e.

something that is meaningful, beyond simple facts and histories. If I may paraphrase Levinas in light of this discussion, the pastor theologian "must return to writing to convey the truth about God, even though it may not ever fully satisfy the righteousness and the holiness of God."[30] This is the call and need of the pastor theologian.

Conclusion

From the evidence of his writings, John functioned as a pastor theologian in that he both created meaningful theology and remained relevant and accessible to the needs of a local congregation. For pastor theologians, our *écriture* is not secondary to our sermons but actually for the betterment of them. Our *écriture* becomes our great text in which we are able to effect theology. This is why pastor theologians are needed in every generation. If Christian theology is reduced to its simplest bullet points, it loses its power to communicate. Our theological *écriture* is not capital-É *Écriture*, but it is an articulation of *Écriture* to many. It is not divinely needed, but it is divinely used.

---

[30]Emmanuel Levinas, *Collected Philosophical Papers*, trans. Alphonso Lingis, Phaenomenologica 100 (Dordrecht: Martinus Nijhoff, 1987), 148.

List of Contributors

Chris Castaldo (PhD, London School of Theology) is lead pastor at New Covenant Church, Naperville, Illinois. He writes on the subject of evangelical renewal among Catholics and Protestants in the contexts of sixteenth-century Italy and early to mid-nineteenth-century Oxon. His most recent book is *Talking with Catholics About the Gospel: A Guide for Evangelicals.* Chris is a fellow of the CPT.

Josh Chatraw (PhD, Southeastern Baptist Theological Seminary) serves as both the executive director of Liberty University's Center for Apologetics & Cultural Engagement and the director for the School of Religion's Theology & Apologetics programs. Josh is a fellow of the CPT. His most recent book is *Apologetics at the Cross.*

Douglas Estes (PhD, University of Nottingham) is the director of the DMin program and assistant professor of New Testament/Practical Theology at South University–Columbia. Previously he served in pastoral ministry for sixteen years. Douglas is a fellow of the CPT. His most recent book is *Questions and Rhetoric in the Greek New Testament: An Essential Reference Resource for Exegesis.*

Gerald Hiestand (PhD candidate, University of Reading) is senior associate pastor at Calvary Memorial Church in Oak Park, Illinois, and the executive director and cofounder of the Center for Pastor Theologians. His most recent book is *The Pastor Theologian: Resurrecting an Ancient Vision.*

Edward W. Klink III (PhD, University of Aberdeen) is the senior pastor of Hope Evangelical Free Church in Rockford, Illinois. Previously he was an assistant pastor in southern California while serving nearly ten years as a faculty member of the Talbot School of Theology. Edward is a fellow of the

CPT. His most recent book is *John* in the Zondervan Exegetical Commentary on the New Testament series.

Joel D. Lawrence (PhD, University of Cambridge) is the senior pastor of Central Baptist Church in St. Paul, Minnesota. Prior to Central, he served on the faculty at Bethel Seminary, teaching theology and ethics. Joel's doctoral work focuses on Bonhoeffer, and he is the author of *Bonhoeffer: A Guide for the Perplexed*. Joel is a fellow of the CPT.

Peter J. Leithart (PhD, University of Cambridge) is the president of the Theopolis Institute in Birmingham, Alabama. Previously, Peter was pastor of Trinity Presbyterian Church, Birmingham, Alabama (1989–1995), and was founding pastor of Trinity Reformed Church, Moscow (2003–2013). From 1998 to 2013 he taught theology and literature at New St. Andrews College, Moscow, Idaho, where he continues to teach as an adjunct senior fellow.

Scott M. Manetsch (PhD, University of Arizona) teaches church history at Trinity Evangelical Divinity School in Deerfield, Illinois, and serves as the associate general editor of the Reformation Commentary on Scripture. He is the author of *Calvin's Company of Pastors: Pastoral Care and the Emerging Reformed Church, 1536–1609*.

Jason A. Nicholls (PhD, Marquette University) is pastor at Redeemer Missionary Church in South Bend, Indiana, where he has served since 2004. He has presented conference papers and published several reviews and a journal essay in the areas of systematic and historical theology. Jason is a fellow of the CPT.

Laurie L. Norris (PhD, Wheaton College) serves as assistant professor of pastoral studies at Moody Bible Institute in Chicago, where she teaches in the areas of spiritual formation and homiletics. She has served her church in various teaching capacities, and also currently serves as research assistant to the senior pastor.

Eric C. Redmond (PhD candidate, Liberty University) currently ministers at Calvary Memorial Church as pastor of adult ministries and teaches at Moody Bible Institute in the Biblical Studies department. He has over fifteen years of ministry experience as a pastor and is the author of *Where Are All the Brothers? Straight Answers to Men's Questions About the Church*.

Philip Graham Ryken (PhD, University of Oxford) is the president of Wheaton College, council member of The Gospel Coalition and former pastor of Philadelphia's Tenth Presbyterian Church. He has written over forty books, including *The Message of Salvation*, *Art for God's Sake* and expository commentaries on Exodus, Ecclesiastes, Jeremiah, Luke and other books of the Bible.

James K. A. Smith (PhD, Villanova University) holds the Gary and Henrietta Byker Chair in Applied Reformed Theology and Worldview at Calvin College. Smith also serves as editor of *Comment* magazine and as a senior fellow for The Colossian Forum. He has written numerous books, most recently *You Are What You Love: The Spiritual Power of Habit*.

Kevin J. Vanhoozer (PhD, University of Cambridge) is research professor of systematic theology at Trinity Evangelical Divinity School in Deerfield, Illinois. Prior to that he served as Blanchard Professor of Theology at Wheaton College and Graduate School (2008–2011) and as senior lecturer in theology and religious studies at New College in the University of Edinburgh (1990–1998), where he also served on the Panel of Doctrine for the Church of Scotland. He is the author of many books, including *The Pastor Theologian as Public Theologian: Reclaiming a Lost Vision*.

Todd Wilson (PhD, University of Cambridge) is the senior pastor of Calvary Memorial Church in Oak Park, Illinois, and cofounder and chairman of the Center for Pastor Theologians. Todd is the author of numerous books, including his most recent, *The Pastor Theologian: Resurrecting an Ancient Vision*.

Name Index

Subject Index

of the cross, 49
of God, 65, 181
women
   in the Bible, 166-67
   in ministry, 163, 166-69
   and theology, 163-65,
    168-69

Word of God, 47, 65, 83-84,
   99, 142
   See also Bible
world, 2, 8, 11, 24, 28, 31-33,
   36, 38, 43, 45, 47, 49, 74,
   106-7, 115-17, 141, 156-57,
   173, 192-93, 197, 200-203

World Series, 19
World War II, 72
worship, 28, 30-32, 48, 82, 102
wrath of God, 18
Yale University, 71
Zurich, 83

Scripture Index